The Swinger in the Mirror

The Swinger in the Mirror
My Secret Life

KIM LEE

Exposit
Jefferson, North Carolina

LIBRARY OF CONGRESS CATALOGUING-IN-PUBLICATION DATA

Names: Lee, Kim, 1970– author.
Title: The swinger in the mirror : my secret life / Kim Lee.
Description: Jefferson, North Carolina : Exposit, 2023 |
Includes bibliographical references and index.
Identifiers: LCCN 2023041669 | ISBN 9781476694238 (paperback : acid free paper) ∞
ISBN 9781476651675 (ebook)
Subjects: LCSH: Lee, Kim, 1970- | Open marriage. |
Non-monogamous relationships. | Group sex.
Classification: LCC HQ980 .L44 2023 | DDC 306.84—dc23/eng/20230911
LC record available at https://lccn.loc.gov/2023041669

BRITISH LIBRARY CATALOGUING DATA ARE AVAILABLE

ISBN (print) 978-1-4766-9423-8
ISBN (ebook) 978-1-4766-5167-5

Front cover photograph by Andrade,
Provoke Photography.

Printed in the United States of America

Exposit is an imprint of McFarland & Company, Inc., Publishers

Exposit
*Box 611, Jefferson, North Carolina 28640
www.expositbooks.com*

To *Kaleb,*
the most important
soul encounter in my life

Table of Contents

Acknowledgments   ix

Author's Note   1

Prologue: 2015   5

1. Family Ties   15
2. Love at Last   22
3. Four-Year Itch   29
4. Weekend Get-Away   35
5. New Church Friends   45
6. First Foursome Experience   54
7. Trouble in Paradise   59
8. Meet the Neighbors   66
9. Women's Retreat   74
10. Our Little Secret   86
11. Downtown Hotel Night   90
12. What Annie Wants, Annie Gets   99
13. Even the Score   108
14. What About *Us*?   114
15. Vegas Weekend   119
16. My BFF   127
17. Red Flags   133
18. Give an Inch, Take a Mile   141
19. Second Vegas Trip   146

Table of Contents

20. Blurred Boundaries   150
21. Surprise Birthday Party   154
22. Sex and Lies   158
23. The Breakup   162
24. I Was a Fool   168
25. The Affair   172
26. Fight or Flight?   178
27. The Aftermath   186
28. A Fresh Start   193
29. Lifestyle 2.0   198
30. Communication 101   208
31. Unfinished Business   215
32. My Emotional Affair   219
33. Day of Reckoning   226
34. Dr. David   231

Epilogue   239
Appendix: Swinging 101 Primer   243
Further Reading   249
Index   251

Acknowledgments

* * *

To Kaleb, my lover, my best friend, and my partner in crime. We've been on this crazy roller coaster ride together for what seems like forever—but I'm not ready to get off just yet. Are you? Throughout this journey, I have learned a lot about you as I have about myself. We've had our ups and downs but through it all, we've managed to stay *together*. I am truly thankful to have had your unwavering support and patience during the writing of this book, even when you stared at me with bewilderment, wondering how I could possibly sit at my computer and write/edit for hours upon hours! But at the same time, I know you looked at me with amazement, admiration and pride at what I've accomplished—thank you for being by my side.

To my editor (and now good friend), Christine Gordon Manley. Where do I begin? First of all, thank you for believing in me when I didn't even believe in myself. I still recall our first telephone intro call and how adamant I was that this would be my first and only book; however, you had other plans for me! I couldn't have done this without your help, honestly. You were my cheerleader, my inspiration and constant reminder that my story was worth sharing and that I *am* a good writer. You gave me the courage, validation, and encouragement to keep writing because you knew I had an important message that I needed to share with the world. Without you and your editorial wizardry, all this wouldn't have been possible. We did it!

To my twin sister. We've been through a lot together, right from the beginning. You've been such an important part of my life and my biggest supporter. Although we haven't shared the same path or journey in life, I know you have (and will) always be there for me and I love you.

N.K., a very big thank you to my close and dearest friend who encouraged me to continue with my writing and to always *dream big*. You have been a part of my personal journey, a witness and support to

Acknowledgments

many of my triumphs and shake-ups along the way. Thank you for helping me to discover the second half of my career life. I couldn't ask for a better friend.

L.L. and Y.Y., my soul sisters. Thank you for listening and supporting me over the years with writing and non-writing stuff. Your feedback and validation of my draft manuscript inspired me to keep going and to work at it until I got it right! Thank you both for being there for me.

To the wonderful people we've met through our LS community, whom we are grateful to now call our friends. I've learned so much from each and every one of you: the personal stories that you've shared of your LS adventures/mishaps, personal relationship struggles and the valuable lessons learned along the way have helped me to look inside of myself and my relationship with Kaleb. Thank you for joining us on our LS journey.

Author's Note

When I first met Kaleb, I desperately wanted to believe that he was my *soul mate*, my one and only. However, over the last two plus decades of our relationship, my thinking has changed a lot. I've finally taken off the blinders to see the weak links in my marriage that I chose not to see for the longest time. I didn't want to admit to myself that Kaleb wasn't my perfect everything as I clung onto this one deep belief—we would be together *forever*. Sadly, my belief in the concept of soul mates slowly unraveled before me. Although I am a hopeless romantic at heart, I can honestly say I no longer subscribe to the notion of finding that *one* person that will meet all of your spiritual, emotional, physical and sexual needs for life.

I now believe that soul mates are merely a myth—a social construct, born out of a figment of our imagination and *expectation* of what we *think* should make us happy. This concept of a perfect, one-stop-shop mate who will make everything in your life better is an oversimplification. It glosses over the tough and messy bits of the human soul, relationships, and life in general. Humans are complex and being in a relationship makes it even more complicated. We individually struggle in our search to find what makes us happy, and this forces us to evolve emotionally and spiritually at every turn. This evolution will inevitably impact upon our relationships as we face doubts and uncertainties in ourselves as well as in our chosen partner(s). And if we don't know exactly what makes us happy, how can we *expect* our "soul mate" to fulfill us in every way?

Can we expect our partner to be perfect and meet all of our needs? Is this realistic? Are we even meant to be with one person … forever? Can we be truly content in a monogamous relationship? For me, I don't think it's possible. Honestly. No one can live up to that, nor should they be expected to. That's partly what attracted Kaleb and I to the Lifestyle (LS)—acknowledging to each other that we couldn't satisfy all of each other's entire needs, emotionally, physically or sexually. We would need to venture outside of our marriage to meet a variety of interesting couples in the Lifestyle who could potentially fulfill some, if not all of these wishes.

What I have come to agree with is the concept of *soul encounters*—randomly meeting important individuals over our lifetime, who satisfy our needs in some capacity and touch us in a special way. Soul encounters aren't necessarily free of the difficulties and complexity that one would find in relationships, but the concept allows for individual change and growth as a result of that experience. As hard as it was to admit to myself, I finally came to accept that Kaleb was not my everything and I wasn't his. On the positive side, that realization took a huge weight off both of us. We downloaded that responsibility to our soul encounters. And that's when the Lifestyle began to take center stage in our lives.

This book is the story of my journey as a closeted swinger and the twists and turns I've taken along the way. Writing about my experiences started out as a need to journal about a heart-breaking moment when my marriage fell apart in early 2011. Although this process was initially meant to help me work through my pain and hurt, it ultimately led me to go deeper into myself and look at the complexity of my relationship with my husband within the context of our Lifestyle (LS) experience. It took me ten years to write my story; much of that time was spent processing how my marriage could fall so far from grace and who was more to blame—Kaleb or me. Knowing what I know now, there were important questions that we should have asked each other before we jumped into the Lifestyle, and not after the fact.

The Lifestyle *should* be seen as a healthy expression of a couple's mutual decision to explore their sexual desires beyond their marital bed in a safe and consensual manner. However, most people don't share this belief. There continues to be a lot of stigma around swinging. The Lifestyle is shrouded in mystery and secrecy, and it is still a taboo subject. Many *vanilla* (non–LS) people view this as an alternative way of living that only *perverted*, *sex-crazed* people engage in. To some, we are a subset of an abnormal and deviant population forced to go underground to fulfill our sexual perversions. Few openly admit that they are swingers because it does not conform to the traditional sanctity of marriage. Kaleb and I never felt entirely comfortable or safe revealing our secret life because we feared judgment and reprisal from mainstream society. Most swingers I've come across tend to keep this secret to themselves—not even family or close friends know. It took me many years before I had the courage to share my truth with my twin sister.

And yet, the Lifestyle industry is a multi-billion-dollar global business. You can find LS resorts, clubs, cruise lines, and websites all over the world. Supply and demand ... the reality is that we're everywhere! Think twice when you look at your co-worker, boss or next-door neighbor ... they may be one of us.

At the time of writing this memoir, Kaleb and I have been swinging for more than 15 years. There are many memorable and salacious stories of LS flings and weekend orgies that I could tell. And there are also important lessons we learned as newbies—the *Dos and Don'ts* of swinging that we accumulated through trial and error over the years. Although it's added greatly to our life in terms of our enjoyment, expression, and pursuit of physical and sexual pleasure, engaging in the Lifestyle has had its downsides as well; it exposed the imperfections in our marriage and forced us to decide if we were willing to stick by each other and work through these issues *together* or go our separate ways.

In the pages that follow, you'll learn more about the underground LS world of hedonistic sexual pleasures and pitfalls—the good, the bad and the ugly (and some very ugly). One thing I need to clarify at the start: this is my story and mine alone. My version of this story may differ from that of my husband's recollection. Even though we embarked on this LS journey together, Kaleb and I have different memories and interpretations of what happened to each of us. This is *my* personal story of how the Lifestyle changed me and our marriage.

To protect my privacy and that of my family, I have written under a pen name, and I have also changed identifiers (names and descriptions) of everyone involved. The LS club and LS website names have been changed as well. All written dialogue is based on my memory and subjective recollection of events. These are my interpretations of how events unfolded and how I perceived the actions and words of the people involved. In my story, I've talked about certain people who have hurt me or spoke of them in a less than positive light; however, this is my interpretation of how I perceived things to have happened between us and more importantly, what I was thinking and feeling at that time. No doubt these people have their own interpretation (and maybe I would be the villain in their story!). We all have our own stories to tell. It is my hope that by sharing mine you'll come to see that all marriages are *imperfect*; however, relationships can still be vibrant, thriving, healthy and even sexy, if both partners put in the effort and communicate honestly with each other. We have the power within to ask for what we need or want from our relationship (and of life in general). Don't let family expectations or cultural or societal norms dictate how you choose to live a *happier* life. Be true to yourself.

There's a poignant quote in the book *Radical Acceptance: Embracing Your Life with the Heart of a Buddha,* by American psychologist and teacher of Buddhist meditation and emotional healing Tara Brach that resonates strongly with my choice to live an alternate lifestyle: "The boundary to what we can accept is the boundary to our freedom" (44). I believe that if we could suspend our fears, assumptions, and judgments—and not set up boundaries to what we *think* is acceptable according to our familial, cultural or societal expectations, we might feel less trapped in our lives.

While my LS journey has evolved over the years, one thing remains true: I *choose* to live a happier, more peaceful and fulfilling life, not dictated or restricted by others' beliefs as to how I should think, feel, speak or behave. I want the freedom to make my own choices in life.

My boundary is *limitless*.

Prologue

2015

* * *

"Do you miss having sex with other women?" I asked Kaleb as we waited for our taxi.

"Yes," my husband replied, "but only under the right circumstances. I enjoy it when you're watching or participating ... then it's great!"

I nodded. "Are you sure you're ready for this?" I asked.

Kaleb grabbed my hand and gave it a squeeze. "I am if you are."

"I'm ready," I replied, and at that moment, our taxi appeared. We slid in quickly and gave the address to the driver. The December night air was crisp, and the roads were lightly covered with snow. The driver drove quickly, as if he could sense the urgency in us.

We drove along the main street before the cab slowed down and turned onto a narrow one-way street. Seconds later, he stopped in front of our destination. No sign was visible, only a large black iron cast door.

"Are we at the right spot?" I whispered to Kaleb.

"Yep, this is the address," the driver, who had clearly overheard me, replied.

I was both nervous and excited. I could see the exhilaration in Kaleb's eyes. He smiled at me and said, "Shall we?" I nodded, and he grabbed my hand as he led me out of the cab.

I gingerly stepped over the snow embankment in my 4" strappy heels, trying to avoid snow getting in between my toes. Once inside, we were directed to a small, closed off waiting area. The door was locked, and a security surveillance camera was mounted above, watching our every move. Seconds later, we heard a loud buzzer, and the door simultaneously unlocked. I smirked, noting how this austere but legal setting had more of a covert vibe than the first illegal underground sex club we checked out in the early 2000s.

5

Prologue

"This is like a prison. No one gets in and no one gets out!" I joked.

We headed to a reception area, where a woman greeted us from behind a Plexiglass wall. Dressed casually in a black T-shirt and jeans, she looked to be in her early 20s. She wore heavy make-up, complete with black liner under her eyes, and an eyebrow piercing. Her sleeve tattoos made her look even more intimidating.

"Membership number?" she asked, not bothering to look up from her computer screen. Kaleb and I looked at each other, waiting for the other to answer.

"Do we need a membership to come in?" Kaleb asked.

She rolled her eyes and let out a sigh at the thought of having to explain about membership. "Look, if you pay the one-time entrance fee, you don't have to sign up for one," she said. At that moment, a young couple entered the reception and lined up behind us.

"We'll pay the one-time fee," Kaleb replied, quickly handing his credit card to her. As she processed the payment, I glanced at the white sign on the wall behind her, outlining the club rules, which included *No Means No* and *Ask Once*. The woman noticed me looking at the sign.

"You know about the rules, right?" she asked.

The puzzled look on our faces answered her question, so she proceeded to give us a quick overview. *Practice Safe Sex... Respect Others' Wishes...* Their *Ask Once* policy meant we couldn't approach a couple again if they weren't interested. In other words, *No Means No*.

Seriously, this needs to be stated on a sign? Wasn't it obvious that if people reject you the first time, then you walk away and try to avoid them in order to save face? I guess there are persistent couples out there who need to be reminded...

I held onto Kaleb's hand as he pulled me through the beaded curtain hanging over the doorway. My eyes adjusted to the darkness as I surveyed the main floor, which had a '70s feel. An L-shaped mahogany bar was to our left, with three purple hanging pendant lights. Every seat at the bar was taken, and only a few tables were available along the back wall.

A small DJ booth was in the back corner, but I didn't see a DJ—only the sound system and strobe lighting to illuminate the dance floor. It wasn't much of a dance floor, around 10' by 10' in dimension, and there was a disco ball twirling above, which added to the retro look. One brave couple, in their late 50s, clutched each other as they slow danced. They didn't seem to notice anyone, suggestively grinding against each other to Marvin Gaye's "Sexual Healing."

The main room was packed with 20 or so couples, standing room only, with a few lucky ones who'd found a seat at the bar. I scanned the room and was relieved I didn't recognize anyone. Most people were in their street clothes; a few couples had nothing on but a towel wrapped around them and a drink in hand. Not something you would see at a regular club.

We ordered some drinks at the bar, and while we waited for our order, I noticed couples continued to slowly funnel down into the main area from the upper levels. It became clear that this was the designated meet-and-greet area to mingle with other couples and potentially make a connection. Couples whispered to each other, trying to assess which couples they would zoom in on.

Drinks in hand, Kaleb pointed to an empty space in the corner where we could stand. As we inched our way along the crowded room, I could feel eyes on us. Couples sizing each other up in this main room before heading to more intimate areas of the club.

"I think we've wandered into the human equivalent of a National Geographic mating ritual special," I said. It was a joke, but the energy was real. During an animal courtship ritual, the interested male attempts to attract the female by exhibiting specific dance moves, belting out sounds, or displaying physical pageantry. Despite feeling this animal energy, I knew the comparison ended there.

"With all due respect to the mighty peacock, at least animals only have to impress one other creature," Kaleb smirked. He was right—a foursome connection was much more complex; there has to be mutual attraction with all parties and *simultaneously*. No matter if one partner proved successful in attracting the other partner, it's game over if the other two are less than impressed.

We took a sip of our drink and continued to canvass the crowd.

"It's busy ... and it's only 9:00 p.m.!" I observed, feeling super awkward. What should we be doing? Our LS experience aside, this was the first time Kaleb and I had intentions of fully engaging at an LS sex club. Our earlier adventure at the illegal underground sex club didn't count— we were newbie voyeurs, at best. I had no idea what to expect tonight, and so I was taking everything in cautiously. It was hard not to feel like this was a meat market, with everyone checking out the quality of the goods before they made their selection. I felt uncomfortable with the attention from both men and women in the room, and I squeezed Kaleb's hand for reassurance.

It was "Young Swingers" night, so the crowd was mostly couples in their 20s and 30s; they were a confident, trendy, and attractive bunch.

Prologue

You could easily spot the older couples, like ourselves—the 40 and 50+ people in the room wore more formal attire of suits and cocktail dresses. We looked like we were trying too hard. These young swingers, on the other hand, weren't dressed to impress; most of them wore jeans and t-shirts or button-down tops, which exuded their relaxed and casual attitude, typical of a hump day social after work.

Although I felt self-conscious about us being older, Kaleb didn't seem to be bothered by the younger crowd. We've been told by other couples that we're fairly attractive and appear much younger than our age. Tonight, Kaleb was looking dapper and handsome, all dressed up. He wore a navy-blue blazer with cream pants and a button-down white crisp dress shirt. It was sexy to see a few curly chest hairs poking out from his shirt. I glanced around the room to see if there were any other interracial couples like us, but I didn't see any. Our size differential also made us stand out. Kaleb stood tall at 6'1", hovering over my petite 5'3" frame. His medium build and broad shoulders made me feel protected and safe when I was with him. Although his wavy brown hair was speckled with a bit of grey around his temple, he still had a boyish look about him, with his short crew cut, fair complexion and clean-shaven face.

As long as I've known Kaleb, he's never lacked confidence in any situation, nor has he required external validation to feel good about himself. Not that he was vain about his looks—he simply didn't care what other people thought of him. I admired that about him. His carefree attitude and self-assured confidence were what first attracted me to him.

I wish I didn't need people's approval—something that was ingrained in me as a child. Appearances and perception were everything. Nothing was more devastating than losing face in Asian culture; God help you, if you did something that was considered inappropriate, embarrassing or—worse—disrespectful of your family's honor.

"Do you think we're too old for this crowd?" I asked.

"Will it really matter once the clothes come off?"

"Probably not."

"If you don't feel comfortable, we can leave," he said reassuringly.

Taking a big gulp of my wine, I reached for his hand and led him to the stairs. "Let's go check out the second floor," I said. At the top of the landing, a young couple in their 20s smiled seductively as they walked past us in the nude and headed into an empty private room. Kaleb and I grinned at each other, wondering if that was a signal for us to join them.

"I guess towels come off up here!" I said. As I looked around, something intriguing caught my eye: a foursome exchange was underway in a private room. One woman laid on top of another woman, caressing and kissing her passionately while their male partners laid beside them, waiting eagerly for their signal to join in on the action. Trying not to make it obvious that we were gawking at this foursome interplay, we began to slowly walk past this room, with our eyes glued to the scene.

We came to the communal locker room and stepped inside. Luckily, no one was in there. Half lockers lined all four sides of the room with two long wooden benches in the middle. Posted above the door was a large white sign that read: *No clothing or outdoor footwear permitted beyond this door!* Kaleb opened the door to locker #16.

"I guess we should get undressed?" I suggested.

"I'll grab some towels for us."

Suddenly, I felt extremely self-conscious and flashed back to my thirteen-year-old self in the girls' changing room, where, with lightning speed, I would tear off my clothes and change into my gym clothes before anyone could get a glimpse of my breast buds. Unlike the other girls, I didn't wear a bra, since there was nothing to fill one. I remember the shame I felt about my prepubescent body.

"Do you need any help?" Kaleb asked, noticing my struggle to pull my tight, non-stretch satin black dress over my shoulders.

"Yes! Get me out of this strait jacket!" I laughed, tugging at my back zipper with annoyance. He gently brushed aside my straightened hair, which grazed the middle of my back, to unzip my dress further down. Then, with one quick tug with his hands, I found myself suddenly standing there exposed, with only my black lace panties on. Kaleb stared at my body with a seductive gaze as I removed my underwear.

Kaleb pulled me in close and whispered, "After all these years, I still find you irresistible!" He caressed my soft rounded breasts, which, thankfully, had blossomed to a pleasing size 32 C. The way Kaleb looked at me at that moment made me feel like the most beautiful woman in the world and, for a moment, I forgot where we were. Then, all of a sudden, my self-consciousness kicked back in, and I quickly grabbed a towel off of the bench and wrapped it around my body before anyone had a chance to walk in. I held my towel firmly in place, making certain it wouldn't fall below my breasts. Kaleb casually removed his dress shirt and slacks as if he were at home, taking his time to fold them neatly before placing them inside our locker. He didn't seem fazed that someone might come in and see him in the buff. He wrapped a white towel around his waist and was ready for action.

I sat on the bench, trying to hold my towel strategically in place, as I

9

struggled with the straps on my new heels. "Why can't I keep them on?" I whined. "I could use all four inches of confidence right about now!"

I reluctantly handed my heels to Kaleb. He locked up our belongings and placed the neon pink key ring coil around his left wrist. "If I lose this key, we're going home naked!" Kaleb teased. I was in no mood for humor. I didn't like the fact that I got all dressed up, only to now have to take everything off … and the thought of walking barefoot on this filthy, grimy carpet made me squeamish. *When was it last steam-cleaned?* I wondered.

"This night is not getting off to a good start!" I muttered, as we walked out of the locker room. "I got to remember to bring my flip flops next time … if there is a *next time.*"

Although the lighting was dim, and I couldn't see the carpet stains, I could feel *something* sticky under my feet as we edged our way along. "Ugghh!" I don't even want to know…

Club Fantasia was not how I envisioned it to be. The website touted this as the largest, hottest, and most elegant Lifestyle nightclub. Other than the young, attractive crowd, I was not impressed.

Although it lacked in décor, Club Fantasia was an interesting physical space; play areas were on the second and third floors and a huge outdoor heated pool was located on the main floor. The second floor offered a number of private rooms located on both sides of the locker room. For those into kink and BDSM (bondage, dominance, sadism, and masochism), they had a back room on this floor called the Dungeon, which was pretty much what you would expect—a leather sex swing hung down from the center of the room, and there was also a king-size bed with restraint cuff/straps attached at each corner. A large table displayed an assortment of sex toys, including whips, ropes, spanking paddles, anal hooks, and muzzle gags.

"Anal hooks?" I smirked at Kaleb.

"No thanks!" he replied.

We slowly surveyed this room with both fascination and trepidation.

"Could you see us in this room?" I whispered.

"I'm game if you are," he replied as he pulled me in close.

"Would you be a Sub or Dom?" I teased.

"Both."

I liked this playful side of Kaleb … it'd been a while since we'd been like this with each other.

An attractive young Asian woman then walked past me, and I did a double take—she was still in street clothes and heading to the locker room. She reminded me of my sister. What would my twin think if she saw me *here*? How many disapproving evil-eyed looks would my father give me? My foray into the Lifestyle was a world away from my oppressive upbringing—a strict Korean household where obedient children followed their parents' rules without question, any mention of sex was forbidden (my father even sent a letter to the principal to exempt us kids from sex ed class), higher education ruled supreme, and medicine was the only profession deemed acceptable.

How did I ever get here?

"Do you want to check out the open bed on the third floor?" Kaleb asked, interrupting my thoughts.

I knew what Kaleb was suggesting. I started having second thoughts about us being here. We hadn't had sex with another couple for over four years—*Were we ready to get back in?* I wasn't sure but I didn't want to disappoint Kaleb, since it was my idea to come in the first place. I nodded, and we slowly edged our way up the stairs. The lighting was dim and foreboding. I took comfort in Kaleb's firm hold of my hand as we entered the third floor's large open play area, much like a mosh pit. A number of couples had already made their way up, crowding around a huge open bed. What were they looking at? As we moved further in, we came upon the main ring event: three couples engaged with each other in various forms of erotic foreplay and sex acts. The XXXL king size mattress was covered in white cotton sheets and situated in the middle of the room. It was standing room only; several couples were watching the erotic show up close and personal. Kaleb and I maneuvered our way in and found a spot near the base of the bed. Standing in front of Kaleb with his arms wrapped around me, my towel suddenly fell down by my waist, exposing my breasts. Unlike the usual self-conscious me, I left my towel hanging... I didn't care. In that moment, I *wanted* to feel comfortable with my body. I allowed myself to be uninhibited and free, like everyone in this sexually charged room.

One particular couple on this center stage bed caught my attention; they were young, mid–20s, fit, attractive, and extremely yummy. She had long, straight blonde hair that fell over her small but perky breasts; her lush curvaceous body was the envy of every woman in the room. Her partner was equally attractive—tall, strong defined legs, broad shoulders, narrow waist, and smooth, sculpted chest. Oblivious to the growing audience around the bed, this gorgeous woman positioned herself on all fours while her partner slowly mounted her from behind.

Prologue

I couldn't stop staring. As he slid onto his back, she climbed on top of him. Placing her hands on his broad shoulders, she began to gyrate her hips, moving slowly at first, then faster and faster, dominating his body fully. They climaxed together, letting out a moan of ecstasy.

We were watching live porn! This was so erotic and getting me off. I turned to Kaleb and gave him a lingering kiss. Without wasting an opportunity, Kaleb asked, "Do you want to lie on the bed?" Before I could answer, he placed his towel down and laid next to this gorgeous couple, who were enthralled in their own passion.

"Okay ... but do you want to grab a few more towels?" I asked. Who knew what *stuff* could be on those bed sheets?

Kaleb quickly slid off the bed and took a couple of towels off of the shelf. He returned to the bed, placing the towels in a neat quadrant before positioning himself on top. He held out his hand to me. I removed my towel, placing it on top of the others and laid next to Kaleb; he pulled me in closer and gave me a soft reassuring kiss. My anxiety disappeared and I forgot about everyone—it was just *us*. I moved slowly down between his legs, gently taking hold of him, and alternating with sensual kisses. Seductively, I licked his cock, moving my tongue around its circumference. I knew this drove him wild. Kaleb closed his eyes, not wanting this dream to end. I became subtly aware that several couples were slowly gathering around to watch our erotic exchange ... and, surprisingly, I didn't mind. Kaleb then pulled me up on top of him, our lips locked in a passionate and lingering kiss, one that I haven't felt in a long time. Kaleb was aroused, and this pleased me.

"Are you glad we came here?" I whispered into his ears. He nodded. He pulled me in towards him and then gently placed me on my back. He caressed my breasts and then guided my legs apart. He sensually kissed my body as he gradually moved further down. I let out a gasp of ecstasy, forgetting about the gorgeous couple lying next to us, who were now watching *us* perform. Slowly, I came to a kneeling position with both my hands in front of me and Kaleb firmly holding my hips from behind. I arched my back, lifting my ass to give him full view and access to my clitoris. He mercilessly teased me with his hard swollen cock, which every so often pressed gently against my inner thighs, making my entire body tingle. I curved my back further, as he tightened his grip on my waist with both hands. Then, without notice, he thrust forcefully inside of me, again and again.

I didn't want this amazing feeling to end.

My trance was broken unexpectedly by a gentle caressing of my right calf. It took me a second to realize it wasn't Kaleb. *Then who?* I glanced back. It was the gorgeous guy next to us! The idea of him touching my body excited me; however, I didn't know how to react to this subtle move. Didn't the rules say he had to get consent before he touched? But I didn't mind his boldness; I was aroused. As Kaleb continued to thrust harder, my attention turned back to this unfamiliar hand slowly making its way up the side of my right leg, finally resting on the outside of my thigh. At the peak of release, Kaleb delivered an intense grunt of euphoria, allowing both our bodies to finally relax back down onto the bed. He gently withdrew and laid on his back. Kaleb held my body tightly against his, looking into my eyes and whispered, "I love you."

As we laid there, the gorgeous couple inched closer to us. I felt a twinge of excitement. I hadn't mentioned this guy's roaming hand to Kaleb. There weren't any introductions; the smile on this guy's face hinted a possible interest.

"Do you want to play?" the man asked. *Of course, I want to play in your sandbox!* I wasn't sure if Kaleb felt the same, but I assumed he would—this woman was hot! LS club hook ups are based purely on appearance and physical visceral compatibility. I was pretty certain that Kaleb was as interested in his female partner as I was in this guy.

"Sure," Kaleb replied. "But using condoms."

"Of course," he replied. Now that the deal was sealed, the male partner slid closer beside me, which prompted Kaleb to do the same with his partner. I felt as if I was hovering from above, watching four bodies melding into one—tits, asses, legs, and arms all entwined. It was hard to tell where one body formed and the contours of the next started. This mysterious man was intriguing; his touch was gentle, yet dominating. He preferred doggy-style and asked me to crouch on all fours, as he had watched me do with Kaleb. After he paused to put on a condom, he mounted me from behind, firmly holding onto my hips. He then grasped my hair with his right hand, as if to hold it back away from my face. As he slowly slid inside of me, he gripped my hair harder, squeezing ever so slightly with each thrust, waiting for my reaction to his rough play. Kaleb had never done this with me, yet, strangely, this bold move aroused me.

As he continued to thrust inside of me, I couldn't help gazing to my right where Kaleb and his partner were. Was he enjoying himself as much as I was? I could see Kaleb slide further down her body, touching and kissing every part of her, gently yet fervently. I felt the familiar mixed emotions: I was jealous, watching this beautiful woman engage with my husband, but, at the same time, I was turned on by it. It's a strange feeling I can't explain, and I know this is something that most women can't relate to, but I enjoy watching Kaleb with other women. It excites and arouses me; the thought of another woman wanting my husband makes him even more desirable to me. As Kaleb released, the woman climaxed.

After Kaleb had removed his condom, tossing it in the wastebasket, he slid next to me and held me tightly. I had a strong urge to make him *mine again*. We laid next to this couple for the next ten minutes, meekly exchanging glances and smiles at each other.

"Well, that was fun!" Kaleb said, breaking the awkward silence. Without names or numbers being swapped, we all then slid off the bed and wrapped a towel around ourselves. No goodbyes or exchange of information needed. It was understood. This anonymity added to the eroticism.

Kaleb and I made our way back down to the second floor and found an available private room. I needed to reconnect with my husband, and I summoned him to join me as I laid seductively on the bed. As he went to close the door, I blurted out, "You can leave the door open. I don't mind."

This was an invitation for any interested couples to watch and/or join us. Kaleb grinned and left the door ajar. He climbed on top of me, pressing his body firmly against mine. I yearned for Kaleb's touch. I needed to reclaim him. He then laid on his back, pulling me on top of him. I gazed into his eyes and kissed him passionately. Our lips released as I slithered down between his legs, kneeling before him. Kaleb eagerly watched as I ferociously licked every part of him, attempting to wipe away the memory of that gorgeous woman he was with only moments ago. I yearned for total control over him.

I could see several men gathering around the doorway, eagerly watching me exact revenge on my helpless man. This voyeuristic show fed into my alter ego. Tonight, I was a goddess—I felt sexy, empowered and in control. I've craved this feeling of power and sexual expression for so long—to ask for and to do what I want (unapologetically) and to allow myself to enjoy my body fully, without being made to feel bad, guilty, repressed, or censured.

Maybe we were ready to get back into the Lifestyle after all...

1

Family Ties

* * *

So how did I end up in the Lifestyle? I've often wondered this. Engaging in foursomes and participating in various sexual activities went against everything my ultra-conservative Asian background had taught me, namely *never* be uninhibited or self-indulgent in our pleasures, or, God forbid, promiscuous.

I grew up being taught a mixture of Eastern philosophies—my father was Confucian and my mother was Buddhist. My father constantly drilled Confucius proverbs into our heads, with endless laminated index cards riddled across our study desk walls, reminding us of the virtues of wisdom, respecting our elders, sacrifice, abstention and self-restraint (basically, think of others before yourself). My mother practiced her Buddhist beliefs more inconspicuously, muttering chants at the home altar, as she shook her burning incense candles over a plate of apples and oranges offered to Buddha. There were a few times my hand was swatted away when I tried to remove an orange before the obligatory 2–3 days of prayers. One important commonality between my father's Confucian teaching and my mother's Buddhist beliefs was the avoidance of self-indulgence—sacrificing and denying our wants and desires for the better good.

All of this was practiced at home—we never visited a Buddhist or Confucian temple. So, I found it incredibly strange when my parents told us, one day out of the blue, we would be attending a Presbyterian church with my aunt and uncle. My sister and I were in our young teens, and, somehow, my relatives had convinced my parents that we needed the Savior Christ to steer us onto a righteous path. My aunt and uncle showed up religiously every Sunday morning, beeping the car horn at 8:30 a.m. sharp, and we'd dash out of the house with our Bible in hand. My sister and I went to their church for the next three years; we even became a core part of the church—we taught Bible lessons to

15

the younger children, and we were actively engaged in the youth choir. My two brothers were somehow exempt from Christ's teachings; it was more important for them to practice Taekwon-Do under my father's tutelage on Sunday mornings.

The boys always seem to have it easier than us girls. My father didn't have the same expectations for them as he had for my sister and me. We were expected to be *more*—have higher grades, be accomplished pianists and achieve greater career aspirations (becoming doctors, of course). It's as if my father had given up on the boys and placed all his eggs in the girls' baskets. Our father expected us to strive for something that we could never attain: perfection. In his mind, my sister and I were destined to be "winners" and nothing less would be acceptable. These high expectations came with a price. Not only did it make us super competitive with each other, it also affected our sense of self-worth, which was intertwined with our achievements and accolades. We believed we were only as good as our last test score. My sister and I excelled at everything we did, but we never felt good enough—our father's approval was always out of reach, no matter how hard we tried.

My sister was more accepting of the rules that the church imposed—she accepted everything without question—which wasn't a surprise to me. She behaved the same way at home. I, on the other hand, questioned why things were the way they were. *Was there really a God? How can you prove he's real? Why do we have to have faith? If I accept all of the church's beliefs and teachings, then would I become good enough?*

Religion wasn't the only reason I felt different from my siblings. I was never as "obedient" as them. Although my brothers and sister hated my parents' authoritarian ways, they didn't complain. They were followers who never questioned the status quo. I, on the other hand, found it difficult to hold my tongue when I felt unjustly treated, letting my emotions and feelings slip out at the most inopportune times. It's not that I wasn't afraid of standing up against my father. I was petrified. My siblings were just more so. We were well-trained not to speak our mind (and to be afraid of consequences, if we did); however, there was a rebellious streak in me, even as a kid, and I would sometimes push the boundaries ... and this got me into trouble every single time.

One late February, my sister and I were doing homework on our beds. We were about 9 years old at the time. Mom had called out to us to help her with dinner, and we knew it was mandatory to always respond with a "Yes, Mom" or "Yes, Dad"—anything less was unacceptable. It was an absolute no-no to respond with "What?!" This time, I slipped up. My twin and I were working on a difficult math problem, and I became agitated that we had to stop what we were doing while our brothers carried on with their stupid video game. My sister rolled her eyes as she got off of her bed to head to the kitchen, but instead of following her, I heard myself yell out, "What, Mom? I'm working on my math."

Just as those words came out of my mouth, I stopped myself and regretted it. My sister froze, meeting my eye. We both knew I would be in big trouble if my father had heard. His appearance in my doorway seconds later verified that he had, and he had "the look" on his face. Fear and trepidation overcame me. Nothing could compare to the wrath of our father—we kids were deathly afraid of him.

"What did you say to your mother?" he demanded. My sister's eyes widened with fear. She stood there quietly, trying to fade into the background, her eyes cast downward, away from my father's glaring ones.

"I'm sorry, I didn't mean to answer with *what*," I pleaded. My apology was useless.

"Get off your bed!" he commanded. He grabbed me by the back of my neck and led me to the living room.

My mother came out of the kitchen. "She didn't mean it" she said, quickly coming to my defense. "It's okay, I don't need her help."

My father didn't listen. The moment he opened the front door, I knew what my punishment would be. I was forced to stand out on the lightly snow-covered porch, barefoot and wearing only a cotton t-shirt and pajama shorts.

"Honey, no," my mother pleaded. Although she tried, she knew it was pointless. Once my father decided something, there was no changing his mind.

Leaving me out in the cold, my father swiftly closed the door without even a glance in my direction. I stood there, as the cold, shrill wind whipped against my legs. The only light was from the ominous full moon. I purposely turned my back to the street, praying that no one could see me and ask why a kid was standing out on a cold February night! What *could* I say? Strangely enough, I felt a need to protect my parents and tried to think up excuses that could reasonably explain it. Outsiders wouldn't understand my parents' strict rules. Appearance was everything in Asian culture—we could never lose face or dignity. Somehow rehearsing my excuses helped distract from the coldness I felt. I deserved this punishment; after all, I was the one who disrespected my mother.

The Swinger in the Mirror

After standing outside for what seemed like an eternity (it was probably less than ten minutes), the front door slowly opened and my mother ushered me inside. My father sat in his armchair, looking up from his glasses. He shot my mother a stern and disapproving look for cutting my punishment time short. He then turned his gaze to me. "Have you learned your lesson?"

"I'll never talk back to Mom again," I promised. Before he could say another word, I ran to my room and climbed into bed. I pulled the covers over my face and wept. My sister sat quietly on her bed, not knowing what to say or how to comfort me. I knew she felt guilty for not helping me, but I understood why she didn't.

That incident showed me how different I was from my sister. Even though she was irritated with my mother asking for our help, she kept her thoughts to herself and automatically obeyed. She didn't dare talk back to my parents—ever. She was the pristine, obedient, and color-inside-the-line type of daughter. I, on the other hand, was not my twin's clone. I was *too bold for my own good*, as my mother often scolded me. "Stay obedient and quiet, like your sister," she would remind me. I thought I was a "good daughter"; I guess I wasn't good enough.

Growing up, displays of affection, emotions, and physical touch were frowned upon in my family. I was not allowed to express to my father that I was feeling sad, hurt, disappointed, or angry—showing emotions or feelings was a sign of *weakness*, in his eyes. As kids, we didn't receive much affection from our parents, nor did we offer it to one another. I can't recall my siblings or I ever giving our father a kiss or him embracing us. Our mother was more receptive of giving and receiving affection, although it was still not a frequent occurrence. My siblings and I would agree that any demonstration of affection was awkward, period.

Sadly, I can't remember my father ever saying "I love you" to me or to my siblings. That was my mother's job. I guess, from his perspective, he expressed his love by simply providing the bare necessities of life—food, shelter, and education, in that order. As the head of the household who commanded utmost respect, my father never cared about what we thought; only his opinion mattered. My siblings and I learned to keep things inside. We didn't even grumble to each other—there was no point.

Early on, my siblings and I quickly learned that affection and sex were undesirable behaviors. Sexual innuendos were avoided at all costs. My father would promptly change the television channel if there was a kissing or (heaven forbid!) sex scene. We changed channels even when our parents weren't in the room. We were well trained minions.

When I was around ten years old, my father was driving us kids somewhere. It was rare for us to be alone with him, which added to the awkwardness of the moment. We were on our best behavior, as usual, sitting in silence and with trepidation that we might do something that would upset him and get us the "look" in his rearview mirror. As we were cruising on the highway, Etta James' song "I Just Wanna Make Love to You" came on the radio. OMG! I wanted to crawl outside of my skin. The idea of physically hurling myself out of the moving car would be far less painful than remaining inside! Much to our relief, my father quickly changed the radio channel, ending the horror of that moment as quickly as it began.

As I entered my teens, it got harder to contain my resentment and brewing independent spirit. *It's my life! I can do whatever I want! Why do I need to follow their rules?* To my mother's dismay, I regularly snuck out of the house late at night to meet my secret high school boyfriend, while my sister tried to remind me how much trouble I would get into. I reassured her that I would be back shortly—no one would find out. However, my mother would often wait by the back door and give me the disapproving look as I entered the house. Luckily, my father was snoring away and never found out about my nightly escapades. If he had, I would surely have been disowned.

It wasn't until I was in my mid–30s that I began to realize that this restrictive upbringing had done so much damage to my sense of self; it had taken away my creative spirit, my voice, and my freedom of expression. I would have these recurrent dreams where I was Mariah Carey or Whitney Houston, belting out songs in front of a sold-out crowd. There were also times I would be standing on top of a mountain, trying to scream at the top of my lungs but nothing came out. Then I would wake up from my dream, noticing my fingers grasping at my throat.

I didn't realize how censored and oppressed I had been living under my father's roof. I didn't know who I was, what my opinions were, what I truly cared about or most importantly, what I wanted out of life. All I knew was that I had to follow what my father wanted of me; how I *should* behave, what to think and how to act. I learned to be a *pleaser*. I wasn't allowed to say what I liked or disliked or what I was feeling or thinking, something that inevitably hindered the development of my identity and sexual expression. I didn't understand the basic concept of physical touch or intimacy, let alone my innermost sexual desires as I matured.

19

Maybe that's why I found the Lifestyle so intriguing ... it allowed me to *re*-discover myself.

When it came time for my sister and I to start college, at age 19, my parents expected us to remain at home and commute three hours to and from school. I somehow managed to convince my parents to let us live on campus—what better way to have more time to study and get better grades! I was proud of myself, actually speaking up to my father and pushing for us to live away from home. He conceded on one condition: we would have to pay our own rent. I happily accepted this deal and began searching for a job. I didn't care that balancing work plus studies would be challenging—my freedom was worth it!

I applied for, and got, a position as a part-time nanny for a family with two children in exchange for room and board. My sister found a similar family arrangement, not too far away from me. We were going to be living on our own for the first time in our lives—this was life changing! I was finally able to breathe and discover who I was as a person, separate from just being a "twin" and a "good daughter."

During this period of independence, I learned that I was a risk taker. I discovered I was also determined, resourceful, and strong-willed. I wasn't afraid to do things on my own, which kind of surprised me given my very sheltered life. Having my own place was my first taste of freedom where I could do whatever/whenever I wanted, without seeking my parents' permission or approval. I could go out at night without needing to sneak around or lie about it—what my parents didn't know, wouldn't hurt them!

This feeling of freedom was intoxicating. It also further illuminated how different I was from my family. My close bond with my twin began to weaken. I came to realize that, despite our shared DNA, she and I were essentially two different people with our own interests, striving to find our identities and passions in life. I purposely began to distance myself from my parents, particularly my father—keeping communication to an as-needed basis. I didn't want to tell my mother anything because I knew it would get back to my father, and then he would try to exert his control over me again... I broke free and there was no way I was going back.

This was the beginning of my estrangement from my father; I began to hate him for all the years he made me feel scared, powerless, voiceless, and insecure about my self-worth and being lovable. As my social circle grew, I discovered that most individuals didn't have this experience with their parents. My anger toward my father continued to grow, and I knew I couldn't be around him.

1. Family Ties

It was during this time that I also started to explore my sexual freedom. My sister started dating her first and only boyfriend (now husband), so I ended up going to various social events on my own. It was strange at first, not having my sister by my side. She preferred to stay at home, studying or spending time with her boyfriend. I developed a progressive view about sexuality and marriage and didn't feel the need to hold on to my virginity. Since sex had always been an off-limits and taboo subject in my family, I didn't feel comfortable sharing my sex life with my sister, as close as she was to me. I felt she might judge my promiscuous ways since we were supposed to be *good girls.*

I remember coming home one weekend to visit my mom during my third year of college. She sat me down at the kitchen table to talk while my father was out. My mother and I didn't have heart-to-heart talks, so I immediately felt uneasy.

"Your sister say you go out a lot," my mother said.

I nodded, "Yeah?"

"I think it no good for bee to visit *too many* flowers. You should stay long with one flower only," she advised.

Her hidden meaning was not lost on me. I rolled my eyes.

"Mom, please!"

Despite cringing at my mother's not-so-subtle lecture, I actually felt that she was right about me needing to find one good guy, like my sister had managed to do. Trust me, I wanted that for myself, too. I just wasn't having any luck in my pursuit of finding the *one.* Much to my relief, my mom never brought it up again.

I guess this phase of my life could be viewed as some kind of rebellious dig at my parents. I was breaking free of my parents' expectations and control over me—of them dictating what I could and couldn't do. *You're no longer the boss of me! I can do whatever I want!* A sexual awakening of sorts—one that would fuel my future curiosity of, and appreciation for, the Lifestyle—this taboo world was a breath of fresh air, welcoming me with open arms into their world that didn't judge, oppress, repress, refrain, or inhibit but allowed for open sexual expression that held no shame or consequences. *Where do I sign up?*

But the world of swapping partners, foursomes, and couple getaways was still years away, as I finished undergrad studies and prepared to start graduate school. I was young, single, and eager to explore life.

And then I met Kaleb.

2

Love at Last

* * *

While undergrad was a time of rebellion for me, in graduate school, I became much more focused and serious about life and my future. I didn't want the casual flings and one-night stands any more. If I was going to be in a relationship, then I wanted to find a guy that would be my one and only soul mate. He would be the *only* man I'd be with sexually for life … so I thought.

Kaleb and I first met at graduate school in the mid–1990s, and it was not love at first sight. I cringed at his barely showing moustache; at the time, only older men in their 50s or 60s—like my father—wore a moustache, not some young guy in his twenties. As Shania Twain so delicately put it, "That Don't Impress Me Much." To be fair, Kaleb wasn't too smitten with me either, initially. He thought I was some kind of Asian pubescent prodigy freak on an entrance scholarship; my youthful appearance and Buddy Holly glasses only reinforced this stereotype.

But our graduate class was small—30 in total—so everyone got to know each other quickly. Two weeks into our program, Kaleb and I were assigned to do a group presentation together, and during our breaks, we would have coffee together. And we'd talk, about ourselves, our families, and even our past relationships. I found Kaleb to be genuinely nice, even sensitive in his demeanor. He was different from the other guys I had dated in the past… Kaleb was expressive and able to articulate his feelings. That was refreshing! He started to grow on me … as did his moustache! That feeling was quickly squashed when I found out from a classmate that Kaleb was getting married the following year. His fiancée, Sheila, moved in with him shortly after our program had started.

Over that first year, Kaleb and I often worked together on assignments and became close friends. I began to see a softer side to him, especially when he spoke about his family. I'd be lying if I said I wasn't falling for him, but I kept it to myself. I knew I had to squash this feeling and fast. He was getting married soon. To my surprise, Kaleb started opening up more about his relationship with Sheila; it wasn't all sunshine and rainbows. He shared that they hadn't been getting along, especially after he had decided to move away for graduate school.

"That's why she decided to join me out here, so we could get our relationship back on track," he explained. Most of their fights centered around each other's families and their diverging life goals. Sheila wanted to get a teaching job in their hometown and raise a family there. Kaleb, on the other hand, pictured himself living in the big city and starting up his own business.

"Why are you guys together, if you fight that much?" I asked him.

"Fighting's the norm. That's the way it is with everyone back home. You stay with each other no matter what," he said.

Kaleb mentioned that he started going out with Sheila when they were both 15. They were each other's first sexual experience. He never questioned if she *wasn't* the one, as he had no other relationships to compare it to, good or bad.

That first summer break, Kaleb and Sheila drove back to their hometown, and I flew back to the city; we didn't communicate at all. Two weeks after returning to school, Kaleb suddenly asked me if I wanted to go for a Sunday drive. Since I didn't have a car, I was thrilled to get off campus and quickly accepted his offer.

"Who else is coming?" I asked.

"It's just us," he replied. To my surprise, Kaleb drove to a local spot, known for making out. I wasn't sure why we had stopped there, but I didn't ask. He parked and we sat in silence, looking straight ahead at the view of the town below. It was a cloudy grey day, but you could still make out the outline of the university chapel in the far distance. Kaleb was acting out of sorts, making me feel nervous. *Why were we alone and why did he bring me here?* Def Leppard's "Pour Some Sugar on Me" rang out softly over the car stereo.

"It looks like it's going to rain soon," I said, trying to end the awkward silence. Then, on cue, gentle pitter patter of rain began to fall on the windshield. Kaleb suddenly turned his body towards me. "It's over between me and Sheila. I broke it off two months ago."

I didn't know what to say, other than, "Oh. I'm sorry."

"It's okay. We weren't right for each other." We remained silent.

Then he reached for my hand. "*You* made me realize that I needed more."

I looked into his eyes.

"I really like you," he said.

I wanted to tell him that I felt the same way, but the words wouldn't come out. Endless questions ran through my head. How could his feelings for Sheila suddenly stop, after eleven years of being together? How could he not love her? Would he want her back? My mouth was dry, and my heart was beating fast. I was scared. Although I had feelings for Kaleb, I didn't want to get hurt.

"Did you hear what I just said?" Kaleb asked.

"Yes, but how do you know you made the right decision?"

"I know I did."

"But *how* do you know?" I pressed.

"Because... I think I'm falling in love with you."

I went quiet. Kaleb pulled me in close. We looked into each other's eyes and I allowed him to kiss me.

I whispered in his ear as he held me tight, "I *think* I'm falling for you, too." I didn't want to say the "L" word, just in case he changed his mind.

We kissed all that afternoon, while Def Leppard played "I Wanna Touch You" on repeat. For once in my life, I wasn't looking for love—it finally found *me*. I wanted to trust him, something I had always found difficult in past relationships. Being with him was easy and uncomplicated; it flowed. Kaleb made me feel safe and secure. At that moment, I knew I had found my soul mate.

In terms of sexual experience, Kaleb and I were worlds apart. I had already been in several two-year plus relationships and had had my fair share of sexual encounters (more than I would care to admit). Kaleb's sexual experience had been linked only to one person.

"How many guys were you with before me?" Kaleb asked, about a month or so into our relationship.

"Dating or sexually?" I asked.

"Sexually."

"Why do you want to know?" I asked, feeling uneasy.

"Just curious."

Although I was afraid that Kaleb might judge me, I told him the truth.

"Wow! You definitely had more than me!" he said.

"Are you bothered by this?"

"Honestly, no. I sort of like that you're experienced. Now you can use your expertise on me," he teased.

He was being good natured about it, but I had genuine concerns.

2. Love at Last

Would Kaleb feel like he was missing out on not having more sexual experiences? He hadn't explored what it felt like to be with more than one partner. That stuck in the back of my mind.

Although we were a new couple, Kaleb and I were extremely comfortable with each other, sharing our deepest and most intimate desires openly. It was effortless, like we could read each other's mind, and everything fell into place, almost too perfectly. We seemed to get each other. We spent countless hours talking about everything—our past, our future career aspirations and goals, and even where we envisioned living once we finished school. I shared things with Kaleb that I had never shared with anyone else. I told him about my dysfunctional family and how my estranged relationship with my father had negatively affected my trust in people, particularly with men.

Kaleb, on the other hand, born and raised in a small, rural town, was extremely close with his parents and his siblings. Although his family didn't display a lot of affection or talk about their feelings, they had a lot of unconditional love for one another. Having said that, they also had no qualms about telling each other how pissed off they felt or if they disagreed with your opinion. Conversations around the dinner table were often boisterous and loud, with everyone trying to speak over each other. You had to shout to be heard, and interruptions were the norm. By contrast, my family ate dinner in complete silence, and no one dared to ask for permission to leave the table before my father finished his meal, not even to go to the bathroom!

I recall the first time I met Kaleb's family, about six months into our relationship. I felt extremely anxious whenever Kaleb and his sisters argued about some matter, trivial in my opinion; however, it ended as soon as it started and laughter would soon follow. It's almost as if they had amnesia and forgot what was said just seconds earlier. These people were light years away from what my family was like—this was refreshing (and yet uncomfortable) to me. No one in his family seemed to get mad or hold a grudge; they just said what they needed to say. Then it was all forgotten and they moved on. So, let me get this straight; you tell someone your opinion/thoughts and even if they disagree with you, you're *not* punished or threatened to be kicked out of the family. Interesting.

We didn't just talk, either. Kaleb and I couldn't keep our hands off each other, having sex every day, sometimes twice a day. And while I was happy, I did notice that our sex life was pretty vanilla, compared to my past relationships. Kaleb and I engaged in foreplay beforehand and then missionary style was our go-to-position. There was no sex talk;

come to think of it, we didn't talk much during sex. My past lovers were more overt in their sexual prowess and eager to introduce me to alternative sexual activities such as light bondage, restraints, and blindfolds, which I admittedly enjoyed. This was the one thing I didn't feel comfortable enough to share with Kaleb just yet. So, we continued with our predictable but pleasant sexual practices. The thought of having sex with someone else wasn't a consideration for either of us at that time.

Although Kaleb and I came from two different worlds—so much so that you wouldn't think we would get along—it worked for us. We even talked about how we would raise our kids, given our own childhoods. Kaleb's permissive upbringing in a Presbyterian household contrasted with my authoritarian and restrictive childhood interlaced with Confucius/Buddhist teachings. We both agreed that neither side was right when it came to raising children. We needed a middle ground to incorporate the best of both worlds into our parenting style. Since this conversation of having kids one day also happened, it was assumed we would get married. Kaleb never thought it was necessary to officially get down on one knee and propose to me in some romantic way. One afternoon, about a year after we'd started going out, we went to a local jeweler and picked out a modest ring on a graduate student's budget and set a date. That was that; we were engaged. I knew that Kaleb was the one for me.

After being engaged for six months, we began sharing more about what turned us on and talked about bringing more sexual excitement into the bedroom. I suggested trying different sexual positions and experimenting with restraints, blindfolds, masturbation, and sex toys. Kaleb was initially taken aback by my kinky side, but he soon embraced my sexual curiosity with intrigue. Then we began to open up more about each other's sexual fantasies, of having sex with someone else or having a threesome.

"How would you feel about having another woman join us?" I asked him one night. This was the first time I voiced my curiosity about being with another woman, and I was worried about his reaction.

"For me?" he asked.

"No, for the both of us," I replied.

"That would be a huge turn on," he said, not flinching at all.

"Really?"

"Yeah, that would be something I'd be okay with. Now, what about a guy joining us? Strictly for you that is. I'd love to watch him bang you," Kaleb said.

"I'd be down with that, too."

Strangely enough, neither of us felt any remote sense of jealousy about the possibility of the other being with someone else.

The frank and open conversations I had with Kaleb about our sex life would horrify my family. It took me many years before I felt comfortable enough to share the truth to my sister about our unconventional lifestyle.

"I have something to tell you," I confided one afternoon while visiting her. At this point, Kaleb and I had been married 17 years. "Kaleb and I have sex with other people."

"What do you mean?" she asked incredulously.

"I like to have sex with other men."

"And Kaleb is okay with this? And you're okay with him having sex with other women?"

"We are both okay with this. We enjoy watching each other with other people."

My sister was speechless. Her reaction was as I'd expected—she was naturally perplexed and concerned with my aberrant Lifestyle choice. This was so far removed from what she expected of me, her twin. To her, I'd deviated from our austere upbringing, having been groomed to be reserved, disciplined, proper, and respectable in the way we carried ourselves; we avoided inappropriate behavior or attention of any kind.

My sister and I had both shared similar experiences until our late teens, but the way that we reconciled our childhoods has been vastly different. It's not my place to share her story. I'll only say that I believe I needed as much distance as possible from my childhood home.

Privately, I began to project my bedroom fantasies out into real life situations. When I went to the grocery store, I began sizing up the men and women there. Could that cute guy in the produce section make me orgasm? I would scan the check-out line to see which attractive woman would most likely be interested in a threesome. There would be the occasional quick, flirtatious longer-than-a-two-second glance at a guy to see if he might respond back. One of three things happened: reciprocated interest, indifference, or bewilderment. I couldn't stop thinking about how it would feel to have different sexual partners; however, I didn't know if this would ever become reality. *Did we have the balls to go through with this, beyond our fantasy role-playing in the bedroom?*

After a year of being engaged, Kaleb was offered a new job and we moved to a small town, up north. We didn't have any family or much of a social network, so we were eager to make new friends. Kaleb became good friends with his co-worker, Kenneth, who was also from the East Coast, so they bonded quickly. Kenneth and his wife, Sandy, had arrived a month prior to us, and they hadn't had a chance to meet many new people. We were all around the same age, in our late twenties. Kenneth was tall and athletic in build, similar to Kaleb. He had ice blue eyes that stood out against his dark brown hair. Sandy was also attractive, with her petite slender frame and strawberry blond mid-length hair. We began hanging out with them every weekend. The four of us always had great banter with each other, and when the booze was flowing, there was plenty of sexual innuendo being thrown around. *Were Kenneth and Sandy interested in a foursome?* I couldn't tell if it was innocent flirting or something more.

I was hesitant to mention my dirty thoughts to Kaleb—I didn't know how he would react to my suggestion of hooking up with his co-worker. So, I stayed quiet, but my curiosity and attraction to both Kenneth and Sandy didn't diminish over time ... just the opposite. I recall one night after the company Christmas party had ended, Kenneth asking if they could crash at our place.

"It's late, and I don't want to drive all the way home," he said. They only lived fifteen minutes away. *Was this Kenneth making a move?*

"Sure, no problem," Kaleb replied. "I'm tired and heading to bed."

"Yeah, it's pretty late," Kenneth replied. Even if he was thinking of doing something, Kaleb just kiboshed it.

Disappointed, I followed Kaleb into the bedroom and shut the door. Kenneth and Sandy slept on the living room futon and left early the next morning. I'll never know if something more could have happened if Kaleb hadn't ended the night prematurely.

Several months later, I decided to share my indecent proposal to Kaleb.

"How would you feel about having a foursome?" I whispered into his ear. Kaleb's eyes and brows widened with anticipation.

"Sure, but who with?" he asked.

"What about Kenneth and Sandy?"

"No. That'd be weird!" he exclaimed.

Although I understood how Kaleb felt about crossing the line with Kenneth, I'd be lying if I said that I wasn't disappointed. This was a dead issue. They weren't biting, and there was no way Kaleb felt comfortable engaging with them. It would be another year or so before this foursome idea would come up again.

3

Four-Year Itch

Kaleb and I had a special relationship right from the start. Not only have I been married to my best friend for more than 20 years (at the time of writing this book), but we've also been business partners for just as long. We have friends who are perplexed and irritated that Kaleb and I could stand to be around each other 24/7, but I think our relationship has essentially worked because we genuinely enjoy each other's company—it's as simple as that. We share similar values and goals, as well as a mutual respect for each other. We understand the importance of allowing each other to be our own person, to grow in the way we need to, without feeling that our partner is holding us back. Neither of us want to feel stifled by our partner or have our activities or interests censored in any way. For example, if I wanted to go on a girls' weekend, I didn't have to ask Kaleb for permission. Likewise, I never told Kaleb what to do and how he should spend his time. We allowed each other the courtesy and reciprocated respect to truly be our own person and pursue interests that served us best, without making the other person feel guilty about it. This mutual respect to allow each other to express ourselves in the most authentic way, complemented the Lifestyle philosophy and set the stage for us to enter it organically. We didn't want to be that couple that harbored resentment or jealousy towards our partner because they were naturally attracted and curious about what it would be like to flirt with the other sex.

Our primary focus on autonomy and trust has been the key element of our marriage and has allowed us to navigate in the Lifestyle. I never doubted Kaleb's unconditional love for me—something that was so important to me, given my precarious relationship with my father. There was such a tremendous comfort in knowing that I was the love of Kaleb's life and he was mine. We were committed to each other, through good times and in bad. We weren't getting into the Lifestyle to find new life partners—we wanted to enjoy the sexual freedom and adventure as a married couple.

The Swinger in the Mirror

After a year and a half of being engaged, Kaleb and I got married on June 20, 1998, at the university chapel, with only our immediate family and some of our professors and classmates in attendance. My mother, who was a seamstress, made my wedding dress, which was a copycat version of Carolyn Bessette's dress when she married John F. Kennedy, Jr. I wore a long, sleek off-white silk sheath dress with a plunging back. I never wanted the big wedding that young girls supposedly dreamed of, with the poofy white taffeta dress and 10 bridesmaids in matching ensemble. Our wedding was perfect—an intimate gathering of 50 guests, which was exactly how we wanted it.

In 1999, Kaleb and I launched our new business venture while I was eight months pregnant. Timing was not the best. We were stressed out—a new baby on the way, no job security whatsoever, and all of our credit cards maxed out.

As Kaleb and I worked tirelessly to give this new business a fighting chance, there was no time left for *us*. Everything was devoted to our new babies: our son and our new company. My relationship with Kaleb was at the bottom of my priorities, left to fend for itself. It was difficult for me to see anything romantic about Kaleb or our relationship. My exhausted eyes only saw him as a business partner, a father, and a roommate, and in that order. Any talk of bringing our sexual fantasies to fruition were put on pause.

I don't recall much of a sex life over that first year and a half of starting the business, so it came as a huge surprise when we found out that we were pregnant with our second child. If it wasn't busy enough, it got even more so, raising two kids while struggling to keep our company afloat. I honestly don't know how we even had time to conceive! Between my desk computer and the fax machine? It didn't take long for all of these stressors to start wreaking havoc on our marriage; we were barely catching our breath, let alone keeping our heads above water.

Before the business and the kids, Kaleb and I always had a rock-solid relationship. I would even be bold enough to say it was unshakeable. We understood each other and never bickered over anything. Now, post-business start-up and two kids later, we were getting on each other nerves, every day. When we fought, we were less than kind or patient with one another. Being a Taurus, I would not give in, and I went to bed annoyed and fed up with his ways. Kaleb was equally as stubborn, and we would stay mad for upwards of a week, only acknowledging one another to address business matters.

Somehow, we managed to weather these first few years and not give up on our marriage. Deep down inside, I knew Kaleb loved me and I loved him; we would get through this together, no matter what. This was non-negotiable in my mind. I didn't want to end up like my mother who came to resent my father after years of living with his stubborn, unyielding, and overbearing ways. We were different from my parents; Kaleb and I knew how to communicate ... or so we thought.

Three years later, in 2002, we seemed to have settled into a new groove with the business and raising two toddlers. The company was slowly gaining momentum, and the kids were becoming less dependent on us. Now in our early 30s, Kaleb and I became your typical young suburban family. This might come as a shock, but we were regular churchgoers and got involved with pastoral duties. Kaleb volunteered as a Sunday school teacher for high school students and I taught the primary classes, just as I had done in my early teens at my uncle and aunt's church. For someone who questioned the existence of God back then, I certainly had come full circle, returning to church life once again. Kaleb and I had a set routine and priorities that we didn't deviate from: work, kids, and church.

Although it was comforting to have everything in its place, I was starting to feel unsettled inside, and I didn't know why. I had everything that I had ever wanted—an established career and the millionaire family—but, somehow, I still wasn't happy. I felt like a robot, going through the same drill, day in and day out. I woke up at 5:00 a.m. every day to tend to my to-do list and tried to go to bed by 10:00 p.m., only to wake up and do it all over again the next day. *Is this as good as it gets?* What happened to our life, the one that was carefree, fun, and spontaneous?

At this point in our relationship, Kaleb and I had been married for four years, and we were mostly coasting on cruise control. Although there have been times over the years when we felt disconnected from each other, this time was different—I felt scared that we wouldn't be as happy as we once were. We were still sexually attracted to each other, but I found myself slowly detaching from him, emotionally. When it came to the business and the kids, we were an awesome tag team, an A+ on our report card. We could read each other's minds and go right into an "action plan," communicating about how we should tackle the day's agenda. When it came to communicating about our relationship, however, we got a D-. We forgot to check in with each other to see if we were okay. It was a stressful time in our marriage, which led to more fighting over the tiniest and stupidest things. We'd nitpick about what the other person needed to do, or forgot to do, simply lashing out when the frustration bubbled over. This wasn't supposed to be us, but we didn't do anything to make it better for the longest time. It was easier to not talk about it and keep motoring ahead. Don't think or feel, just do. Eventually, though, I had to speak up.

"I don't feel good about us. We're always fighting," I said, one evening, in bed, trying to hold back tears.

It was reassuring when Kaleb turned towards me and embraced me tightly.

"I know. I feel the same way," he said.

"How do we make things better?" I asked.

"Let's get away, the two of us. Maybe a trip down south would help."

I nodded. We had to work on us and put mommy/daddy/business duties on hold. I was worried. If we didn't figure *us* out, I knew we would be in serious trouble. I missed Kaleb. I missed the old me—the one that was spontaneous, fun, and carefree. Where did she disappear to? But, more importantly, would she ever return?

So, we booked a last-minute, five-day trip to the Dominican Republic. We left the kids with my parents, and I told my staff that I was inaccessible for the week. I couldn't wait to board the plane and have a moment of freedom. No kids, no work, no responsibilities ... only the two of us.

We spent our days on the beach, drinking whatever and whenever we wanted. This was exactly what we needed to unwind. Nothing to pull away our attention, other than being in the moment together. We didn't have deadlines to worry about, emails or voicemails to check, or a never-ending to-do list to distract us. We pinky swore that we wouldn't talk about work or the kids. It felt good lying in Kaleb's arms on our stretched-out beach towel, gazing at the cloudless sky and watching the waves gently crawling to shore. We'd stare into each other's eyes and playfully kiss ... over and over again. That was nice. I missed him looking at me in that loving and desirable way. I couldn't get enough.

"Promise me, you'll always look at me like that, even when we're home," I said.

We vowed to make our relationship a priority and keep the chemistry between us alive. Often times, couples believe *loving their partner* is the same thing as *being in love* with them. I often hear people say they love their partner because they have been there from the start; they love their partner because they go way back and have history together. Maybe this description is how the majority of people define love, based on a sense of comfort and familiarity they share. There's nothing wrong with this. But for me, I don't only want to say I love Kaleb because I'm comfortable being with him; I want to say I'm *in love* with him. I want to feel passion in our love. And this trip helped me to see that Kaleb and I still had the spark—we were still *in love*.

Although our love and passion hadn't disappeared, it was buried by everyday life stressors. When we returned from our trip, sadly it didn't take long for us to slip back into our old ways, week by week. Work, kids, church ... and then repeat. One day, I decided that I would change things up.

I greeted him at the door with a long lingering French kiss, reminding him of how it was on our trip, just a month ago.

Kaleb grinned. "I think we need to put the kids to bed early tonight," he murmured.

Exactly at 9:00 p.m., we locked the bedroom door in case the kids suddenly decided to barge in. Earlier that afternoon, I went through my bottom drawer and pulled out a lacy black bra and matching thong panties that I had bought a few years ago. The outfit still had the tags attached. I was in the mood to tease and seduce tonight. I went into our bathroom and changed into my sex outfit, complete with fishnet stockings and black stiletto heels. This should get Kaleb's attention. I was excited to see his reaction... I wanted him to *desire* me, like a sexy hot babe he'd picked up at a bar.

"Take off your clothes and lie on the bed," I instructed from the bathroom. "I have a surprise for you."

"I like surprises," he replied, playfully.

As I peered out from the bathroom door, I could see Kaleb lying naked on the bed, with his eyes closed, stroking himself in anticipation.

"Are you ready?" I asked.

"I'm *so* ready!"

I slowly strutted out into full view.

"Wow! Babe, you look amazing!" he exclaimed.

"You like?" I teased.

"How can I not love that?"

Encouraged by his energy, I took out a black blindfold from the top drawer of Kaleb's nightstand. I had found it the other week when I was searching for batteries for one of the kids' toys—it had been left there from years ago, forgotten and hidden away by knick-knacks stuffed into this drawer.

I wanted to take control of the moment and have Kaleb's undivided attention. I was going to seductively tease him as long as I could, taking pleasure in knowing that he was dying to take off my lingerie and get some action ... but I wouldn't allow him to. I was going to make him wait and beg for it.

I climbed on top and straddled him, placing the blindfold gently over his eyes. I began to run my fingers lightly across his chest hair, pausing to kiss him and gently bite his lower lip. Kaleb let out a needy moan. I continued to move down his chest with my lips, alternating between a swirling wet lick and a gentle bite of his nipple. Kaleb reached out to grab any part of me, but I gently placed his hands back down by his side.

"I'm in charge," I said. I continued to kiss his stomach, licking and kissing my way down to his inner thighs. His body twitched. Working in tandem with each stroke, I used my tongue to gently swirl around his shaft, licking it slowly up and down and between my fingers. Kaleb let out a moan and, once again, reached out to touch my body—this time with success. His hands followed the curve of my hips down to my fishnet stocking covering my buttocks and thighs. I could tell Kaleb couldn't wait any longer, and he whipped off his blindfold. He pulled me in to him.

"Tell me what you want," Kaleb whispered.

"I want to watch you with another woman," I said. I could feel myself close to climaxing, but I held back to keep this moment going.

"Tell me what I'm doing to her?" he asked.

"You're taking her from behind, fucking her hard."

"And what are you doing?"

"Playing with myself."

"Then what?"

Before I could answer, I felt myself climax and I cried out. Kaleb followed my lead. My body relaxed, and I laid on top of his chest, trying to catch my breath.

"That was amazing!" I whispered. Kaleb nodded and smiled.

"Why don't we do this more often when it feels this good?" I asked.

"I honestly don't know."

"Babe, I don't want us to be that couple who coasts through marriage. I want to feel *alive* when I'm with you."

"What do you suggest we do?" he asked.

"I might have an idea," I said with a devilish grin.

Enough with just daydreaming—I was ready to make our foursome fantasies a reality. Would Kaleb be on board, too?

4

Weekend Get-Away

Five years into our marriage, threesome/foursome imagery had become a regular part of our foreplay. Kaleb and I would take turns describing a MFM (male-female-male) or FMF scene or a foursome, and the fantasy certainly enhanced our sex life. Now, I wanted to move from fantasy to reality. Upon reflecting, our fantasies might have opened Pandora's box—Kaleb and I were navigating through uncharted territory. Like the saying goes: "be careful what you wish for." We had no clue what was in store for us; we thought the hardest part of the Lifestyle was going to be finding an attractive couple to engage with. Boy, were we ever naive!

"Let's go to Georgetown this weekend," Kaleb suggested one afternoon.

"Why?" I asked. Georgetown was about three hours away—far enough that it wasn't a regular occurrence but close enough that we'd sometimes venture into the city when we wanted a bit of an adventure. I was curious what Kaleb had in mind.

"What if we went to a sex club?" he said.

"Huh?" I said. I was caught off guard. I knew that we would eventually explore this hedonistic world at some point, but attributing a specific weekend to it made it more real. It was all talk up until now. It's one thing to talk about fantasies, it's another to enact them.

"Are you having second thoughts about being with other people?" Kaleb asked.

"No, it's not that. I am excited, but I'm also feeling a bit anxious."

"Anxious?"

"Well … what if we bump into someone we know?" I asked. Sure, the chances weren't high, given how far away Georgetown was … but the thought of seeing someone there we knew made my stomach clench.

"We don't have to go if you feel uncomfortable. We can do other things in the city. I just want to spend time with you," Kaleb said reassuringly.

"No, I *am* curious to know more about the club scene. I guess I'm afraid that playing with another person or couple might change things between us ... and that scares me," I admitted.

Kaleb reached out and embraced me. "Babe, nothing will ever change our relationship. This LS stuff is purely for fun and nothing more."

His words reassured me.

"I think we should go. I'll call the babysitter," I said.

The day before we were to leave, I still had some reservations about what would happen.

"I'm not ready to have sex with another couple, if that's what you're hoping for," I blurted out to Kaleb, the morning before we were to leave.

He smiled at me. "I have no expectations. Let's just check it out and see how it goes."

"Okay."

We got on the road after lunch. In the car ride, I was quiet and deep in thought. Despite Kaleb's reassurance of this trip being chill and adult time away, my anxiety level was going through the roof; I had no idea what to expect. All we knew was that these clubs were underground (this was back in 2003...LS clubs became legalized in our state in 2005). Anxiety aside, I did find the illegal aspect appealing—there was an element of danger, which was a huge turn on.

Since it was our first weekend away from the kids in a long time, we decided to splurge on a swankier downtown hotel. We checked into the Four Seasons Hotel and upgraded to their one-bedroom suite, in case we had unexpected "visitors."

"When do you think we should head to the club?" I shouted out to Kaleb from the bathroom.

"I don't want to get there too early," Kaleb replied.

"10:00 p.m.?" I suggested.

"Okay, but let's grab a bite first. I'm starving!"

We headed down to the hotel restaurant, but I didn't have much of an appetite. I felt too nervous. After dinner, we went back up to the room. I had no clue how to dress for a sex club. When you're planning on hooking up with a couple, do you aim for the sexy vixen or a more casual look? I grabbed a black deep V-neck top and a pair of dark blue jeans from the closet.

"You're changing again?" Kaleb asked.

"I can't wear what I had on at dinner!"

"Why not?"

"It's not *sexy* enough," I replied, stepping out of the bathroom, modeling my new choice of attire. "What do you think? Too low-cut?"

"No, not at all. You look great!" he replied.

I was going for a casual but sexy look. Kaleb kept on his long sleeve patterned shirt and a pair of black slacks that he had on at dinner.

"How do we ever find this underground club?" I asked.

"I don't know. Maybe we can ask our driver."

We left our hotel room promptly at 10:00 p.m. and hopped into a waiting cab.

"Do you know of any swingers' clubs nearby?" Kaleb asked. He wasn't even embarrassed in the slightest. I, on the other hand, turned towards the window, trying to hide my face.

But the cab driver didn't even bat an eyelash. He must be used to hearing this question from out-of-town visitors. "I've heard of a place but it's illegal... The Peacock Club."

"Do you want to go there?" Kaleb asked me.

Looking to him for reassurance, Kaleb squeezed my hand.

"Umm ... sure, okay," I replied.

We didn't know the layout of the city that well, so we had no clue where he was taking us. He drove 30 minutes outside of the downtown core. Kaleb held my hand, occasionally squeezing it as to say, "Don't worry, I've got you." We eventually ended up at an industrial park area. The street was dimly lit, and the cab stopped in front of a reddish brick building, which stood out against the factory buildings and heavy equipment machines parked on the fringes. The building had no signage and was only showcased by a black heavy double steel door. Two burly guys were standing out front, having a smoke. Were they bouncers or patrons? I stepped out of the cab tentatively. *Where had this driver taken us?*

"Maybe we made a mistake coming here," I whispered to Kaleb. What if these guys jumped Kaleb and dragged me off somewhere? What if this club was really a human trafficking ring? Inside my head, a narrative played out of me getting drugged and then waking up in some locked room to work as a sex slave! *What would my sister say if she knew I was here?* Kaleb, of course, appeared cool and collected, even eager in his demeanor. If he had any concerns or fears, it didn't show.

"Let's go inside and check it out. I'm sure it's all good," he said, as he grasped my hand and led me through the large door. We were greeted by a lady at the front booth.

"Entrance fee is $50 per couple," she said dryly. There was no pleasantry or small talk, simply a transactional exchange.

Kaleb handed her a credit card. The lady pointed at the *CASH ONLY* sign. I guess they didn't want any paper trail. Kaleb handed her a $50 bill, and she proceeded to place neon orange bands on our wrists. This reminded me of being at an amusement park and feeling the thrill and exhilaration of going on my favorite "ride."

A burly man in his late 50s, dressed in a cheap polyester brown suit and tie, suddenly emerged from the back room, as if on cue. He greeted us with a big smile, probably eager to recruit new members.

"You're not an undercover cop, are you?" he asked in a half joking, half serious tone. Kaleb and I looked at each other.

"Ah…" Kaleb stammered.

"Just kidding … but you can never be too sure," he chuckled. "This is your first time, right?"

"Yeah, we're visiting from out of town," Kaleb replied.

"Do you want a tour? We're offering a discount membership to new couples," he said.

"Sure, why not?" Kaleb said.

The club had supposedly undergone recent renovations. He led us up to the second floor, usually *reserved for members only*. I talked myself into thinking I was on an investigative assignment, doing a feature story on the city's underground sex scene, to offset the awkward feeling of being there.

Once upstairs, Kaleb and I looked around with wonderment. I couldn't believe we were actually here … not as observers but as participants. We had stepped into the *other world*. This was not like any ordinary club. At the top of the stairs, we were greeted by a much friendlier hostess, a blonde attractive woman in her mid-twenties. Her DD cup size breasts spilled out of her tight white tank top, and her long legs were accentuated by her micro black miniskirt and stiletto heels.

"Hello, welcome!" she said. She gave the manager a wink and smile. "Andre must be giving you the tour."

"You can store your belongings and valuables in here before you head into the play room," the manager said, pointing to the half lockers, adjacent to the reception desk. *Play room?* I thought.

"We supply everything you need … at no charge." A stack of neatly folded white towels lined the cubby-hole, and a large plastic bowl of condoms and lubrication sat on the reception desk. It appeared that we were the only ones up here, as it was still too early for the regulars. There was soft mood lighting and jazz music playing in the background. I'm not sure what I expected to see, but everything looked so pristine, tidy, and organized, like an upscale spa. The manager then showed us the private rooms and pointed to the communal shower, large enough to fit up to 10 people, he boasted.

"You could have an orgy in that shower!" I laughed.

"Let me show you the best spot!" the manager said. He led us down the hall into a spacious room that had eight queen-sized beds, four of which were placed side-by-side with a three-foot aisle separating the other four beds across from them. Beds were made up with white crisp sheets but no pillows. Mirrors lined the entire four walls and ceiling, which reminded me of a fight scene out of Bruce Lee's *Enter the Dragon* movie. You could watch yourself and others from all angles!

"Now this is where things could get real freaky!" the manager said with a smirk. "I've seen up to 20 couples in this room at one time." Kaleb and I shot each other a look of bewilderment.

We then headed to another room at the back. I noticed a white 6' × 4' × 6' booth, big enough for one person, in the corner.

"What's that?" I asked inquisitively. As I walked closer to inspect this odd contraption, I noticed a door into this booth. There were also four small cut-out holes (each 4" in diameter), two to the left of the door and two to the right, spaced two feet apart from one another., and about three feet off the ground. I opened the door and stuck my head inside. I turned back and gave Kaleb a puzzled look.

He grinned. "You don't know what that is, do you?"

"No, what is it for?" I asked.

"It's a *glory hole*."

"Huh? What's that?" I asked.

The manager jumped in and explained that a male or female could enter the booth and wait for the guy(s) to position in front of a hole, sticking their penis inside of it. Then the person standing on the inside of the booth would perform oral sex on the recipient on the other side. The fascinating part about this was that the guys on the outside had no clue of the gender of the person performing the act on them—I guess most didn't mind either way.

I found it all kinky, yet fascinating at the same time. Here we were, inside an illegal sex club, taking in everything this manager was telling us. This place was inviting us with open arms to explore the hedonistic side of our sexual desires, which were mere thoughts a week ago. Now, here was our chance to act out everything we had ever fantasized about. But were we ready? The jury was still out...

After the 20-minute tour, the manager walked us back down to the main bar area and dance floor. It was after 11:00 p.m. but still not much of a crowd. I guess this was early by club standards. Several couples gathered around the bar, chatting with each other. They looked like your average run-of-the-mill type people, not how I had imagined swingers to be. They seemed *normal*. They could have been your neighbors, friends, co-workers … even fellow parishioners in church. Dressed casually in street clothes, they chatted as if they were at a pub on a Friday night.

The music was cranked up, pumping a rhythmic bass throughout the club. Kaleb and I stood at the end of the bar, trying to get the bartender's attention, but no luck. The bartender ignored us. Out of the corner of my eye, I noticed an older couple, in their late 50s, looking our way. The older gentleman smiled and winked. I looked back to see if he was trying to get someone's attention. No one was behind us. Wait a minute! Was he sending *me* a signal?

"Kaleb, that guy just winked at me," I whispered and discretely directed my eyes to the couple at the three o'clock position.

"Maybe they want to hook up with us," Kaleb chuckled.

I fidgeted with my fingers. Could they see right through us that we were newbies and didn't have a clue what we were doing?

"What should we do?"

Kaleb gently squeezed my hand. "Nothing."

To my relief, the manager walked up to us at that moment.

"Sorry, Fridays are slow. Here's a card to come back tomorrow for free!" he said.

"Yeah, maybe," I said.

"Hey, I can't seem to get the bartender's attention for a drink," Kaleb complained to the manager.

"We're not licensed to *sell* drinks."

"Huh?" Kaleb replied.

"You have to go down the street to the convenience store to buy your booze. The bartender will write your number on your wrist band to keep track of your stuff in the fridge," the manager explained.

"Will you be okay by yourself if I go get a bottle of wine?" I didn't want Kaleb to leave my side, but I desperately needed a drink.

"I'll be fine," I reassured him. Kaleb gave me a kiss on the lips before he left. I took a seat at the bar, trying not to look terribly uncomfortable. My heart was beating faster and my face was flushed … and I hadn't had anything to drink yet. Could people sense my self-consciousness? Ten minutes passed and Kaleb was still not back. I was just getting ready to escape to the bathroom to hide out when he walked in with a brown paper bag and handed it to the bartender.

"Cheers!" I said, taking a big gulp, once my drink was handed to me. *Look cool! Stay calm!* I repeated my mantra in my head.

As the night progressed, a few more couples trickled into the main bar area. There were only a handful of younger couples in their 30s, like us—most were middle-aged or older white couples in their 50s and 60s. It didn't help that these couples reminded me a bit of Kaleb's parents. Yikes! None of the younger couples caught my eye either. Kaleb and I hadn't talked about our own expectations for the night. I was happy to be there to observe and take everything in. I didn't know if Kaleb felt the same. Was he was hoping to get some action? I'm not saying that I wasn't intrigued and aroused at the thought of being approached by an attractive couple. I didn't know how things would unfold, which made me feel uneasy. Who's supposed to do what and when?

My inner monologue was interrupted by an interesting connection unfolding nearby. Couple A was making moves on Couple B. (It appeared the women started things off.) Couple A woman leaned over to strike up a conversation with Couple B woman. Then, they invited their male partners to join in on the conversation. Flirtatious smiles, laughing, and clinking of wine glasses followed. Bingo! A mating match was secured between Couple A and Couple B. Then the four of them made their way upstairs, walking beside their new partner. So, this is how it was done! Seemed pretty straightforward. Note to self: approach the female partner first to initiate a conversation. Then the guys will follow the ladies' lead.

Kaleb and I found a table and continued to people watch as we sipped on our glasses of wine. We tried to act casual, like we've done this a million times before. Maybe our reserved behavior came off as stand-offish. Or our quiet demeanor gave off newbie energy ... whatever it was, no one approached us.

Looking back now as an experienced swinger, I could see how green we must have looked to these people. They could spot us a mile away! When Kaleb and I started our LS journey, we had no clue what the Life-style was all about. Knowing what we know now, we generally stay away from newbies or couples who aren't married or in a long-term relationship—in my opinion, they don't know each other well enough to navigate properly in the Lifestyle. These couples haven't acquired the years of experience to feel secure enough in their own relationship. Put another way, they haven't worked through their shit yet and this potentially could lead to *drama*. Kaleb and I are in this for the fun, not to teach these couples about their relationship and what *not* to do when it comes to swapping.

After another half hour or so of sitting and drinking, I noticed an attractive couple in their mid-thirties approaching us. I hadn't noticed them before. The man introduced himself and asked if he and his wife could join us. Wait a minute! Wasn't the woman supposed to take the lead? This must be a new approach.

Kaleb replied, "Sure."

While he went to call on his wife, I quickly whispered to Kaleb, "What if they expect us to have sex?" Kaleb didn't have a chance to reply before they sat down at our table.

We all smiled timidly. To calm my nerves, I told myself there was nothing to worry about. They seemed like a nice couple, newbies just like us. The wife was quiet, often deferring to her husband to do most of the talking. I started firing off questions, as if this couple was applying for a job. I thought I should know everything about them, if they were going to get inside our pants.

"What do you do for work? Where do you live? How long have you been married? What do you do for fun outside of the Lifestyle? How many kids do you have and what are their ages? How long have you been in the Lifestyle and what brought you guys into it?"

The wife smiled meekly, looking uneasy with this Spanish Inquisition. Did she even want to be here? Or did her husband persuade her to do this? That thought did cross my mind. The husband told us that he was an engineer and his wife was a stay-at-home mother to their two young children.

"My father is an engineer, too," I said, as if this commonality would bond us in some way. I felt uneasy, and it probably showed. It didn't help seeing Kaleb relaxed, occasionally nodding and smiling, leaving me to handle the interview.

This couple looked like they were your typical suburban family with young kids, no different than us. It's funny how you mentally picture what swingers might look like—hardcore sex fiends with leather, chains, piercings, and tattoos. But they live amongst us, with regular jobs, families, and vanilla friends—projecting ordinary lives on the surface.

As the conversation started to dwindle, the silence became awkward. Now what? *Kaleb, jump in any time now!* I tried to communicate telepathically. We all politely smiled at each other, waiting for someone to say or do something. We likely all looked like a deer in headlights. Then the husband suddenly stood up, which cued the wife to do the same.

"It was nice meeting you both," he said and thanked us for our time. The interview was officially over. We watched them casually walk away, trying their luck with another couple at the bar. Although I was relieved nothing had happened with them, I must admit it felt like a rejection. I was a bit offended, like we weren't interesting or good enough for them. One thing's for sure, you have to develop thick skin in the Lifestyle and learn not take things personally. Couples don't connect for a variety of reasons—you shouldn't feel badly if things don't work out. Of course, we didn't know this then ... hence my hurt feelings. This would be our first but not our last mismatch.

Kaleb went back to the bar to get a refill on our drinks to repair our bruised egos. While sitting at our table, I noticed that same guy in his late fifties checking me out again from the back corner. He made no attempt to hide his interest. He was handsome and stylishly dressed in a suit with an open, white-collared shirt. I never thought I'd be attracted to someone older, but I was. His wife, an attractive, petite brunette in her early thirties, returned from the restroom.

Feeling uncomfortable at this man's continuing attention, I decided to head to the restroom. As I stood washing my hands, that same petite brunette woman walked in and smiled at me.

"Hello," she said warmly. *Hadn't she just used the restroom five minutes ago? Wait a minute—maybe her partner sent her in to recruit us?*

That thought made me panic. I politely smiled back and replied, "Hello," and then quickly left the restroom. *Why didn't I say something more?* I clearly forgot to follow the rules of engagement for successful match mating where the women first initiate conversation. I could have sealed the deal by accepting this woman's invitation to connect further. Another missed opportunity!

I sat back down at our table, where Kaleb was waiting with our drinks.

"That couple is checking you out," he said.

"I know. I noticed them when you were at the bar. I think his wife was trying to engage with me in the restroom," I said.

"Did she say anything to you?" he asked excitedly.

"No, we smiled at each other, and then I left."

"Oh."

"You know I'm not good at making small talk."

The couple maintained their gaze in our direction, hoping that we would ask them to come over. Kaleb and I sipped on our drinks and waited. I'm not sure what we were waiting for, exactly. Honestly, I think someone would have had to hit us on the head with a mallet to get our attention. The couple then headed upstairs. It was now close to 1:00 a.m. and Kaleb and I decided to call it a night.

"What did you think?" Kaleb asked, as we rode in the taxi back to our hotel.

"It was ... *interesting*," I replied.

"What did you find most interesting?"

"Well, the glory hole was an eye opener!" I said. "I also didn't expect the orgy shower and private rooms either! What about you?"

"The best part for me was people watching," he replied.

"I'm glad you suggested we go tonight," I whispered. Kaleb leaned in and kissed me.

"Even though nothing happened, I'm not disappointed."

"Are you sure?" I asked.

"I'm sure. This was a good start," he replied.

We decided to spend the rest of the weekend in our room. We made love and laid in bed, reminiscing about being at the club. The ambiance, the people, the coupling rituals, the private rooms ... all of it was so intriguing!

This first experience only further piqued our curiosity and interest in learning more about the LS world. We approached the question of this lifestyle being a good fit for us in the same manner that we made other important decisions in our lives; that was, debating the pros and cons. The obvious pros included meeting interesting people, connecting us emotionally and sexually, diversifying our sexual experiences, and giving us a social outlet. The negatives were feelings of insecurity and jealousy potentially surfacing.

By the end of that weekend, Kaleb and I decided that the pros outweighed the cons. We were officially ready to dive into the Lifestyle headfirst and eat the proverbial forbidden fruit.

"Let's give it a try. What do we have to lose?" Kaleb asked.

I didn't realize how these words would come back to haunt us.

5

New Church Friends

* * *

After our eye-opening and sexual awakening weekend, Kaleb and I were curious to find out more about the Lifestyle, especially since many of the couples we saw at the sex club looked, well, average! They were just like us, looking to meet other like-minded couples and fulfill sexual fantasies in a non-judgmental environment.

Although Kaleb and I were excited about the possibility of exploring this other world further, we didn't immediately get involved with the LS community. We needed more time; perhaps deep down inside, we had our own doubts and fears of the unknown and what LS might bring into our relationship. So, we decided to let things happen organically. It would be a full two years after our underground experience before we met our first monogamous LS couple at—where else?—church.

One Sunday afternoon in July 2005 (around the seven-year itch mark), the kids and I attended a church barbeque. Kaleb had taken off to the golf course right after service had ended. While standing in line with the kids, I turned back and was surprised to see that Steve Foster and his children were standing behind us. I knew that the Foster family had moved into the neighborhood a few months back and had two young children around the same age as ours, but we hadn't yet had a chance to formally introduce ourselves. I caught Steve's attention and gave him a smile. Steve was slim and fit, slightly shorter in stature than Kaleb, likely around 5'10". He had brown wavy hair with a few greys speckled throughout. Steve greeted me with a warm smile. He was attractive for an older guy; I placed him in his early fifties (fifteen years my senior).

"Hello, I'm Steve," he said.

"I'm Kim, and this is Samantha and Lucas." The kids smiled meekly, continuing to focus on eating their hot dogs and chips.

"It's nice to meet you! These are my two little ones, Michelle and Michael," he replied. They were equally as shy with the introductions and began tugging at their father to move to the picnic table.

"My husband, Kaleb, had to leave but I would love to introduce him next Sunday at coffee hour," I said.

"Natalie—my wife—isn't here either. She wasn't feeling well," Steve said. "Would you like to join us?"

"Sure, thank you," I replied.

As we walked towards a picnic table, the four kids suddenly ran off to a nearby swing set. I discovered that the Fosters didn't live far from us, and our kids would attend the same school in September. Steve seemed like a nice guy, engaging and easy to talk to. As we continued to chat, it's funny how my mind went *there*. Were they in the Lifestyle? What was he like in bed? Since we've seen this other side of life, regular conversation with people became tainted with random and intrusive speculation of their sexual prowess.

"Did you want anything from the dessert table?" Steve asked, interrupting my dirty thoughts.

"Ahh ... no, I'm good, thanks," I replied. Did he notice me mentally undressing him? If I had to rank male sexual partners in the past 15 years of swinging, Steve would undoubtedly be in the top five. Not only did he have an attractive face, but his tall and athletic physique was exactly what I looked for in a man.

The following Sunday, after service, I led Kaleb to the coffee table where Steve and the woman I presumed was Natalie were standing.

"Is this the *Steve* you were fantasizing about last night?" Kaleb teased.

"Shush! We're in church!" I blushed.

Natalie was an attractive Vietnamese woman in her early forties with a petite slender frame and jet-black long straight hair. What struck me most was her beautiful smile and gorgeous almond shaped hazel eyes. I've never met an Asian woman with such light eyes before. I tried not to stare at her but it was hard not to. *Did Kaleb find her as attractive as I did?*

In my early twenties, I had come across a number of beautiful women of all ethnicities but I hadn't given much thought to the concept of bisexuality. I appreciated a woman's femininity and captivating beauty; their soft features, curvature, and how they generally presented themselves. I hadn't realized (or admitted to myself) at that time that I was *attracted* to these women on some level. It wasn't even in my consciousness to question my sexuality at that point. I was heterosexual; I merely appreciated a woman's beauty. Then, coming into my early thirties, I started to become more aware of my sexual attraction to women. Looking back at the underground club, I was intrigued by the petite brunette in the restroom more so than her partner. I'd felt nervous and shy when she spoke to me, rendering me speechless. I think my discomfort had more to do with my unexpected sexual attraction to this beautiful woman than the unknown prospect of a foursome hookup.

I didn't want to admit to myself that I was sexually attracted to Natalie. Part of that hesitation had to do with the fact that she was Asian, like me. Homosexuality is a taboo subject in the Asian culture. I told myself that I simply regarded her as a sister, thereby, not allowing myself to overstep the boundaries of our strict code of conduct.

"It's nice to finally meet you!" Natalie said. "Steve told me you guys had a great time at the barbeque. I wished I had been there."

"It's too bad that you and Kaleb missed it. The kids got along really well," I said.

"Maybe we could do dinner some night and get to know each other better," she suggested.

As we sipped on our coffee, Steve and Natalie shared their love story; they had met in Hong Kong, which is where Natalie had lived most of her life, and they were both in pharmaceutical sales. Steve had relocated there from the UK, heading up the company's sales division.

"So, you were Natalie's boss?" I asked.

"You could say that," Steve replied.

"It got serious after a few months of dating," Natalie explained. "When people found out, let's say it was the office gossip of the year."

"That's when we both decided to leave the company and look for work over here," Steve said.

Ten years together and two kids later, they'd moved around the country a fair bit before settling down in our neighborhood.

I was a bit taken aback. I couldn't help but think about how they'd started dating, crossing boundaries between boss and employee. Was I being too judgy? Probably. I admit hearing that part of their story made me question their moral compass to some extent.

But I tried to let it go. That was ten years ago, after all! Maybe I was too quick to pass judgment on them. The more time we spent with them that summer, the more I liked them; we both did. Steve and Natalie were like us—easy-going, good senses of humor, and great conversationalists. Even our kids hit it off, always taking off to the backyard or basement to play together.

The Swinger in the Mirror

Although Kaleb and I didn't let on, we were secretly crushing on them; we would talk dirty during sex about having a foursome. We had no clue if Steve and Natalie were even into that. Kaleb and I kept this secret to ourselves, not wanting to overstep any boundaries. We were happy that we finally met a couple that we had a lot in common with—being biracial for one and, secondly, our kids were the same ages. We began spending more and more time at each other's homes, enjoying drinks, dinners, and late nights. Sexual overtures and *friendly* exchange became a regular part of our interactions. Maybe we were all testing the water...

Toward the end of the summer, both families decided to book a two-night stay at an outdoor water park resort. We had adjoining rooms, one for the kids and one for the adults. There were two queen beds in each room. We brought a couple of bottles of wine to enjoy once the kids were off to bed. That first night, we had more to drink than we should have. Natalie made occasional flirtatious comments to Kaleb. Steve was equally as playful in his banter with me. Then, Steve made a bold yet seamless move upon returning from the bathroom; he went from sitting beside Natalie to planting himself right next to me on the couch. *Were they giving us the green light?* However, we carried on as if nothing happened ... we had to be sure that Steve and Natalie wanted something *more*. I'm not sure what more they could have done to make it obvious, but we didn't take the bait.

At 1:00 a.m., I decided to call it a night. "It's getting late. The kids will be up at 7:00 a.m.," I said, yawning.

"Yeah, we should get some shut-eye," Kaleb said.

I remember falling asleep quickly and Kaleb cuddling into me from behind. But around 4:00 a.m., I was woken by a sound. Kaleb and I were on opposite sides of our bed with our backs turned to each other. I saw a shadowy figure slowly move across the room. I assumed either Natalie or Steve had to go to the bathroom, but, suddenly, I felt a hand softly brush up against the right side of my face. I tried to focus my eyes to see who could be kneeling by the side of my bed. It was Steve. What was he doing out of bed? And why was he caressing my face? I laid still, trying to pretend I was asleep. I could feel the warmth of his breath close to my face. I didn't know what to do. I froze.

He continued to gently stroke my face, and then I felt his fingers slowly glide down my neck and the left side of my body. Where was he heading? I was nervous, yet slightly aroused. This sensual moment then ended abruptly; Steve lifted his hand and turned away, heading back to his bed. I was utterly confused. I didn't dare move an inch, directing my eyes towards the clock radio ... it was 4:09 a.m.. My mind raced, trying to understand what had just happened. I reached over to touch Kaleb to make sure it wasn't a dream. I wrapped my arms tightly around him, but he was in deep sleep and snoring faintly. I cuddled into Kaleb and eventually drifted off to sleep, only to wake up a few hours later to loud voices coming from the kids' room.

As I rolled out of bed and got the coffee pot on, I noticed the other three adults were still asleep. I looked at Steve. Would he feel uncomfortable about last night, too? I decided to prepare breakfast for the kids. The clanging of the dishes soon woke everyone up.

"Morning, how did everyone sleep?" Steve asked. He acted like nothing had happened—just three hours earlier. Kaleb and Natalie seemed normal, too. We continued with the rest of the family trip, and nothing was brought up. *Was I dreaming?*

A month later, I decided to bring up that night. I felt anxious telling Kaleb; would he get upset at Steve and at me for not telling him sooner?

"Remember when we were at the resort with Steve and Natalie?" I asked hesitantly.

"Yeah."

"Well ... in the middle of the night, Steve came by my side of the bed and started caressing my face," I said. "But he didn't do anything else," I quickly added. I waited for Kaleb to say something.

"Did you hear what I said?"

"Yeah, I heard," he replied.

"Well?"

"Well, what?" he said.

"You're not upset?"

"No, why would I be? Steve was probably sleepwalking or something," Kaleb surmised.

"Maybe." I ended the conversation there, not wanting to make more of the situation. To this day, I still don't know if Steve was acting intentionally or he actually had no clue what he had done. Regardless, that chance encounter stirred something inside of me... I was intrigued by him more than ever.

Kaleb and I began spending pretty much every weekend with the Fosters. Steve was becoming much more overt in his flirtation with me, and Natalie seemed to follow his lead. Yet no one had the nerve to say what we were all thinking: *you take my partner and I'll take yours.* The sexual tension steadily increased, especially when the drinks were flowing. Our foyer greetings changed from a quick hug and cheek kisses to longer embraces and a second longer kiss on the lips.

I can't put a finger on the exact day when we officially became a foursome; there was no talk or discussion, it just happened. It all started with the guys sitting close on the couch with the other partner, caressing legs under the dining table, or gently rubbing tight shoulders. Then it progressed to more overt behaviors. Often, the night ended with everyone in the hot tub, clothes strewn across the lawn furniture. More drinking led to more kissing and heavy petting, but no one had the balls to do more. It was exciting and sexually liberating to know that Kaleb was completely comfortable with me making out with another man and likewise for him. Neither of us felt guilty about flirting and acting on our impulses.

After a few months of friends-with-benefit actions, Natalie suggested a downtown date night at a popular Moroccan restaurant. The dimly lit dining area had several low tables with vibrant colored cushions and pillows for seating on the floor. Baskets of bread, olives, couscous, and tagines fanned out on our table.

Steve sat next to me, which prompted Kaleb to move closer to Natalie. We ordered a bottle of wine and were giddy with the excitement of the night to come, pondering if the four of us would dare to take it to the next level. *Would tonight be the night?*

""Eating with your hands is so sensual," I said, and the other three grinned at me in reply.

Steve then placed his hand on my right thigh, caressing it gently. I could feel Kaleb watching us. *Was he jealous?* Taking his cue from Steve, Kaleb placed his arm around Natalie's shoulders. It was happening—we were coupling in public! As the music turned up, four voluptuous belly dancers pranced quickly into the dining area, seducing us with their rhythmic hip swaying and eye-catching rhinestone fitted bras, beaded belts, and flowy chiffon skirts. The dancers began scanning the room to invite patrons up to join them, extending their hands to Natalie and myself.

"Oh no! I'm not going up!" I said, hiding my face against Steve's neck. I didn't feel comfortable having attention on me. Natalie, on the other hand, was in the mood to dance. She grabbed my hand and led me onto the dance floor with her.

"I can't," I whispered to Natalie.

"Don't worry, it'll be fun!" she said reassuringly. The dancers paired up with each of us and began swaying their hips, directing us to follow their moves.

5. New Church Friends

Natalie was a natural! She swayed her hips seductively, impressing her dance partner. I tried my best to follow my partner's lead but, honestly, I just looked awkward. Then Natalie stood in front of me and to my surprise, she held onto my hips with both hands, guiding them in sync with her movements. Slowly, she slid her hands sensually up the side of my body, caressing my breasts. I've never had a woman touch me, especially in public. Although I felt embarrassed, I was also drawn to her. As the song came to an end, we released from our embrace, and Natalie gave me a quick kiss on the lips.

"Thanks," she said with a wink.

In that moment, I realized that I was as attracted to Natalie as I was to Steve. There was something unique and captivating about her sensual touch, something I hadn't felt before with a man.

As unexpected as my time on the dance floor was, sadly, the rest of the night was anti-climactic. Our meals came, and we had normal dinner conversations. No more flirtation, no suggestive overtures. Nothing. It was almost like the sexual energy disappeared instantaneously. As the dinner service came to an end, there was the awkward five-second lull in the conversation. I was hoping *someone* would suggest a night cap at a nearby hotel, but no such luck. The bill was paid, and we all walked out to the front of the restaurant; we said our good-byes with a hug and a side peck on the cheek. I was confused by the turn of events. Kaleb was just as puzzled.

"What happened tonight?" he blurted out on the drive home.

"I don't know. It was weird," I replied.

"It got pretty hot and then it just petered out," he said.

"I know. I was hoping you would suggest going to a hotel or something."

"Well, I was waiting for Steve. When he didn't, I assumed they weren't interested in doing more tonight."

"I wish someone had spoken up," I said.

"You and Steve were getting pretty cozy," Kaleb smiled.

"Yeah, he's an attractive guy. What about you and Natalie?"

"She's full of energy! I like that about her," he replied.

"Do you think they would be interested in a foursome?" I asked.

"Probably but who knows?"

"I'll see if I can find a way to talk to Natalie, bring it up somehow," I suggested.

I didn't have to wait long. The following week, we were invited over to their place for drinks.

"We should bring it up tonight, if they don't," Kaleb said, as we pulled up in their driveway.

Natalie greeted us at the front door. "You guys are late. We're already on our second drink!"

"Sorry, we had to put the kids to bed first," I said. We went into the family room where Steve was comfortably seated on the couch with a glass of wine.

"Is this seat taken?" I winked as I sat down next to Steve. He shifted closer to me and gave me a quick kiss. Natalie handed us our glasses of wine before sitting next to Kaleb on the other end of the couch. Then there was an awkward silence in the room; no one wanted to bring up the abrupt ending to our dinner downtown.

"So ... what did you think of the Moroccan restaurant?" I asked, trying to make small talk.

"It was good," Steve replied. "You liked the food, didn't you Natalie?"

"Oh yeah, it was delicious!" Natalie said.

More awkward silence. We all took a sip of our drink simultaneously.

"Were you guys thinking of staying downtown longer and doing something else?" Kaleb came right out and asked.

"What do you mean?" Natalie asked, with a smile.

"I don't know. Continuing the fun at a hotel or something," he replied.

"That would have been cool with us," Natalie replied.

"Us too. It was pretty hot and heavy at the start and then it just fizzled out," I added.

"We got the impression that you guys weren't feeling it," Steve said.

"Really?" Kaleb asked. "How so?"

"After we came back to the table, you seemed more serious, Kaleb," Natalie remarked.

I couldn't help but chuckle to myself. I've mentioned this before to Kaleb about his frown lines making him look angry, even if it wasn't the case.

"No, I was fine, really. I enjoyed watching you and Kim dance. It was super hot!" Kaleb said.

"Babe, you do get that angry look on your face at times," I teased.

"I honestly thought you were upset with me for dancing so close with Kim," Natalie said. "It's hard to read you sometimes."

"I'm sorry. I didn't mean to give off that vibe."

"Maybe you should get rid of your frown lines with Botox, it might help!" I laughed.

"I can't believe my face is getting me in trouble," Kaleb chuckled.

"We were disappointed the night ended early. We should have said something then," Steve said.

We cleared up the misunderstanding between us and agreed to be clearer about our feelings. I decided to put it out there and state our intentions.

"We like you guys ... a lot. I think we have good chemistry together," I said.

I took a deep breath. *Oh, fuck it, just ask them, Kim...* "Are you interested in a foursome?"

Natalie and Steve looked at each other.

"I thought you'd never ask!" Steve smiled.

"Oh good!" I replied. "It would have been super awkward if we'd misread your signals."

"We've never done a foursome before, but we'd be comfortable exploring it with you guys," Natalie added.

"I'm glad we're talking about this. It seemed like there was a white elephant in the room, and no one wanted to go there," I said.

"We didn't know how you guys felt, so we didn't want to say anything too soon," Natalie replied.

"So, everyone is all on the same page?" Kaleb asked.

We all nodded in agreement. My heart started to race. Would tonight be the night to finally act out our fantasies?

Turns out, no. "Sorry guys, I have an early morning meeting," Steve announced, standing up.

"Yeah, we should head out. It's getting late," Kaleb added.

"Natalie and I will plan something fun soon," I said on our way out the door.

Although I was slightly disappointed that we couldn't have our inaugural hookup that night, it was probably a good thing to wait. It would give us (and them) a chance to think about what this foursome would look like and what we wanted from it. This was new territory for all of us. But it *was* going to happen...

6

First Foursome Experience

*   *   *

"Figures," I muttered to Kaleb over coffee one morning, about two weeks after our chat with Natalie and Steve. "We finally clear the air and now our work and family schedules keep getting in the way!"

"I'm sure we'll nail down a date," Kaleb replied. "At least they're interested!"

Natalie and I finally came up with a plan to do a week-long trip down to the Caribbean. The only problem was that the kids would be with us.

"Do you think we could carve out some adult fun time?" Natalie asked.

"Sure! We could do the same setup we had at that water park resort, kids all in one room and us in the other," I suggested. "We'll just have to be careful and discreet."

"Okay, let's book it!"

On the plane ride down, we sat with our own spouses, acting proper and *vanilla*-ish. When no one was looking, we would give our *other* partner a wink or devilish smile to show our interest.

After the kids had gone to bed, our first night there, the adults had plans to have some fun of our own. We opened a bottle of rosé and sat on the couch, getting cozy and chatting away. But, once again, no one was making a move. *Oh no, not this again*, I thought. But, then, to my surprise, Kaleb suddenly stood up and began to unbutton his shirt and unclasp his belt.

"Enough of the pleasantries, let's do this!" he asserted.

He reached out for Natalie's hand and slowly led her to our bed. Following their lead, Steve and I got up and we laid on their bed. Natalie unbuttoned her blouse and took off her skirt, exposing her slender toned body in a nude bra and matching panties. She looked hot! (My choice of underclothing was not as sexy—a white jockey bikini and sport bra.)

Steve excused himself to go to the bathroom, and I found myself watching Kaleb slowly remove Natalie's bra and guide her to the edge of the bed to help her slide her panties off. He then took hold of her face and started to kiss her lips passionately. She embraced him tightly and returned his kiss, caressing his broad shoulders and chest. As I watched this erotic scene unfold, I was surprised I didn't feel at all jealous. Instead, I was turned on seeing them together. This was all so new to me. I was intrigued and couldn't take my eyes off them, but my attention was suddenly diverted to hands caressing my breasts from behind. Steve had returned and was slowly kissing my neck. Our eyes locked and he kissed me deeply. He then gently laid me on my back as he knelt between my legs. I elevated my hips slightly so that Steve could remove my panties.

How surreal that the four of us were finally swapping all the way! What was more surprising was how natural everything seemed. No drama, no upset. I loved the spontaneity and self-indulgence of the moment. I could express my sexual urges with another man, yet, at the same time, get off watching Kaleb with another woman. This was sexual stimulation overload. I was hooked. This was the moment we officially entered the Lifestyle.

Steve's hands were all over me, touching, playing, and rousing all parts of me in our erotic foreplay. Although I was savoring his every touch, I couldn't help but glance over to see what Kaleb and Natalie were doing. Natalie's moaning was hard to ignore. Kaleb was giving her oral from behind as she knelt on all four. This visual was making me so aroused! I wanted—no, I *needed* Steve to be inside of me ... now. But Kaleb and I hadn't talked out the details of how we would be having sex in terms of what was or wasn't allowed. Unfortunately, we had not yet formulated **Rule #4** (talk about details before we act) and **Rule #9** (always use a condom). Were we allowed to have full swap? Or was this going to be soft play? Were we using condoms or not? Both Kaleb and Steve had had vasectomies years ago but was it safe to have sex with Steve and Natalie without using one? What about STIs? These were important questions that should have been addressed between Kaleb and me, and the four of us, before we landed on these beds. Both parties had been married for a while and we had never hooked up like this before. I think we all assumed it was safe to *not* use one—at least that's what we all wanted to believe. We were living in the moment and acting like cliché teenagers—*act now, think later.*

The Swinger in the Mirror

I continued to watch Kaleb and Natalie, and I didn't have to wonder about Kaleb's interpretation of any rules for long. It excited and aroused me to hear Natalie moan as he entered her. I couldn't believe it! I was watching my husband screw another woman, and I was enjoying it. Lying on my back with my eyes closed, I felt Steve slide further down to pleasure me. As his body hovered over mine, I stared into his eyes, which appeared soft yet intense with passion. Steve wanted to take his time and make sure I was enjoying his every touch. His approach was different from what I was used to. Kaleb was much more assertive in bed, which I also loved; rough sex was part of the sensuality of our love making. Steve, on the other hand, was gentler and more sensual.

After a while, Steve slowly inched his body up along mine and kissed my lips intensely as he entered me. I looked over and noticed Kaleb watching us ... which made this moment much more arousing. Although Kaleb and I were physically apart at that moment, the sexual and emotional connection between us was palpable ... we were both on a high, getting off on this voyeuristic experience together. It was intense. Steve let out a loud grunt as he released.

While Steve was in the bathroom, Natalie suddenly got up and climbed next to me, cuddling into me under the sheets. I felt excited, yet also nervous. Natalie's soft hands gently caressed my breasts first and then glided all over my body. It felt natural being with her. I kissed her back. Although I enjoyed being with a man, there's something amazing and beautiful about experiencing the sensuality of a woman—the scent of her body, the softness of her skin, her tenderness and vulnerability.

While this was my first time being with a woman, it wasn't the first time another woman had shown interest in me. In my mid-twenties when I was in graduate school, I had my first *womance* with a classmate of mine, Stella. She was an attractive divorcée in her mid-forties. I found her engaging and full of positive energy, which made me gravitate towards her. I looked up to Stella, given that she was mature, experienced, and seemed to have everything going for her. I didn't think anything more of our relationship other than that she was a cool person to hang around.

When I confided in her about being interested in Kaleb, her reaction surprised me. She wasn't supportive of me pursuing him, almost to the point of being annoyed every time I brought up his name. I was aware of Stella's increasing attention; however, I brushed it off as her wanting to be close friends. Then, one day while we were chatting on the phone, Stella suddenly asked me if I was ever sexually attracted to a woman. I went quiet—I didn't know how to respond. Was she subtly asking if I was interested in *her*? But wait a minute, wasn't she straight? She had been in a long-term common-law relationship with a man ever since I had known her, so her question threw me off completely. I told her that I never thought about being with a woman sexually and left it at that. After I got off the phone, our conversation stayed with me ... how did I *really* feel about being intimate with a woman?

Stella's question forced me to look deeper within myself. When I look back through my life, there were times I paid attention to certain women, either friends or strangers in passing. I waived it off as simply appreciating the beauty of the female form and nothing more. I've always found women were generally more attractive than the men I've come across. At that time, I hadn't thought of wanting to be in a relationship or sexually intimate with a woman. I had always been with a man, emotionally and sexually.

The more I thought about who I was attracted to sexually, the more I realized that there were more layers to me as a person. Maybe I wasn't as straight as I would have myself to believe. Stella never brought that topic up again and neither did I. Our friendship sadly ended abruptly when Kaleb and I officially became a couple.

As Natalie continued to caress my body and kiss me tenderly, the boys watched us intently as we pleasured each other. I motioned them to join us on the bed. Kaleb slid next to me. There was such intensity in his kiss, more than I've ever felt before. Natalie and Steve were engrossed with each other. With the four of us on the bed together, naturally there was a swapping and meshing of hands, legs, body parts, groping, touching, kissing, and licking ... it was a pure foursome in action, with various partners and positions in play—Kaleb and I, Steve and Natalie, Steve and I, Natalie and Kaleb, and then back to girl-on-girl. (There was no male-on-male interaction as Kaleb and Steve are both straight.)

Suddenly, Kaleb slid off the bed and reached for my hand; he led me back to our bed—the look in his eyes was intense.

"I'm going to have you all to myself!" he said.

"I'm all yours," I whispered in his ear. I wanted Kaleb to devour me. Watching each other with someone else took it to a new level of eroticism. Never have I felt such a powerful urge to reconnect and feel as one with him. Kaleb felt the same intensity. We had forgotten about Natalie and Steve on their bed. We were both on such a high and addicted to this amazing feeling!

Kaleb and I made love until the early morning, finally drifting off to sleep against the warmth of each other's bodies. We were awoken by the sound of the cartoon TV show blaring from the kids' room next door. Only two hours of sleep ... but well worth it! The four of us got up and quickly threw on our clothes. We went into automatic parent mode and got our kids dressed and ready for breakfast. It felt somewhat awkward, as we all acted as if last night's sexual utopia never happened.

Kaleb and I didn't talk much about that night either, other than to say that it was a lot of fun. Because we had never been in this situation before, we didn't realize that we should have communicated more and about *everything*—before, during, and after the episode. Important conversation should have included not only talking about what we each wanted to get from this foursome experience sexually and fantasy wise, but also about defining the boundaries, what was okay to do and what was out of bounds in terms of sexual acts. Equally as important, we hadn't discussed with Natalie and Steve if we were all on the same page in terms of each couple's expectations. Our basic belief at the time was that there was no need for any discussion amongst the four of us. We all enjoyed the experience. No one was cheating; everyone was playing together in one room, and we saw what the other partner was doing ... and so it was all good, so we thought.

7

Trouble in Paradise

* * *

After returning from our family vacation, we continued to hang with Natalie and Steve on a regular basis over the next year and a half; however, we only had a handful of times we actually hooked up. It's not that we didn't want to have sex with them more often, it's just that no one planned anything, so we let things *happen* when everyone was in the mood.

The first few times we played in a foursome were amazing; being with a different partner was exciting, hot, and sexy. Like with anything, though, the novelty wore off. Saying that, Kaleb and I never got bored of watching each other play with the *other* partner—that was the cherry on top for us. The most enjoyable part of our "I'm going to reclaim you" sex afterwards was the dirty talk we shared; recounting details of what we saw each other doing with the other partner was a major turn on. It was a love-hate juxtaposition of emotions, teetering between feeling slightly jealous and possessive with sexual arousal, on speed. For us, our experience with Natalie and Steve wasn't so much about being in a foursome per se as it was about us watching each other being sexually pleasured by someone else. It was extremely important for Kaleb and I to come back to each other and reconnect physically and, more importantly, emotionally by sharing our experiences with each other as we made love. Being voyeurs is a huge part of the eroticism of the Lifestyle, and that's why we have always enjoyed sharing a sexual experience in the same room, from day one.

About three months into our foursome relationship, Steve and Natalie asked us a question, one night while we were at their place.

"Would you be okay if we played in separate rooms?" Natalie asked.

"It might heighten the experience for everyone," Steve suggested.

I was not prepared for this. My visceral gut reaction was *No, thanks. We like it the way it is.* If we went to separate rooms, I would feel "cheated" out of this voyeur experience.

The Swinger in the Mirror

But it's always been hard for me to say no and not to give someone what they've asked for; that's the pleaser in me. Even to this day, I still need to remind myself to put my needs first before others during LS moments.

Feeling uneasy, I looked to Kaleb. I was hoping he would say no on our behalf.

"What do you think, babe?" I said, deferring to him. To my surprise, Kaleb didn't object and replied, "Sure, sounds good."

I assumed that by concurring, Kaleb *wanted* to be alone with Natalie. I felt hurt and disappointed that he didn't telepathically pick up on my true feelings. I wish we had taken a moment to ourselves to discuss what we wanted as a couple—that was our first mistake in the Lifestyle. Instead, we complacently agreed to do it *their* way.

Steve then took my hand and led me down to their basement, and I followed. Natalie took Kaleb up to their bedroom. I remember feeling strange that Steve and I were alone for the very first time. Although we'd already had sex a number of times by this point, his presence made me feel nervous. As he prepared a drink for me, I kept thinking about Kaleb and what he was doing with Natalie. I missed Kaleb not being there beside me. *He should be here ... we should be here together.*

During these moments of separation, I felt I no longer belonged to Kaleb. It changed the sexual synergy for me. Kaleb and I were supposed to be in this erotic play together to heighten our sexual experience as a couple. Although I didn't like this separation, I chose to squash my gut feelings, but deep down inside, something was gnawing at me—why were we playing apart if this was not what either of us wanted? Why were we putting Steve and Natalie's needs before our own?

This has been a repeat pattern for me: I don't trust or listen to my inner voice. Instead, I convince myself to believe that it's more important to make others happy than to do what makes me happy. I didn't want to disappoint Steve and Natalie (and perhaps Kaleb) if they were okay with the separate arrangement. I had convinced myself throughout my life that my feelings didn't matter so why say anything? My self-worth was tied to pleasing people and not wanting to disappoint them in any way. My incessant need to please and avoid disappointing others often left me feeling shafted when it came to getting what I wanted during LS hookups.

When Steve and I were having sex on the basement couch, I honestly didn't fully enjoy the moment with him; Kaleb's absence took away the appeal of it. I felt guilty, like I was somehow cheating on Kaleb. In order to fully engage sexually with Steve, my mind exited my body. Now I realize that I was *dissociating,* as we say in psychology. In order to squash my inner voice and discomfort, I separated the two parts of me: the "good girl/pleaser/dutiful wife" versus the "bad daughter/tramp/naughty vixen," with the latter character dominating my persona during erotic moments with Steve. I convinced myself that this new *monogamous* set-up with Steve and Natalie was fine, as long as Kaleb and I were both having *fun.*

But it was not fine. And I wasn't sure that I had actually had fun.

* * *

"I have to tell you something," Kaleb sighed, looking up from his phone. "I've been feeling anxious all day." I stopped stirring the pot of stew I was making for supper and gave him my attention. His tone told me that something was off, but I wasn't sure what…

"What's wrong?" I asked.

He motioned to the kitchen table and we both sat.

"Natalie called me this morning."

I was surprised by this. Typically, it was always Natalie and I who communicated, not the boys or with our partner. I tried to act unaffected and replied, "Oh."

"She called me from her hotel in New York … she said she missed me," Kaleb added.

"She said what?" I snapped. Anger flooded through me, and I had to remind myself that Natalie was the one who had broken a trust rule, not Kaleb. I could hear him out.

We'd been seeing Natalie and Steve for about six months by this point, but our encounters were always the four of us, under the same roof. It was supposed to be just physical and sexual, not involving emotions and feelings.

"She asked me … to join her there," he hesitantly added.

"What?!" Now, my blood was boiling! *How could a friend betray me like that?* I thought the four of us understood the parameters … we kept our "play" inside the bedroom and nothing more. Clearly, Natalie didn't understand our rules.

"Why would she ask you that?" I demanded. I admit I was losing control over my emotions here and projecting anger onto Kaleb.

"I don't know! Ask her yourself!" Kaleb snapped back.

"I'm sorry. I don't mean to take it out on you," I said softly, reaching over to touch Kaleb's arm. "I'm just confused and upset that she did this."

"I'm just as confused. I didn't see this coming," Kaleb replied.

"Do you think Steve knows about this?" I asked.

"No. She told me to keep it a secret, from him ... and from you too."

"Oh, I see."

"I was going to tell you sooner but I wanted to wait until I got home. You know I can never keep anything from you."

"I believe you," I said, reaching out to give him a hug.

Natalie had crossed the line. She betrayed my trust and I had to confront her. It made me ask myself why I had a tendency to go out of my way to not hurt others or overstep their boundaries only for them not to extend the same courtesy to me. *Could I ever trust her again?*

I ran upstairs and called Natalie from our bedroom. I was hoping she would tell me it was a mistake or at the very least, a misunderstanding. I wanted to give her the benefit of the doubt, but deep down inside, I knew she couldn't right her wrongs.

Natalie picked up after several rings and was surprised to hear from me.

"Can you come over? I need to talk," I asked.

"I'm in New York right now but I'll be back tomorrow morning," she replied. "What's wrong?"

"I don't want to say over the phone," I said.

"Okay ... this sounds serious. Should I be worried?" she asked.

"Come over tomorrow afternoon, and we'll talk then, okay?"

The next day as I waited for Natalie, my mind raced. Feelings of anger were gradually replaced by anxiety and dread of how I would start this conversation and if it would end well. *Do I come right out and accuse her? Would she deny it to my face? Or would she apologize? How could she explain herself and would I even believe her?*

"Do you want me to stay when you guys talk?" Kaleb asked.

"I think it's better if we talked alone," I replied.

The doorbell rang, which cued Kaleb to head upstairs to the bedroom. I took a deep breath before I walked to the foyer. I opened the door and Natalie greeted me with a big smile, not knowing what was going to happen. She gave me a hug, although I didn't reciprocate it. She released me from the embrace and saw the serious look on my face.

"Okay, tell me what's going on? I can tell something's off."

"Let's go downstairs." I led her down to the basement and we sat on the couch.

"Did you call Kaleb yesterday?" I blurted out.

Natalie looked surprised. She hadn't expected Kaleb to tell me.

"And ask him to stay with you in New York?" I continued.

"Uh ... yeah, I did," she replied.

I looked away, trying to not let her see my seething anger at her callous response.

"You know how much I hate travelling alone. Steve was busy, so I thought Kaleb would like to join me. I didn't mean anything by it."

"On what planet do you think it would be okay to ask your friend's husband, to go away with you?" I exclaimed.

"Well, given our *situation*, I thought it would be okay. For god's sake, we're having sex with each other's husbands, what difference would a trip make?" she asked, indignantly.

I wanted to scream at the top of my lungs, *What the fuck were you thinking? You can't go behind my back and do what you want with my husband!*

This conversation was going nowhere. She had nothing to defend her actions. Her responses were disappointing and maddening—no sense of accountability or respect for our friendship. Natalie couldn't understand why I was upset—in her mind, she hadn't done anything wrong.

Looking back on it, the four of us should have communicated our expectations way be*fore* we leapt into the bedroom. Here you have four people with differing needs, each acting out their sexual fantasies, individually and as a couple. You never know if one person is capable of stepping out of line and affecting the interchange of the other three. Natalie's misstep of going outside of the boundaries of a foursome made me realized that engaging in the Lifestyle was not all fun and games; there was potentially a darker side to it. I didn't realize back then how swinging could become *complicated* fast ... white lies, secrets, cheating and emotional fallout as a result of this hedonistic entanglement.

You go on the assumption that everyone is following the same rules—respecting and honoring the other couple's relationship. The sexual experiences are supposed to add to a relationship, not to tear it apart. Although the LS world would appear to be full of chaos and a madhouse from an outsider's view, there are still rules to abide by. It isn't a free-for-all. If secrets and mistrust were the rules rather than the exception, then Kaleb and I would not have chosen to go down this LS path.

How could Kaleb and I continue with our foursome with Natalie and Steve if I couldn't trust my so-called *friend*? This friendship we had seemed to complicate things. But was it a mistake for Kaleb and me to expect a close friendship to form within this foursome? Or were we supposed to treat this scenario for what it was, purely a sexual transaction and keep friendship totally out of it? To this day, I still don't know 100 percent what the right answer should be.

With these thoughts swirling inside my head, I was beginning to doubt our friendship and foursome with Natalie and Steve. I took a deep breath and heard myself say, "I don't think this is going to work."

Natalie was stunned. She didn't expect me to go there. She could tell I was dead serious by my tone and facial expression. She began to back-pedal.

"I'm sorry. You're right, I shouldn't have crossed the boundaries," she said.

I was surprised that she owned up to it. At least, that was a start.

"I was really hurt by what you did," I said.

"I didn't mean to," she said. "I promise, there won't be any more contact with Kaleb or hotel invitations," she continued. "It was a bad judgment call."

Despite her apology and remorseful tone, I didn't know if I could trust Natalie again. But I didn't want to give up on our friendship or this foursome just yet. I wanted to give her the benefit of the doubt so things could go back to the way it was. We tried to engage like before and pretend things were okay between us, however, it wasn't the same for me (or Kaleb). Natalie's betrayal had changed everything. Kaleb and I began to spend less time with them and we drifted apart over the next month or so, to the point of a platonic friendship. No one said anything about the estrangement and eventual ending of the foursome; we just *uncoupled* gradually over time.

On a few occasions, Steve and Natalie invited us to their place to *hang* like we had before but I wasn't comfortable resuming our foursome and Kaleb felt the same way. We'd make up some excuse as to why we couldn't go over. The fate of our friendship eventually went down the same path, gradually petering off. From start to finish, our friendship and foursome swapping with Natalie and Steve lasted in total two years. As far as I was concerned, our experience with foursomes was done, sealed and shut forever. This had left a very bad taste in my mouth.

In processing, I didn't feel this situation with Natalie affected my trust or relationship with Kaleb. It wasn't him that I didn't trust; it was Natalie. Kaleb didn't have to tell me what Natalie had said, he could have kept it to himself and I'd be none the wiser. Although I did trust Kaleb, there was a small part of me that wondered if he had somehow encouraged Natalie's advances. *Was he more into Natalie than he admitted to me in terms of the intimacy and emotional relationship they shared? Did he lead her on in some way, making her feel more for him? What was Kaleb's role in all of this?* I was afraid to bring up this conversation with Kaleb or dig any deeper. I probably should have talked to him ... but I never did bring it up.

Why didn't I? Good question. Maybe I didn't want to know the answer at the time; it was easier to put the blame all on *her*, which allowed me to carry on with the allusion of our p*erfect* marriage.

Did I feel disappointed about our friendship and foursome ending with Natalie and Steve? Yes and no. I didn't actually miss them. I *was* sad, however, that we no longer had another like-minded couple to spend *special* moments with on the weekends. That left a big hole in our social calendar over the next two years.

Then we met Annie and Tom Jennings, our new neighbors.

8

Meet the Neighbors

* * *

After pulling the plug on our relationship with Natalie and Steve, Kaleb and I went back to *normal* life. We made a conscious decision to stop swinging ... at least for a while. Our experience with Natalie and Steve taught us that although the Lifestyle had some fun and sexy times, there was also a thorny and complicated side to it that we didn't foresee— particularly around developing real emotions and attachments with your LS partner. If you play with fire, you're likely to get burned, right? Kaleb and I got too close to the fire ... and we got singed by the flankers.

Both Kaleb and I were able to compartmentalize and disconnect the physical act of sex from the emotions. We could have sex with other people, but we made love only with each other. I think Natalie mistook her feelings of physical closeness with Kaleb as an actual connection and something deeper in meaning. To us, it was a casual hookup and nothing more.

Kaleb has always been honest with me. At this point in our relationship, I'd never questioned where his loyalties laid. There were never any secrets between us, or that's what I wanted to believe to be true. I was so certain that Kaleb and I had the perfect relationship. In my mind, our foundation was strong and unshakeable. I never thought it could ever waver; boy, was I wrong!

Two years after our relationship with the Fosters ended, Annie and Tom entered our lives. One late November evening, our doorbell rang. I was upstairs getting changed, so Kaleb answered it. When I was done, I peered down from the top of the stairs and saw an attractive woman in her mid-thirties talking to Kaleb in our foyer. She had piercing blue eyes that stood out from her long light brown hair. Her super slim figure was accentuated by her black yoga pants and form-fitting white quilted hoodie.

"Hi, my name is Annie Jennings. We're new to the neighborhood."

"Welcome!" Kaleb greeted her.

8. Meet the Neighbors

"Thank you. We're hosting a *Get to Know Your Neighbor* party at our place on December 5, and we'd love for your family to come!" She handed what looked to be a homemade invitation to Kaleb.

"I'll definitely mention it to my wife. Kim's upstairs so hopefully you'll get a chance to meet her another time," Kaleb said.

"I hope you guys can make it. This neighborhood could use some community spirit so please spread the word," she said enthusiastically.

As the door closed, I made my way down the stairs. "Who was that?" I asked.

"Our new friendly neighbor," Kaleb said, with a smirk. "Annie Jennings lives down the street and she's invited us to their Christmas party." He handed me the invitation.

I thought it was strange of her, a newcomer, to suddenly organize such a big event without knowing anyone in the neighborhood. Sure, we all kept to ourselves but we did offer the cursory *hello* and *how-are-you* greetings when we saw each other, which was friendly enough ... at least I thought.

"So who's this Martha Stewart wannabe?" I asked sarcastically.

"Now, you be nice," Kaleb chided. "I think we should go. I'm sure I've seen kids who look to be around Samantha and Lucas' age a few times that I've driven by their place. It'll be nice for them to have some friends to play with."

I rolled my eyes. "I guess we could go over for a bit." Normally, I was usually more into meeting new people than Kaleb, but oddly this time, I wasn't feeling it. I couldn't put my finger on it but my gut instincts were telling me to be careful with Annie. Was I jealous of her amazing *neighborly* idea of boosting community spirit? After all, we had moved into the area four years ago and still didn't know any of our neighbors' names. I marked down the Jennings' party on the fridge calendar, placing a big question mark beside Annie's name. *Who was this Annie? And what was her deal?* I'd find out in two weeks.

On the night of the party, our family walked over to the Jennings' house, which was down the street from ours. It was a beautiful crisp night and the roads were bare. As we rounded the corner, we came upon a beautiful view of their home. Brilliant red and white Christmas lights strung across their roof lines and around the large front windows; an evergreen wreath with a large red bow hung on their front door. It was picturesque and inviting.

Kaleb rang the doorbell. Annie opened the door, greeting us with a big smile.

The Swinger in the Mirror

"Hi, I'm Kim, and this is Samantha and Lucas," I said introducing myself.

To my surprise, she gave me a hug, like we were old friends. She then introduced her husband, Tom, who was equally as warm and inviting. As we moved into their atrium, our eyes were mesmerized by their 20-foot Balsam fir Christmas tree, decorated with brilliant white lights and red and gold ornaments perfectly strewn throughout. The kids were in awe of how gigantic this tree was compared to our 7-foot artificial one.

Tom took our coats and offered to get us some cocktails. As Kaleb and I stood with the kids, we looked around their home, which looked like it came out of a page of the *Architectural Digest* magazine. The interior of their home was well staged, with stylish modern furniture and accents juxtaposed against exposed wooden beam ceilings and a rustic black cast iron wood-burning fireplace.

Annie ushered her two kids, Jane and Brody, in from the family room.

"Guys, this is Samantha and Lucas and their parents, Kim and Kaleb. Say hello to our neighbors," she said. Jane was 10 years old, a year older than Samantha but it didn't take long for these two to connect and go up to Jane's bedroom to play. Lucas and Brody were both 12 and quickly bonded over PlayStation games. After the kids scattered off, Annie and Tom gave us a tour of their lovely home. As we made our way along, Annie introduced us to *our* neighbors, who lived directly across from us. We've known them for a few years but never really spoke to them at length until tonight's party.

The party had a good turnout, with more than 25 families attending. The Jennings were hospitable, and everyone seemed to be having a good time. Surprisingly, I was, too. There was plenty of food and drinks flowing, and everyone was in a festive mood. I had pegged Annie as an attention monger, but I soon realized that she was in fact very sweet and thoughtful ... my intuition about her was completely wrong.

In the months after the party, Annie and I started hanging out, often meeting up for coffee and scheduling playdates for the kids. Annie was an interesting person. She had diverse interests and hobbies, including gardening, painting, and interior design. She had formerly been an interior designer but gave up her career in order to raise a family. Tom, on the other hand, was out of the home most of the week, helping his father run their real estate brokerage firm. As we spent more time together, I began confiding more in Annie than I did with my sister; we shared collective experiences living in the same neighborhood, our kids going to the same school, and running in the same social circle.

"You're spending a lot of time with Annie," Kaleb said one morning at breakfast.

"We have a lot in common. It's nice having someone to talk to," I said.

"I guess you found your new BFF," he teased.

I hated that term—we weren't in grade school—but Kaleb was right about Annie and I becoming close. I knew that I was letting my guard down when it came to opening up and trusting Annie. This is not typically me; I usually keep people at a distance, never allowing myself to get too close to *anyone*. I don't like feeling exposed and vulnerable to being hurt and disappointed ... clearly things that stem from my relationship with my parents. Yet, somehow, I felt comfortable letting Annie in. Deep down inside, I liked having someone close by to share my daily ups and downs with—a role that my sister couldn't fulfill since she lived in a different country and time zone.

Over the next six months, not only was I spending more time with Annie, but Kaleb and I also gradually found ourselves with the Jennings couple on most Friday and Saturday nights. I had some déjà vu, flashing back to nights with Natalie and Steve! Honestly, we didn't plan it this way; we were simply happy to be back socializing again after a two-year hiatus. We weren't looking for a new foursome—just friends and nothing more ... so, we thought.

By the end of June, I recalled everyone feeling excited that the school year was finally coming to an end and we didn't have to worry about homework and the kids' activities. It was convenient, living a few houses down from each other. The kids got along; the adults relaxed in the basement bar and chatted over a bottle of wine. It was great hanging together and decompressing after a stressful work week. Over the summer, we became regular fixtures at each other's homes. It actually felt weird when the four of us weren't together; Annie and Tom were fast becoming an important part of our social life. As scary as it was to admit to myself, I was cherishing my friendship with Annie.

That Labor Day weekend, we decided to host an end of the summer barbeque to celebrate the kids returning to school. As it was getting late into the evening, Samantha and Lucas asked if they could go over and sleep at the Jennings' house.

"Please, mommy?" Lucas and Samantha pleaded in unison. I looked at Annie.

"That's totally fine with us! Our nanny can watch the kids," Annie reassured. "Plus, we can hang here longer."

"That's an excellent idea!" Kaleb exclaimed, opening up another bottle of wine. The kids all left our house, and we carried on with the laughter, conversation, and drinking. As the evening wore on (and the glasses of wine were consumed), my inhibition started to break down.

"Come to the bathroom with me," I told Annie.

"Is this a girlfriend bonding moment?" Annie laughed.

"Yeah, sort of," I said with a grin.

We didn't feel shy sitting on the toilet in front of each, chatting as we peed.

"It's nice that the boys get along so well," Annie said.

"Yeah, they sure love their sports!" I said.

"I'm really glad our families met. Even the kids get along so well," she said. I flushed the toilet and turned on the faucet. As I washed my hands, I looked up into the mirror and noticed Annie looking at me.

"What?" I laughed.

"You look nice tonight."

"Oh ... thanks," I replied, feeling awkward at her compliment.

Annie paused and continued to look at me.

"Stop. You're making me feel self-conscious!" I said. "Do I have something on my face?"

"Sorry, I can't help staring. You're very attractive," she replied. She inched closer towards me, making me feel confused yet also intrigued.

Before I knew what was happening, Annie kissed me on the lips. I didn't see that coming! Although it was unexpected, it was strangely familiar. The softness of Annie's lips brought back memories of Natalie.

Annie pressed her body up against mine. I didn't pull away from her. Our lips locked and we continued to embrace. I felt aroused. We could have been in the bathroom for 5 minutes or it could have been an hour, I had no idea. Time stood still. As we released from our embrace, we looked into each other's eyes. Then, the giggles started. I couldn't believe I'd kissed my best friend!

"This might be a weird question but do you think the boys might enjoy watching us kiss?" Annie asked.

"I don't know but let's find out!" I replied.

We walked out of the bathroom, hand in hand. Tom and Kaleb carried on chatting about golf clubs as Annie and I planted ourselves on the couch. Annie pulled me in close to her and we carried on where we left off in the bathroom. Although I initially wanted to give the boys a show, I soon forgot they were there. I found myself mesmerized by Annie's beautiful ice blue eyes. I held her face in my hands and kissed her sensually. My body was tingling during this passionate exchange. I could sense that Annie felt the same as she grabbed hold of my waist and began to caress my breasts through my blouse.

Tom stopped mid-sentence, watching in disbelief. For some reason, Kaleb seemed less surprised by our sudden erotic display.

After a few minutes of kissing, Annie stood up and took my hand, guiding me towards Tom. She directed me to sit on his lap facing him. She then went over to Kaleb and did the same. As if on cue, we each began touching and fondling our new partner. Tom and Kaleb didn't have a clue where this all had come from, but they certainly weren't complaining. Although this interchange was amazing and pleasurable, there was a "hit pause" moment for me. It was wildly strange to watch myself be all over Tom while my husband had oral sex with my best friend.

It was just after 3:00 a.m. when Annie and Tom went home. We had some fun that evening, but we didn't end up in bed with each other. I'm glad we didn't go any further; sex would have been too much at this point. It was a surreal and intense night. After they left, I couldn't wait to have my way with Kaleb. We made love repeatedly throughout the early morning; each moment of consciousness stirred a need for our bodies to intertwine and connect again and again.

I woke up at noon feeling exhausted. I vaguely remembered the doorbell ringing a few hours earlier and Kaleb rushing out of bed to answer the door. The Jennings' nanny had walked Samantha and Lucas back. I slipped out of bed quietly and headed down to the kitchen to make lunch for the kids.

I came back up to the bedroom with a tray of coffee and laid it on the nightstand. Kaleb was deep asleep but began to stir when I climbed under the sheets and cuddled into him. I gently stroked his face. Thinking back on our evening with Annie and Tom, I started to feel uneasy. *Had we made a mistake?*

Kaleb turned over and embraced me. "Morning," he whispered.

"I got you coffee."

"I could use some," he smiled.

"What did you think of last night?" I asked.

"It was pretty wild ... in a good way," Kaleb replied.

"Yeah, it was totally unexpected." I cast my eyes down and went quiet.

"What's wrong?" Kaleb asked, pulling me in close to him. He knew me well enough to know something was bothering me.

"Do you have any regrets ... being with them?" I asked.

"Not really. Why? Do you?"

"I'm worried it's going to change things between Annie and me," I replied. "And the four of us."

"Nothing's going to change," he said.

"You don't know that."

"Then talk to Annie," he suggested." I know how important she is to you."

I nodded.

"I just don't want our friendship to be ruined because of this ... like before."

"You should definitely talk to her," Kaleb affirmed.

I grabbed my phone from the nightstand.

"Hey Annie," I texted, waiting for her to respond. It didn't take long for a reply.

"Morning. How are you feeling? You okay with last night?" she texted. Annie seemed to be reading my mind.

"We're fine. Last night was ... interesting," I texted back.

"Are we still good, you and me? And us four?" she typed back. I was relieved to know that she was just as worried as me about our friendship being affected.

"Yes, of course, why wouldn't we be?" I replied.

"To tell you the truth, I feel more connected now to you and Kaleb," she texted.

"I feel the same way with you and Tom," I replied.

"I'm glad," she texted.

"What about you and me kissing?" I hesitantly texted. I hoped Annie wasn't freaked out by our girl-on-girl action.

"I liked it. Did you?" Annie messaged.

"Yeah, it was all good," I replied.

It didn't appear that Annie had any regrets about us being together or swapping our partners.

"I'm curious to see where this new experience takes us next," Annie texted.

"Me too."

Although this experience was new and exhilarating, I was also worried. I hadn't told Annie about our past foursome experience with Natalie and Steve. I was scared this would end up like it did with them.

8. Meet the Neighbors

We shared a sexual experience that took us beyond friendship and there was no going back from it, yet I was cautiously hopeful it would somehow turn out differently.

The four of us got together the following weekend and got caught up on our week over a drink. No one seemed to want to bring up what had happened *that* night. It was an unspoken thing, yet everyone could feel the sexual energy surging. There was playful flirting and suggestive banter thrown around, but that was about it. Our next sexual tryst wouldn't repeat itself for another few months.

Our basement experience with Annie and Tom revved up our sex life. During the two years post–Natalie and Steve, Kaleb and I were less sexual and passionate in the bedroom. We were going through a dry spell ... until Annie and Tom brought it all back. We had forgotten how much fun it was to hang with another couple. Should we consider a foursome with Annie and Tom?

Or were we heading down the same path as we had with Natalie and Steve?

9

Women's Retreat

* * *

"I've been feeling *stuck* at home lately. I told Tom that I need to get away for a few days and do something for myself," Annie confided, one day over coffee. It'd been a couple of weeks since the Labor Day BBQ and Annie had come over while the kids were at school.

"What did you have in mind?" I asked.

"I was checking out a weekend retreat north of here. It's for women who want to feel more empowered in their life," Annie said, pausing to take a sip of coffee. "Sexually," she finished, looking at me.

"Oh?" I said, genuinely curious.

"Yeah, like achieving pleasure with female climax and orgasms. Also, they talk about intimacy in relationships, self-esteem, and body image issues."

"That sounds pretty cool!"

"I could use a friend. Come with me!" Annie said.

It didn't take much convincing, as I was keenly interested to learn more about women empowerment and sexual exploration. We signed up that day. This three-day getaway would also give us some girl bonding time, which we were both excited about. To cut down on costs, we agreed to share accommodations.

Two weeks later, I was on the road, heading to the retreat lodge, which was an hour away. Annie and I were driving up separately due to our schedules. It wasn't a long drive, yet it was far enough to feel like I was getting away on a mini-trip. I was happy to have this bit of time to myself—no kids, no responsibilities, and electronically unplugged. Although I felt guilty about leaving the kids with Kaleb, I also realized that I needed to do something for me *for once*.

I arrived at the lodge and checked in. Our room looked dated, with burgundy velvet curtain panels and floral wallpaper in pink. There was one queen bed, which we were sharing to cut down on costs. I didn't give it much thought.

9. Women's Retreat

Annie arrived, and after we got freshened up, we headed downstairs to the reception room. We were met by the facilitator, Lynne, who was a woman in her mid-sixties. She had a calm and serene nature about her, which made me feel better about our weekend ahead. After we were given our itinerary and a brief introduction, we had the rest of the evening off, so Annie and I decided to venture out and explore the beautiful grounds. While out, we noticed a hot tub in the back of the lodge.

"Let's get changed and have a glass of wine in there!" Annie suggested.

"Sure," I agreed. I thought this might be a good chance to bring up a possible foursome and gage her reaction to it.

We sat in the hot tub, drinking away. One glass, two glasses, three glasses … we were on our way to drunk, happy and giggly. We were having so much fun that I forgot to bring up the foursome idea, and before I knew it, we were heading back to our room to get ready for bed.

We climbed into bed, chatting away like kids at summer camp.

"What do you think tomorrow will be like?" I asked.

"I don't know, but it should be interesting. Everyone in this group seems nice," Annie replied.

"I'm sure we'll learn a lot."

"Is there a particular seminar you want to sign up for?" Annie asked.

"I was thinking about doing that orgasm workshop," I said.

"Really?"

"Well, it's been years since I've had one! I can't remember the last one with Kaleb—maybe before the kids were born," I said.

Annie looked surprised to hear me say this. We'd never talked about sex or intimacy issues with our spouses before. There was something about the dark and being away that had lowered our inhibitions. (The alcohol probably helped, too.)

""I used to cum easily with Kaleb," I added, "but now I can only climax with Barney."

"Huh? Who's Barney?" Annie asked.

"My purple vibrator," I said. "Barney's not only for kids," I said, trying to keep a straight face. Then, Annie and I burst out laughing.

"But seriously, I know what you mean," Annie said. She paused. "I'm embarrassed to admit this but I've never had an orgasm. I don't even know what it feels like."

"What? Not even once?" I asked.

"Not *ever.*"

The Swinger in the Mirror

I was taken aback. I couldn't imagine never experiencing an orgasm. I didn't know whether Annie's situation or mine was worse—not having ever experienced an orgasm or not being able to feel one ever again after knowing what it did feel like. I decided I was the winner in this battle of the Who Has It Worst... You can't miss what you never had, right?

"Maybe there's something wrong with me or I'm not doing it right. Either way, I can't cum," Annie said. A long pause followed before she spoke again. "I've never shared this with anyone, not even Tom."

"Tom doesn't know?" I asked incredulously.

"No," Annie said quietly.

"You've been faking it all along? Wow! You must be good at orgasmic moaning!"

I had meant that to break the ice and comfort her, but it was obvious that this was a sensitive topic for Annie. She remained silent for a moment. "Please don't mention this to Kaleb. I don't want it getting back to Tom. He would be hurt by this."

"I promise, I won't say anything to Kaleb," I said.

"Thank you."

"Maybe it's not *us*," I suggested. "Maybe it's the guys—their technique or positioning. I don't know."

"Well, that's the real reason why I wanted to come to this retreat. I was hoping it could help me *somehow*," Annie said.

"I hope for my sake too," I replied.

We stopped talking then as we both tried to sleep. But sleep was not coming easily to me that night. An hour passed and I found myself still wide awake. Annie seemed to be in the same boat, repeatedly changing positions on her side of the bed. A slither of moonlight peeked between the curtain panels, allowing me to faintly make out the outline of Annie's body. It brought me back to the scene in the basement bathroom ... *of us kissing passionately*. I could feel my heart beating faster. I had an urge to move my body closer to hers. There was something sensual being in the darkness, which heightened my sense of touch, taste, smell, and sound. *Should I make a move? What if she rejects me?*

My thoughts were suddenly interrupted with the gentle touch of her hand on my arm under the sheets. I didn't flinch. She probably touched me by accident as she tossed and turned. But then, I heard the bed creak as her body shifted towards me and came closer.

I could feel the warmth of her breath on my face. The sexual energy between us was intense. I was experiencing the same attraction to

Annie that I felt with Natalie when we were first together. Annie slowly leaned into me and kissed my lips. I held onto her body, tightly.

It was strange not having Kaleb around; we were usually together in the same room during play. Yet it didn't cross my mind that he might be bothered by me kissing Annie so passionately without him being there. Was I breaking our **Rule #7** (find a moment to check-in with each other to confirm if it's okay to hook up)? I had convinced myself that it was perfectly fine to kiss a woman, more so than if I had done the same with a man; the latter would constitute cheating. This present scenario was *different*; I was with Annie, my best friend. I also overlooked **Rule #5** (don't make assumptions). I was assuming that Kaleb wouldn't mind me being with Annie since most men enjoyed girl-on-girl action. Maybe this was a double standard on my part, but I was using this rationale to proceed.

"Can I touch you?" Annie whispered, as her hand grazed my breast. I responded by holding her face and kissing her lips. Our hands caressed every inch of one another's bodies. Annie then slipped under the sheets and embraced my body. *Oh my gosh! It's happening!*

Annie softly kissed my breasts, as she slowly moved her way down my stomach ... lower and lower until I gasped and moaned with pleasure. Her warm soft tongue lingered against my clit. *Now* I felt like I was cheating, yet I didn't want her to stop. I felt the most relaxed I've ever been with a woman, which surprised me. Although Natalie and I had fondled and kissed, we never had oral sex. This was a first for me. Annie was amazing with her gentle and attentive ways. Anatomically speaking, a man and woman's tongue are pretty much the same; however, there was a subtle difference about *this* experience. It felt more natural, the emotional connectedness between our minds and bodies.

Even though I had experienced being with Natalie and now with Annie, I didn't own up to the fact that I clearly wasn't *straight*. I didn't want to admit to myself that I enjoyed being with a woman as much as I did with a man. I was in denial. The concept of bisexuality wasn't in my head space at that time... I didn't know how it applied to my situation. Coming from an Asian immigrant family, I was made to believe that we were all heterosexual; it was a God-given fact. Growing up back in the '80s and '90s, I didn't know anyone who was gay, lesbian, or bisexual (and those were the only terms I knew of back then). It wasn't as discussed as it is today. The distinction between gender and sexuality were foreign to my generation, unlike the growing movement and acceptance of the 2SLGBTQSIA+ community today. I assumed that if someone was straight, then they would always be straight ... there was no self-discovery and coming out of the closet at a later point. There was a rigid, black-and-white concept of sexuality back then; either you're straight or you're not—there was no in between.

In my early twenties, when I was freely exploring a less inhibited sexual lifestyle, I kept my activities to men only. This would have been the perfect time in my life for exploration, but I was too afraid to admit this to myself or anyone because of the social stigma, especially in Asian culture. I didn't want to be judged and looked at as being different. So, I buried my feelings. I didn't allow myself to be truly honest with how I felt about other women. I was *supposed* to be heterosexual genetically; I'm no different than my identical twin sister and she's straight ... therefore so was I, right?

As I had more encounters with women, I found that I wanted to share what I was feeling inside and naturally, my instinct was to tell the closest person in my life—my twin. This happened in the same conversation when I told her that Kaleb and I were having sex with other people. I was really nervous about telling her that I was not straight; I didn't know how she would react, maybe even more shocked than me telling her that we were swingers. *Would she judge me that I liked being with women? Would she think less of me or act differently?* Although my sister was surprised to hear that I was attracted to females, she seemed supportive and accepting of who I was. While I still feel a bit reluctant to this day speaking about my bisexual experiences, being a part of the LS community has allowed me to let my walls down and be truer to myself. My honest and candid conversations with other bisexual women, usually after play, was the biggest contributing factor to me becoming more accepting of my sexuality and understanding the different layers to me. I'm still working on accepting who I am, but I'm slowly getting there.

Back in the room with Annie, I wasn't thinking about labels; it was all about immediate pleasure. I let out a moan as Annie gently kissed my body from below the sheet, slowly making her way back up to my neck and eventually up to my lips.

"You're yummy!" Annie said, with a grin on her face like a Cheshire Cat.

We both couldn't help but laugh. I gave her a quick peck on the lips. I looked at the time ... it was 1:20 a.m.

"Maybe we should try to get some sleep?" I suggested.

Annie cuddled into me as we laid in bed, but I couldn't fall asleep. I was still processing what had happened. Annie and I just shared a passionate moment together ... and now here we were spooning in bed. A million thoughts raced into my mind. *Was this moment a one-off or something we both wanted to continue to explore? How would Kaleb react to me telling him? Would he feel upset that I played without him?*

The next morning, I woke up with Annie holding me, her arms wrapped around my waist. As I slowly shifted my body, she awoke.

"Morning," she whispered.

"Sorry, I didn't mean to wake you. How did you sleep?" I asked.

"Slept like a baby," she replied with a grin.

"Me too," I said. *Was she going to say anything about last night?* I wasn't going to bring it up if she didn't.

"Shall we get ready and go down for breakfast?" Annie asked.

"Sure." I could feel an awkwardness between us in that moment. I didn't regret what we did last night—and I hoped the same was true for Annie.

As we descended down the stairs, we could hear the chatter below in the dining hall. At the entrance of the room stood a large 5' × 5' white easel, outlining the agenda for the weekend.

"Boy, there's lots we need to do to un-leash this inner goddess in us," Annie chuckled. Some items on the board included: Body Image Issues, Building Self-Confidence and Self-Acceptance, You and Your Sexuality, Trusting Your Body, Enhancing Intimacy in Your Relationship, and Empowering Your Inner Voice.

"Did you see the last one? Make Friends with Your Vagina?" Annie said, laughing.

"These are all interesting!" I said. Then my eyes opened wide with amazement. Group Session: How to Self-Pleasure and Achieve an Orgasm.

"What? How am I supposed to orgasm in front of other women when I can't even do it with Kaleb in the privacy of our bedroom!" I chuckled.

"I think you can also do a one-on-one session," Annie replied. "It looks like no one's signed up for that yet."

"Hmmm ... at least, it's more private," I said.

The past five years had been frustrating and demoralizing for me, not being able to achieve an orgasm. It wasn't that I didn't experience pleasure having sex with Kaleb—I just had trouble climaxing with him *inside of me*. I only came with external stimulation from a vibrator. We would have amazing foreplay and sex, and Kaleb would cum. I would then reach into my nightstand and grab my vibrator to finish off. While it did the job, I missed the closeness and intimacy I felt with Kaleb when we climaxed together, one after the other; we used to be able to satisfy each other fully during sex. Now it was *different*. It was more than just stress and trying to relax in the moment. Nothing worked, not even different sex positions, karma sutra, or smoking pot. I even withheld sex from Kaleb for two whole weeks, expecting it would trigger an orgasmic tsunami within me; however, the only surge that happened came from Kaleb—it was one of his biggest releases ever! I was hopeful that I might be able to orgasm with a different sex partner, but I was wrong—it was the same with Steve. Over time, I came to accept that I could no longer climax during intercourse ... *with anyone.* I honestly believed there was something wrong with me ... my body was failing me, and I wasn't even 40. I was desperate to fix my problem and willing to try just about anything.

"I think I'm going to sign up for the 1:00 p.m. session. Hopefully, she can work miracles," I said. "What about you?"

"I don't know. I don't think anything's going to help me," Annie replied.

"If you don't try, how will you know?"

"I just don't feel comfortable with some stranger touching me..."

This made me question signing up. *How was she going to help me orgasm? What was this therapist going to do?* Despite my fear of what was going to happen in this session, I was desperate to change my situation. I was anxious yet intrigued.

"Let me know how it goes with you. If it works, then *maybe*," Annie said.

"Sure, let me be the guinea pig," I smirked.

After an intensive morning of sessions, I was ready for a lunch break. As I ate alone, I began to think and worry about my upcoming session with the therapist at 1:00 p.m. I had no idea what to expect.

After lunch, I went upstairs to the second floor and gently knocked on the door. A young woman opened the door and greeted me with a warm smile.

"Hi, I'm Tina. You must be my next appointment," she said.

She was an attractive woman, roughly mid–30s, with wavy blondish hair tied up in a ponytail and wearing black yoga pants and a white cotton top. I noticed an interesting tattoo along her right forearm that read *Embrace your uniqueness.* Tina had a calming soft aura about her, which put me at ease. She explained that the session would allow me to feel less anxious and inhibited about my body. She would guide me on how to allow myself to "let go" in order to orgasm. She garnered consent to touch my body with her hands; she would suggest hand movements in addition to guiding her hands over mine when touching my clitoris and vagina. Tina explained that, if I consented, she would be inserting two of her fingers inside of me to allow more relaxation of my vaginal muscles.

I was speechless. This woman was going to physically help me orgasm, yet my husband hasn't been able to? This should be interesting! But I was game to try, so I gave my consent. Tina then left the room so I could undress. Once I had removed all my clothes, I laid on my stomach on the massage table, as she had requested and covered myself with the thin white sheet.

"Can I come in?" Tina asked, knocking on the door.

"Yes, come in." I said anxiously.

Tina entered the room and stood by my head.

"Don't be nervous, you'll be okay," she smiled warmly. "You're in good hands."

"I know. Thank you."

She lowered the white sheet down to my feet, exposing me completely. She started off by massaging some oil in the palm of her hands, gently placing them on my upper back. She slowly pressed down and kneaded across my shoulders and then worked down to my arms. She then moved down my back and onto my waist and hips. As she worked her way down to my inner thighs, I tensed up. *Where was she headed?*

"I would like for you now to turn over onto your back."

"Oh. Okay." I slowly turned over. Exposed and vulnerable, I closed my eyes to ease my anxiety. I could hear Tina shake the oil from the bottle and rub her hands together. Then the warmth of her touch, gently massaging in the oil into my tense shoulders slowly dissipated my uneasiness. She slowly made her way towards my breasts, caressing them. I tried not to think of this as sexual, but it was hard not to. So sensual and relaxing ... this reminded me of the way I felt being with Annie the previous night. I decided to keep my eyes closed throughout so I could focus on my therapist's touch instead of her visual presence.

Tina moved down my stomach, towards my inner thighs, massaging gently. She worked on them for a good ten minutes, going up and down both thighs.

"Is it okay for me to use my fingers to gently massage your labia?" she asked. I nodded. *Could this be happening?*

She continued to massage my inner thighs and slowly inched her way down to my vagina. I could feel her fingers gently working on the perimeter and slowly moving inwards.

Although she was gentle, there was a functionality to the movements of her fingers. To my surprise, Tina then took hold of my right hand.

"Here, I would like you to slowly insert your index and middle fingers inside … like this," she said. Her hand gently held onto my wrist, as she guided me to move my fingers in and out, in unison with her. I could feel myself slowly getting wetter.

As I began to build up pace and vigor, I was surprised to find my breath becoming more rapid and shallow. I consciously tried slowing down my finger movements (and breath), but Tina noticed the rhythmic change. She placed her hand soothingly over mine and continued to guide my fingers in and out, maintaining the quick rhythmic pace. This sensation was getting more and more intense. It felt *familiar* … could I be on the verge of coming?

Although I was excited (and relieved) that my body was physiologically still capable of having an orgasm, I found myself fighting it. I was terrified to let myself go … to feel utterly out of control. My body tensed up, trying to keep in whatever I was holding back.

"It's okay to let go," Tina reassured me, sensing my reluctance. "Allow yourself to feel what you're feeling."

"I don't know if I can."

"It's okay, you are allowed to feel pleasure."

Her reassurance and acceptance were comforting. I wanted to release my inhibitions.

"It's okay, you can let go," she repeated softly. "Let your body relax and feel good."

As we continued our rhythmic hand movements together, I could sense something different happening within my body. There was a deep sexual energy surging inside of me that I couldn't explain or control. Then a visceral urge to release overtook me.

"I'm going to come…"

"Let go," she repeatedly softly.

No! Hold it in! Whatever you do, don't scream, don't come, I chastised myself. But I was slowly losing this fight. I no longer had control over what was about to happen—I was going to climax, here and now, right in front of this stranger! A surge moved through my body—my legs began to shake involuntarily, ending in a rhythmic pulsating and tight sensation in my vaginal muscles. My pelvis elevated as the intensity reached a crescendo.

I shuddered and let out a cry of ecstasy. It was indescribable. My body awoke from a state of dormancy and I finally felt alive again.

As I came down from my high, my body went limp and all the energy suddenly drained out of me.

Tina stroked my arm gently to bring me back to the present. "How are you feeling?"

I couldn't answer, simply nodding. I was in disbelief at what had just happened. At this seismic moment, I realized that my inability to orgasm all these years had nothing to do with Kaleb. This was all about me—my past emotional wounds around sex and intimacy that have stayed with me. I had been afraid of my body ... to get in touch with it, to truly feel pleasure, and to love it with all of its imperfections. Growing up, I hadn't been permitted to fully express my emotions or embrace the experience of enjoying sexual pleasure. Most of my life, I'd worn chains that kept telling me that it wasn't okay to ask for what I wanted or express who I was. I had to be what others wanted me to be ... *a good girl*. I had to refrain from feeling, thinking, and being, which manifested into my caged sexual energy.

In this moment, I realized that I had to change how I thought about myself and about self-indulgence; I no longer had to feel guilty, embarrassed, or weighed down by feelings of shame around my body or for having sexual desires. This moment allowed me to find a deeper connection to my own power within and to discover that I needed to be true to myself in my journey as a sexual being. I deserved to enjoy pleasure in its purest form. I didn't need to feel dirty or bad about it.

"How was your orgasm?" Tina asked.

"It was liberating," I said.

"This is exactly what this massage was meant for ... to let down your inhibitions and find your pleasure center," she explained.

"I can't believe I came ... and in front of you, too."

"Thank you for allowing me to help you."

"I felt safe with you. Thank *you*," I said.

I slowly got dressed and made my way back down to the main room. I felt euphoric, like a weight had been lifted off my shoulders. I finally understood what was holding me back from climaxing ... *me.* It wasn't a physiological problem; it stemmed from my own deep wounds. Allowing myself to climax was about letting go of a lot of things: the shame around submitting to feelings of sexual pleasure ... others' expectations ... and negative messaging that I had internalized from my parents ("think of others, not about your own needs").

The Swinger in the Mirror

I rounded the corner and bumped into Annie who had come from our room.

"Hey you! Did you finish your massage? How was it?" Annie asked.

"I don't know what to say other than it was *powerful*," I said.

"That good?" she asked.

"I didn't realize how much I had pent up inside of me, sexually and emotionally. It was such an amazing experience! You really should sign up for it."

"I don't know," Annie said.

"Well, there's always tomorrow if you change your mind."

"Are you going to the afternoon sessions?" Annie asked, changing the subject. I decided not to push it—Annie's journey was her journey. I had my own to focus on.

"Can't wait!" I said excitedly. "I'll meet you in class."

The other sessions were informative and helpful too. I particularly enjoyed Empowering Your Inner Voice and Building Self-Confidence and Self-Acceptance sessions, where we explored the psychology of our emotions and how they affect our behaviors, even in the bedroom. The entire weekend was an eye-opening experience. I'm a perfection-ist, self-critical, and a people pleaser. I'd been taught by my parents to conform to societal norms and do the *right thing*, at least in public. I was even repeatedly slapped on my left hand for writing or using chop-sticks with it. This was not acceptable practice in my culture. Ironically, my parents' attempt to discourage my *natural tendencies* served to push them underground, only to surface years later in my becoming bidex-trous as well as bisexual ... and in that order.

This weekend experience was life-changing; I learned that I had to be true to myself in my journey of discovering my sexuality, as well as in all other parts of my life. It showed me that I want to feel alive, free, and more whole in my intimate relationships. I wanted to explore my sex-uality further; there was more erotic energy to draw out from within myself. I had to free myself of the shame I carried around when it came to embracing my body, feeling pleasure with sex and getting in touch with my inner desires, including with both men and women. I no lon-ger wanted to feel afraid to ask for what I wanted or to hide or apologize for who I was. I needed to show myself more compassion and to shift from *doing* what others wanted of me to *being* who I truly was. I was on my way to become a more sexually confident woman—one that I was meant to be. This came down to learning to unconditionally trust and love myself *more*.

When I arrived home, Kaleb was happy to see me and gave me a big hug.

"I missed you," he said.

"I missed you and the kids, too."

Kaleb was interested to hear about my weekend, and I was excited to share my new liberated beliefs with him.

"Will my *goddess* come out tonight when the kids go to bed?" Kaleb asked with eagerness.

"She might ... only if you're a good boy," I teased back.

Despite my openness in relaying about my massage experience and everything I learned at the retreat, I was hesitant to tell Kaleb about Annie and our first night together. Would he be mad that I had done it without him being present? I'd never had sex with a woman before. I felt guilty because I felt like I had cheated on him. But I knew I had to tell Kaleb everything.

"There's something I need to tell you," I said.

"What is it?"

"That first night... Annie and I slept in the same bed and things kind of happened."

"What do you mean?"

"We kissed."

"That's good, no?" Kaleb asked.

"It was good ... then Annie and I did other stuff." I told Kaleb what had happened, and to my surprise, he wasn't upset at all.

"You're not mad?"

"Why would I be?"

"I was afraid you would feel that I had cheated on you since you weren't there."

"Yeah, I wish I had been there! Watching the two of you would have been pretty hot!"

I was speechless. I didn't expect Kaleb to react this way, let alone feel horny about it.

"Let's get ready for bed," I winked. "I feel the *goddess* coming out."

10

Our Little Secret

A month after the retreat, Annie called me and asked if Kaleb and I wanted to come over for an impromptu drink. It was a school night, which made the request a little unusual, but Tom was out of town for a couple of days for business and she wanted some company.

"Is it going to be *weird*, just the three of us?" I asked.

"Why? ...it's only drinks," Annie replied.

"Will Tom be bothered? I don't want him to feel like we left him out."

"It's not a big deal. I wasn't going to tell him anyway," Annie replied. She reassured me that it would be fine and not to overthink it.

"Okay, sure, we'll come over," I agreed.

So around 9:00 p.m. that night, we walked over to Annie and Tom's place. My parents just so happened to be visiting that week and could keep an eye on the kids.

"My kids are already in bed and asleep," Annie said, greeting us. "What can I get you to drink?"

"A glass of white wine, thanks," I said.

"Same for me," Kaleb replied. We all lounged cozily on the couch in their family room, watching the logs burning in the fireplace. Kaleb sat on one side of the couch and Annie sat on the other end; I decided to plant myself in between them. I suddenly felt like the third wheel.

"Too bad Tom's away," I said.

"Yeah, he's always busy with work," Annie said, rolling her eyes.

We continued to chat about our day. I could tell our dynamic was off, more stifled than usual in the way we talked. There was no sexual teasing or flirtation that we'd become accustomed to when it was the four of us. Instead, it was a normal, vanilla conversation.

Annie took a big gulp of wine. "Well, I'm ready for another drink!

Anyone else?" Both Kaleb and I nodded, even though there was still some left in our glass. Maybe drinking would lessen the awkwardness.

By the third drink, I would say we were all feeling more our usual selves. Annie moved closer by me and suddenly leaned in to give me a lingering kiss. This was the first time Annie and I had connected in this way since the retreat weekend. We hadn't talked about that night so I'd assumed she wasn't interested in carrying on, sexually, with me.

"I didn't expect that," I whispered to her.

"Sorry, did you mind me kissing you?" Annie asked.

"No, not at all. I'm glad you did," I said, retuning the kiss. Kaleb grinned with approval. He leaned back into the couch and enjoyed the sensual performance. I then took hold of Kaleb's neck and pulled him in for a kiss. I could feel Annie's hands caressing my body as I made out with Kaleb. She then got up and maneuvered herself between us, forcing us apart as she leaned her body against Kaleb. I didn't feel jealous at all. Instead, I felt turned on that Kaleb and I were sharing this sensual moment together ... *and with Annie.* It got more heated as Annie and I took turns kissing Kaleb, vying for his attention.

"You know I've never had an orgasm before," Annie voiced to Kaleb. "I was shocked to hear her bring this up, given how uncomfortable she was talking to me about her sex life."

"Maybe you guys could help me?"

"Ah ... sure," Kaleb replied, not knowing what more to say.

"How so?" I interjected.

Annie led both Kaleb and me off the couch, directing us to lie down on the white rug by the fireplace. Kaleb and I took turns kissing Annie. We didn't miss out on our opportunity to kiss and grope each other as well. The moment was extremely erotic and sensual. Clothes slowly came off until the three of us were lying naked on the rug, all intertwined together in this erotic foreplay.

I then began to lick her clitoris. I lost myself in this moment, loving every second that Kaleb was watching me as I pleasured her. I inserted my fingers to gently massage the inside of her clit, practicing the technique that Tina had shown me. Annie gasped but I could tell she was holding back. Like me, she wasn't allowing herself to be free with her body. Yet her moans were saying something entirely different. I gently directed Kaleb to join in, taking his hand and guiding his fingers inside of her. He became aroused as he massaged her clit. As he quickened his pace, her breath got heavier and louder.

"Do you feel it?" I whispered in her ear.

She couldn't form words. I don't know what prompted me, but I encouraged Kaleb to get on top of Annie, thinking that his hard cock penetrating her would help release her inhibition. I didn't even think about Kaleb not wearing a condom. We weren't planning on having sex; it was supposed to be only drinks. I got carried away by the moment and let this tryst happen.

Soon after Kaleb began riding her, Annie suddenly let out a gasp of pleasure, griping firmly onto his arms as her body quivered. She continued to moan with pleasure after he withdrew.

I couldn't believe what just happened! My husband fucked my best friend (which I encouraged), and she had her first orgasm *in front of us*. You can't make this shit up! Although it was incredible that we were able to help Annie release, I felt mixed emotions. Up to this point, our foursome had only engaged in oral sex, including my encounter with Annie.

I didn't know how to process this moment. I felt confused and emotional. Tom and I hadn't had sex yet, but I was okay encouraging Kaleb and Annie? Our erotic moment got the best of me, and now I regretted my part in urging them to have sex. Although it was good that Annie was able to have her orgasm, this intimate moment should have been with her own husband, not with mine.

Kaleb then rolled onto his side to lay next to me. He kissed me softly and held me tightly. He whispered in my ear, "I didn't come." That made me feel better, knowing that he reserved that only for me. I needed his reassurance at that moment.

I sat up and looked over at Annie, who had her back turned to us, trying to hide her tears.

"Are you okay?" I asked.

"Yeah, I'm fine. Just feeling a bit emotional," she told me. "I can't believe I *actually* came."

"Everything happened so fast," I said in disbelief.

"I know, I didn't get a chance to think—my body just took over," she said.

I reached over to Annie and gave her a hug. I was happy for her ... *truly*.

"I know you've been struggling with this for a while," I said.

"You guys are awesome. I mean that," Annie said.

The three of us laid on the rug together, with Kaleb in between us. Staring off into the fire, we were all in our own heads, saying nothing. *Should we have done what we did ... and without Tom?* I felt guilty.

"Will Tom be upset with what we did tonight?" I asked.

"Not if he doesn't know!" Annie exclaimed. Kaleb and I looked at each other, not expecting her to say that.

"You're not going to tell him?" I asked.

"No, I think we should keep this our little secret," Annie said.

"Keep what a secret? Us fooling around without him? Or that you had your first orgasm with Kaleb?" I asked perplexedly.

"Both. Tom would be hurt and upset if he knew about tonight."

"Annie, it's not right to keep this from him," I said.

"If we tell him, we risk losing what the four of us have," Annie argued. "There's no need to create a situation ... unnecessarily."

"I think we should be honest with him," Kaleb voiced. I agreed with Kaleb. It felt wrong keeping this from Tom. Kaleb and I had formed a friendship with him and it didn't feel right not to let him know.

Annie felt differently. She reassured us that we would never do this again and, therefore, there was no need to say anything. Full stop.

"Okay, I guess you know your husband best," I eventually agreed.

This was the first time Annie convinced us that a secret wouldn't hurt anybody. Looking back now, I realize that this was the beginning of us falling for Annie's manipulative antics, against our better judgment. Kaleb and I knew that keeping this from Tom was wrong, but we didn't want to stir up any trouble for their relationship or possibly end our foursome. We felt conflicted but gave into Annie's wishes anyway.

11

Downtown Hotel Night

True to our word, Kaleb and I remained silent about our three-some tryst. And so did Annie. We all carried on like it never happened. While I didn't talk about that night, I did catch myself replaying that moment of them having sex. It still bothered me. It wasn't so much the act of sex that upset me, as it was the timing and logistics of it. It should have happened in a foursome scenario where Tom and I engaged at the same time as Annie and Kaleb. The score was now 1–0 for Annie but who's keeping track, right? I told myself to let it go and trust that things would even out … Tom and I would have our *moment* soon enough.

About two weeks later, I received my routine text from Annie the second the kids got onto the school bus.

"So what are we doing tomorrow night?"

"I don't know, the usual I guess. Your place or ours?" I replied.

"Let's change it up and do something different."

"Like what?"

"Let's go downtown and find a bar lounge to have dinner and drinks. Maybe dancing after?" Annie suggested. "Why don't you guys drop off Samantha and Lucas at our place, and they can spend the night here with Phillipa."

I smiled. Annie and Tom having a live-in nanny sure made sponta-neous adventures easier. I happily accepted her offer. I couldn't remember the last time Kaleb and I got dressed up and went downtown.

The next evening, I found myself excited for the evening's festivi-ties. We'd walked the kids over to Annie and Tom's earlier in the after-noon so I could have extra time to get ready. Kaleb enjoyed it when I got dressed up and did my hair and make-up; it was a nice change to see me in something other than my go-to home attire—T-shirt, sweatpants, and my hair up in a ponytail.

"Do you like this black cocktail dress?" I asked Kaleb. "Or too much cleavage?"

"There's never too much boob!" Kaleb replied with a smile. I felt bold and beautiful as I stepped into my black heels.

As I was putting the final touches to my make-up, Kaleb grabbed me from behind, kissing my neck seductively. "You look amazing!"

I missed that look from him, like I was the only girl in the world. We were constantly in business work mode or engrossed in parental duties. Those fleeting moments of being in lust with each other, like in the early days of dating, didn't happen often, so I cherished this moment with his eyes all on me.

Annie and Tom drove into our driveway around 4:30 p.m., hoping to beat the Friday rush hour traffic downtown. Annie jumped out of the front passenger side and greeted us both with a hug and kiss on the lips.

"You look great!" I told her. She wore a white satin halter top and black leather pants.

"What about me?" Tom teased, as he peered out from the driver's seat.

"You look devilishly handsome," I reassured.

"You don't look too shabby either," Tom remarked.

"Why don't you sit in front with Tom? Kaleb and I can take the back seat," Annie winked.

As we backed out of the driveway, Tom took hold of my hand and leaned in for a quick peck. I noticed in my rearview mirror Annie and Kaleb already cozying up to one another and making out. I didn't mind seeing this, oddly enough. The four of us were becoming comfortable with each other, and I felt excited to spend time with my *other* partner. Annie had made reservations at a trendy restaurant. She loved organizing and was great at scoping out hip places.

As the hostess seated us at our table, Annie coaxed Tom and I to sit beside each other while she and Kaleb sat across from us. I could see Annie and Kaleb holding hands under the table. I shifted closer towards Tom and placed my hand on his lap. If they were going to display PDA, then I guess Tom and I should follow suit!

As the evening progressed, we ramped up the flirting, giggling, and playful glances. We ordered one cocktail after another and shared a bottle of wine with dinner. Drinking was a huge part of our foursome experience—just as it had been with Natalie and Steve. We seemed to be liquored up every time we were together; I guess it allowed us to step out of our comfort zone and become bold enough to make the moves on each other's mate.

"Where should we go now?" Annie asked, after we'd settled our bill.

"I don't want to go home yet," Kaleb replied. "The night's still young."

"Let's go to the Velvet Lounge. We can have drinks and dance the night away!" Annie suggested.

We all agreed and jumped into a cab. The club was busy, but Annie managed to get a table for us; she had connections with the manager, who was a high school friend of hers. Tom ordered a round of cocktails.

"I sure need this, after a stressful work week!" I said. "I want to let loose tonight."

That's likely the reason why Kaleb and I gravitated towards this four-some experience: it allowed us to feel young, spontaneous and alive. There was also the allure and excitement of breaking rules and doing things that we *shouldn't* be doing. We enjoyed our friends-with-benefit relationship with Annie and Tom; they were our perfect partners in crime. Looking back on it, they were looking for the same things as us—freedom, excitement, and fun. Kaleb and I were exhilarated feeling young and carefree again. *Why would we ever want to stop feeling this way?*

Annie and I got on the dance floor and seductively moved with the music. I had hoped that she would initiate something with me; however, she headed back to our table when the song ended. She didn't seem to want to engage with me in any way more than as a friend. *Hmmm ... what's up with that?* To my disappointment, Annie went over to Kaleb, pulling him out of his seat and up onto the dance floor. Her eyes were only on Kaleb, her partner for the night. She wrapped her arms around his neck and clung onto him as they swayed to Madonna's "Crazy for You." Tom and I sat this one out.

I was jealous of Kaleb dancing with Annie, not because he was with another woman (that was a turn on watching them) but because Annie hadn't looked at me in the same way as she did with Kaleb as they danced close together, gazing into each other's eyes. I nuzzled into Tom's shoulder, seeking attention and comfort from him. I leaned my head into his chest, aroused by the woody and earthy smell of his cologne. I could feel the warmth of his breath on my neck, as if he was coming in for a kiss, but I was wrong. Tom held me close to him and we snuggled. Kaleb and Annie came back to the table when their song finished.

Then, out of the blue, Kaleb suggested we get a hotel for the night.

"Let's have some *fun!* It's after midnight, and the kids are asleep ... what's the rush back?"

Was *fun* code for sex? I didn't see that coming! Had he and Annie discussed this hotel arrangement while they were dancing?

"That's a great idea! There's a hotel down the road," Annie suggested.

Tom quickly agreed, too, so we grabbed a cab to the hotel. I felt embarrassed and self-conscious as we walked into the empty lobby without any baggage. Kaleb and Tom approached the reception desk, while Annie and I stood back. I kept my back turned to the front desk clerk, trying to hide my identity.

"How many nights will you be staying?" I heard the clerk ask. *More like hours*, I thought.

"One night," Kaleb replied.

"Will that be two rooms?" asked the clerk.

"No, one suite please with two queen beds," Tom quickly added. The clerk looked up from his computer screen. There was no doubt the clerk knew exactly what we were up to. One night only, two couples in one room, and no baggage. I'm sure he'd seen this before.

The clerk handed Kaleb the key, and we headed off toward our room. I couldn't believe I was going to finally have sex with Tom. Kaleb opened the door, which led into the living room part of the suite. There was a faint cigarette and musty carpet odor in the room. Annie and I gave each other a disgusted look.

"Okay, so it isn't fancy," I said, leaving the obvious unspoken. *It'll do for tonight.*

The bedroom was to the left of the living room and there were two beds, as Tom had requested. Annie and I went to the bathroom to freshen up. As I was trying to unzip my black dress, Annie stood behind me and to my surprise, she began to kiss my right shoulder. She continued to unzip me and slowly lift off my dress, leaving me standing in my black lace bra, panties, and stilettos. I returned the favor, undressing her as we continued to kiss each other. I didn't want us to stop.

Suddenly, Annie broke from our kiss. "We should get back to the boys," she suggested.

"Oh, okay," I replied, disappointed.

Was I moving too fast? Or did Annie not want to take it further with me? Maybe she didn't feel the same way? Annie walked out of the bathroom, and I followed behind. Tom and Kaleb were stretched out on each bed, with only their boxers on, a look of sheer delight spread on their face seeing us in our lingerie.

The Swinger in the Mirror

"Come here!" Kaleb said to me.

I slowly made my way to him, soon forgetting about Annie and what had happened in the bathroom. As I leaned over to kiss him, I stuck out my buttocks and arched my back, making sure to expose my black lacy thong to Annie and Tom.

"Whew! That's hot!" Tom exclaimed.

Kaleb held my face with both hands and brought me in closer to him, kissing me with passion. As we continued to kiss, I slowly straddled him.

"I like this side of you!" Kaleb said. His fully erect penis wanted all of me *now*.

"Not yet," I teased. I slid off to his side and began to seductively caress my breasts and play with myself. Kaleb looked surprised at how bold and playful I was, a side of me he hadn't seen in a long time. While I was enjoying myself, teasing my husband, I admit that this performance was partly for Annie, to showcase what she was missing.

Kaleb attempted to reach out and touch me, but I backed away.

"Uh-uh!" I said, as I pushed his hands away. "Keep your hands down by your side," I commanded. I lingered over his chest, kissing it softly and then inched my way down, hovering over his groin area.

I looked over at Annie, catching her smile. She accepted the unspoken invitation and approached. She began to caress my back and kiss the nape of my neck, which sent shivers down my body. Kaleb and Tom watched in anticipation as Annie continued to tease me with her tongue and lingering kisses. Annie and I were loving this moment—holding our husbands captive, as they waited with bated breath for our next move. Annie slowly made her way down my body. I moaned in ecstasy, hoping she was enjoying this as much as I was.

Annie then turned her attention to Kaleb, kissing his lips softly and pressing firmly against his body.

"Come with me, big boy," Annie whispered into Kaleb's ear, as she pulled him up from the bed and led him to the adjacent bed. It was time to be with our new partner.

Tom laid down next to me. I closed my eyes as we kissed passionately. I pretended he was Kaleb, which aroused me even more. I couldn't help but glance over to Kaleb and Annie, their lips locked and hands all over each other. Just as I had felt when I saw Kaleb and Natalie together, it was arousing to watch my husband with another woman. Even though we were on separate beds, I felt connected to Kaleb, as we watched each other touch and stimulate our partners.

11. Downtown Hotel Night

As I caught Kaleb looking over at us, Annie's hand quickly turned his face back to her attention.

"Are you jealous? You keep looking over at them," Annie whispered to him.

"No, it turns me on when I watch her," Kaleb replied.

"I want you to look *only* at me," Annie instructed him. She then got up from the bed and took hold of Kaleb's hands.

"We're going to the other room," Annie announced. Kaleb obediently followed her to the living room, leaving Tom and I alone in the bedroom.

We're not going to watch each other have sex? Just as I'd been uncomfortable when Natalie wanted to be alone with Kaleb, I had reservations with this arrangement. I desperately wanted to shout out, *Hey! Don't leave!* but I didn't. This was one of those moments when Kaleb and I should have taken a moment to talk privately before we did anything ... we should have followed **Rule #4** (talk about details before you act). We were making the same mistake we made with Natalie and Steve. We hadn't discussed any boundaries of our sexual play, either. *Why hadn't we learned from our mistakes with Natalie and Steve?* I honestly don't know. Maybe it was a combination of not thinking in the moment and also taking a casual, reactive approach to situations instead of a preemptive move to assert our needs first as a couple ... but we clearly didn't think about us again, and that's where we've gotten ourselves in trouble over the years.

Tom quickly turned my attention back to him by guiding my hand down to his stiff cock.

"Oh!" I grinned, immediately forgetting about Kaleb and Annie.

"Where were we?" Tom asked, playfully.

I gave him a lingering kiss. "I want you to be inside of me," I pleaded. All these months of flirting and now, Tom and I were going to finally have sex.

But wait a minute! What about condoms? Was Tom planning on going bareback? I know that Kaleb didn't have any condoms on him so he likely wasn't going to use one either. The four of us hadn't had this discussion yet. I could have (and should have) asked Tom to wear a condom to be safe; however, my libido was taking center stage at that moment. I felt like history was repeating itself. Just like with Natalie and Steve, the four of us hadn't talked about boundaries, rules or the logistics before playing. *Would it have been the smart and responsible thing to do?* Probably. Instead of adopting a *think-before-you-act* approach, we went into full *doing* mode ... yet again.

The Swinger in the Mirror

Tom was great in bed, better than I had hoped for. It was definitely worth the wait! Afterward, we cuddled. We could hear Annie and Kaleb enjoying each other in the next room.

"I guess they're still at it," I smirked. Tom held my face and kissed me.

"I'm sorry I came so quickly. I couldn't help myself. You turn me on so much," Tom expressed. I grinned at him.

"You know how to make a girl feel good," I teased.

"I truly mean it."

"Thank you. I'm attracted to you, too," I told him.

"I wished you had come, too. Was there anything I could have done better to help you?" he said. Tom was such a caring and thoughtful lover.

"I enjoyed myself, honestly. I loved everything about it," I said. "But I usually don't come *easily* ... not even with Kaleb."

"I appreciate you telling me. I wouldn't want a girl to fake it with me."

I guess Annie's orgasmic moaning was very convincing. Poor guy.

I enjoyed being alone with Tom, especially how attentive he was to my needs. But I preferred all of us being in the same room—that would have been better. I wished I could be a fly on the wall to see what Kaleb and Annie were doing. The last couple of years I've watched Kaleb struggle to climax during sex; it was taking him way longer and took physically more out of him, to release than before. Although Kaleb had no problems becoming erect, he was becoming increasingly frustrated not being able to *pull the trigger* despite his efforts. He was especially discouraged that he hadn't been able to cum inside of me in the last few years, which was what I most enjoyed during intimacy. I wondered if he was experiencing the same with Annie. *Could he get hard with her? Was he getting frustrated? Wait a minute! What if he did cum with her?* I felt despair at the thought. Kaleb once confided to me that, although he enjoyed being with Annie, he wasn't particularly attracted to her; she wasn't his type.

"You know that I prefer brunettes over blondes," he had told me.

"Annie's very attractive!" I voiced.

"I'm not saying she's not. I just prefer *you*!" Kaleb grinned.

By the sounds of their groaning and moaning, Annie and Kaleb seemed like they were doing just fine. I could feel a bit of jealousy slowly creeping up inside of me... I didn't like that feeling. *Why was I being like this when I wasn't the jealous type?*

While waiting for them to finish, Tom and I searched for our clothes and got dressed. We laid on the bed and Tom made small talk about his work, although I didn't pay much attention. I kept my ears to the noise level next to us. I pretended to listen to what he was saying, occasionally smiling and nodding my head.

The moaning eventually stopped. Kaleb must have finished. Ten minutes later, they emerged from the other room, fully dressed. We stared at them as they came in, looking coy and embarrassed, like we had caught them in the act of doing something they shouldn't have been doing.

"Sorry, we didn't realize you guys were waiting for us," Kaleb said.

"No worries, it's all good," Tom replied.

"We should get going, it's getting late," I told Kaleb. "Plus, we still need to pick up the kids." Kaleb nodded.

"Leave them with us. They can all have breakfast together," Annie piped in.

"Thanks," I said. "I'll drop by your place after breakfast then."

"Well, that was fun! We should do it again real soon," Tom said, giving me a wink.

We gathered our stuff and left the hotel room. As the four of us walked through the lobby, the front desk clerk looked up from his computer, smirking like he was right all along about us doing a quick hookup. *Not likely we'll stay at this hotel again!*

As Tom drove home, it was awkwardly quiet in the car; no one said a word. Annie was in the front passenger seat this time, while Kaleb and I sat in the back. The vibe was different from when we were driving down 10 hours earlier.

"Home sweet home!" Tom said, as he drove up our driveway. Annie and Tom got out of the car, and we exchanged hugs and kisses.

When we got up to our bedroom, we noticed it was 3:00 a.m.—much later than I thought. I couldn't wait to take my make-up off and climb into bed. I was exhausted and wanted to sleep, but Kaleb had other plans. He unzipped his pants, letting them fall to his ankles. Without saying a word, he pulled my body close to him and turned me around to stand facing the bed. He lifted up my dress and pulled my panties down.

"Bend over," he commanded.

"Babe, it's late," I tried to protest, but it was a weak attempt. Seeing Kaleb want me so bad was a turn on.

"I *said* bend over," he repeated. This time, I obeyed.

He knelt down on his knees and began to massage my clit slowly, moving my legs further apart.

"Now, it's my turn to have you," he said.

I relished this moment... I had all of Kaleb now. Holding me tightly as we laid in bed, Kaleb whispered, "It feels so good to finally cum tonight." I was surprised to hear him say this.

"Didn't you cum with Annie?" I asked.

"No. I couldn't even get hard with her tonight," he said. "I had way too much to drink."

Was it really the alcohol? Kaleb had no problems getting hard with me before we swapped partners. Maybe he was right—he wasn't into *her*.

"Oh ... was she bothered?" I asked.

"Probably, but she didn't let on."

Although I felt badly for Annie, my possessive self also felt relieved that she didn't have him completely tonight. I knew that it was selfish of me to feel this way, but I was glad Kaleb was still *mine* ... at least for the moment.

12

What Annie Wants, Annie Gets

* * *

The next morning, the alarm went off at 8:00 a.m. *Ugh, I forgot to turn it off!* We'd only gotten four hours of sleep. I looked over to see if the alarm had woken Kaleb, but he appeared to still be asleep. *Damn, I forgot I had agreed to pick up the kids from Annie's.*

I stumbled out of bed and managed to get myself dressed and head over to their place. I didn't see Annie or Tom, only the nanny, which was fine as I didn't want to linger anyway. I was exhausted but last night's nightcap was worth it! After I got the kids back home and settled in front of the television, I crawled back into bed. As I cuddled into Kaleb's backside, he slowly turned over to me and began kissing me softly.

"Morning," he said, pulling me in closer.

"How did you sleep?" I asked.

"Not good."

"Maybe we can have a power nap this afternoon," I suggested.

Kaleb's eyelids began to close and he dozed off. But I was wide awake and in full conversation mode. I couldn't get last night out of my head, thinking about what Kaleb and Annie were doing in the other room.

I poked Kaleb, abruptly waking him. "Did you have fun last night?" I had to know.

Kaleb struggled to keep his eyes open. "Uh huh," he mumbled.

"How was it with Annie?" I asked.

"It was fine."

"Fine good, or fine okay?" I prodded.

"I'm barely awake, babe," he pleaded. "Can we talk about this later?"

"Why can't we talk about it now?" I asked, impatiently. Kaleb could sense the *need* in my voice.

"Okay, what do you want to talk about?" he asked. He sat up in bed, stretching out his arms and yawning.

"Did you enjoy last night?" I asked.

"It was, uh, good," he replied.

"How *good*?"

"Not as good as you think," he answered.

"Why are you being so vague?" I knew I was likely irritating him, but I couldn't let it go.

"What do you want me to tell you? That I couldn't get a hard on?" he snapped.

"I'm sorry, I was just curious," I said, taken aback by his tone.

"Look, honestly, other than oral, nothing happened," he said. "We didn't have sex, if that's what you want to know."

I felt bad now, bringing this up. "Oh."

"What about you guys? Did you have fun?" Kaleb asked, trying to change the topic.

I went quiet.

"I guess you had sex then," he said with a look of disappointment on his face.

"Are you upset that we did?"

"No, not really. I just wished I was able to get hard."

"Do you regret going to the hotel last night?" I asked.

"I wouldn't say I regretted it ... the night didn't go the way I had expected, is all," he explained. "And it kind of sucked that we weren't in the same room."

I nodded in agreement. "I didn't expect you guys to leave," I said.

"I didn't either, but she wanted to be alone in the other room."

"It felt weird when you left."

"I wish we had stayed," he explained. "Maybe I wouldn't have had a problem getting hard if I had watched you or touched your body."

Last night wasn't *exactly* what Kaleb and I expected or wanted for our first foursome play with Annie and Tom. Although sex with Tom was great, Kaleb and I didn't get the voyeur experience we wanted as a couple, which would have heightened the eroticism of that moment. For us, a true foursome required all four participants to engage at the same time *and* in the same physical space, drawing sexual energy from the exchange; there was something intensely erotic about watching your spouse being enraptured by another partner. And then there was the issue of Kaleb not being able to perform with Annie. *Was she upset? Would she bring it up with me?*

"Aren't you attracted to her?" I asked Kaleb.

"I thought I was. I had no trouble that night with the three of us. But last night, no matter what she did, I couldn't get hard," he explained.

Hearing this made me feel more guilty that Tom and I clicked sexually and he got his happy ending. I didn't share this with Kaleb.

"Maybe you had too much to drink," I reassured him.

"Yeah, maybe. I'll cut back next time," he replied.

I couldn't help but wonder if that would really make a difference. What if he still couldn't perform? *Would Kaleb end this foursome?*

My cell phone pinged, jolting me from these racing thoughts back to the present.

"It's Annie," I told Kaleb.

I hope Annie doesn't bring up about what happened with Kaleb, I thought. *What would I say to her? What could I say?*

"Do you guys have plans next Saturday?" she messaged. *Phew!*

"Nope. Why?" I texted back.

"I'm throwing a dinner party, and I wanted to invite you guys," she messaged.

"Let me check with Kaleb, but it should be okay," I typed back.

I normally would be excited about a dinner party (and play after) but I wasn't. I wondered if Kaleb would have the same problem with Annie. *What then?*

It seemed that our social calendar pretty much revolved around Annie and Tom. Getting together with them was becoming more and more planned. There was no spontaneity or last-minute decision to do something exciting; last night's adventure was not our norm. It was also starting to bother me that everything was scheduled by Annie. It was getting to a point where we sort of felt guilty if we didn't say yes to whatever she suggested. It became somewhat of an expectation to hang with them every weekend. Although they were a lot of fun to be around, there was a big part of me that hated this expectation and feeling obliged to agree every time she asked us over. I didn't know how to say no to Annie, to anything she asked of me.

There I was again with my need to please and not wanting to disappoint people! As a child, my father instilled in me a sense of guilt and even fear whenever I didn't do what was asked of me. Kaleb couldn't relate to this; he didn't feel guilty if he didn't meet up to people's expectations—it was their issue, not his. If Kaleb didn't want to do something, he'd speak up; however, when it came to planning socials with Annie and Tom, he left it up to me and went with the flow.

It was difficult to maintain our regular "vanilla" friendships during this monogamous foursome relationship, causing us to lose touch with many of our closest friends. During that time, I didn't realize that we were neglecting them. When they'd ask us to go out on a particular weekend, I already knew we'd have to decline because we would likely be hanging with Annie and Tom. I made up some excuse and suggested that we'd touch base the following month, knowing full well that we would still be busy. A close friend once asked me, "Have you guys gone MIA? You're never around!" It was easier to avoid their calls or texts than have to tell them repeatedly that we were unavailable, *yet again.*

We became completely absorbed and some would say even, *addicted* to our relationship with Annie and Tom. They made us feel like teenagers again, ready to let loose and party when we clocked out on Fridays at 5:00 p.m. Lots of flirtation, drinks flowing, and laughter, which was then capped off with a late-night tryst. And hit repeat, week-end after weekend. It even felt weird if we missed a weekend. Looking back, Kaleb and I were bored with our life; we were stressed with work and dealing with family responsibilities, with nothing fun to look forward to. Kaleb and I needed a distraction. Then Annie and Tom came along. It was perfect timing.

"We're free on Saturday!" I texted back fifteen minutes later.

"By the way, I've invited Melissa and Doug to join us," she messaged back. Melissa was a former co-worker and the four of them had known each other for years.

"I can't wait to meet them!" I typed.

"Don't get any ideas! They're leaving after dinner," she messaged with a smiley face emoji, hinting that there was 0 percent chance of us three couples *hanging* together.

"That didn't even cross my mind," I typed back, with a winking emoji. She sounded possessive in her tone, reminding us that she wasn't planning on sharing us.

"We can do drinks after the kids go to bed. Phillipa agreed to work for us that night." Annie inserted a winking emoji—having drinks was synonymous with getting it on.

That Saturday afternoon, we told the kids that we were going over to Annie and Tom's place for a dinner party.

"Why can't we come, too?" Samantha whined.

"No kids are going. Plus, you haven't seen grandma and grandpa in a while," I said.

"I don't want to go over there. Why can't we all stay home and watch a movie?" Lucas suggested.

12. What Annie Wants, Annie Gets

"Oh babe. Annie is making a special dinner for the adults," I tried to explain. "We'll watch a movie tomorrow, okay? I promise."

"You always go over there!" Lucas exclaimed.

I felt guilty leaving the kids every weekend, and now they were complaining. The adult voice in me said we should stay home with them more often, skip a weekend or two, if we were *good parents*. However, the teenager voice didn't want to stop having fun. *Didn't we deserve it after a hard week of work?* As a compromise, Kaleb suggested asking Annie if their kids could do a sleep over at our place, provided Phillipa could come as well.

"That's a brilliant idea! Then the kids could keep each other company," Annie messaged back. "Phillipa will bring the kids over to your place after they finish dinner."

Kaleb and I walked quickly over to Annie and Tom's house, getting there around 7:00 p.m. After being at their place so often, we automatically let ourselves in through the front door and made our way to the family room, where we found Melissa and Doug sitting on the couch by the fireplace. They looked up when we entered the room.

"Hi, I'm Kim, and this is my husband, Kaleb," I said. They stood up and greeted us with a hug.

"I'm Melissa, and this is Doug," she replied.

Then Tom entered the room, with a drink in hand for Doug.

"Good, I see you guys made introductions," Tom said. "What would you like me to get for you?"

"Glass of wine for me, please," I replied.

"And you'll have a scotch neat, right?" Tom asked. Kaleb smiled and nodded.

Annie was busy in the kitchen, getting dinner prepared.

"Do you need any help, Annie?" I asked, peeking into the kitchen. "Or better yet, a drink?"

"Thanks, but I'm almost done and ready to serve," she replied. "Could you ask everyone to get seated?" I summoned the others to the dining room.

Annie was the perfect host. She had prepared an elegant dining table, which was set with a fresh floral centerpiece and two white candles; crystal wine glasses and white China plates were neatly positioned on the white sheer floor-length tablecloth, accompanied by silver cutlery and neatly rolled white cloth napkins.

"Wow! The table looks stunning," I voiced.

"Something smells amazing, too!" Kaleb added.

"I hope you all like prime rib," Annie replied. We nodded with enthusiasm.

Annie truly outdid herself, serving us a four-course meal that rivalled any Michelin star restaurant. That's one thing about Annie: when she did something, she did it 100 percent. It was all-or-nothing with her.

"That was delicious! I couldn't eat another bite," Melissa exclaimed.

"We hate to eat and run, but we have to pick up Susie from the babysitter's," Doug explained, after a phone call had pulled him away from the table moments earlier.

"Everything okay?" Tom asked.

"Yeah, she's fine. She wants us to come home," Doug replied. "She says her tummy hurts, but I think she misses us."

We all got up from the dining table, and Melissa and Doug put on their coats.

"It was nice meeting you guys. I hope we can see you both again soon," I said. Kaleb echoed the same sentiment.

"Yes, it was lovely meeting you both," Melissa replied, as she gave Kaleb and I a hug.

"Sorry, Annie, that we couldn't stay longer but you know how it is with kids," Doug said.

"We get it," Annie replied. "These things happen, unfortunately."

After the good-bye hugs and kisses, Annie closed the door behind them.

We made our way back to the family room and sat on the couch.

"Too bad they had to leave early," I said. "They seemed like a nice couple."

"They're awesome people," Tom said.

"Well, the timing couldn't have worked out any better!" Annie exclaimed. "Now we get to *hang out*, just the four of us." Annie winked.

"Who needs a touch up on drinks?" Tom asked, hoping to prime us for the night of play ahead. Kaleb and I nodded.

Tom brought us our usual selection, a scotch on the rocks for Kaleb and a glass of Riesling for me. As the evening progressed, I felt a pressing need to bring up our hotel experience. We needed to have a candid conversation of what we each wanted to get out of this foursome and make sure we were all on the same page.

"Did you guys have fun last weekend at the hotel?" I started off.

"Yeah, it was great!" Annie said. "What about you guys?"

"We had a good time..." Kaleb replied. Annie could sense some reluctance in his voice.

"You sound like you were about to add a *but*," Annie said, with a nervous laugh.

"No, it *was* good ... but to be honest, it would have been better if we were all in the same room, playing *together*," Kaleb replied. I nodded in agreement.

"How would that be better?" Annie asked, with a perplexed look.

"Well, Kim and I enjoy watching each other having sex. It's a huge turn on," Kaleb explained. "We were hoping that you guys were into that, too."

"That doesn't work for me. I'm not comfortable with all of us being in the same room," Annie was quick to assert. Tom remained quiet.

Kaleb and I looked at each other, not knowing how to respond. What could we say? This was how she felt, and she stated it in no uncertain terms.

"Look, I don't want Tom to watch me have sex or vice versa. That doesn't turn us on," Annie explained.

"How do *you* feel about it, Tom?" I asked.

"Uh, it's up to Annie. If she prefers to be in another room, then that's fine with me," Tom said.

Tom's reaction here was not so surprising, given that he always went along with whatever she told him when it came to social plans. Hearing Annie strongly voice her displeasure with playing in the same room made it harder for Kaleb and me to push back with what we wanted. We didn't want to upset Annie and force her to do anything that made her feel uncomfortable; in order to be sympathetic of her feelings, we had to forgo our own needs. So, while I was reluctant to agree to this separate play arrangement, I found myself caving. That was our second mistake with Annie and Tom (the first being that we allowed it to happen in the first place, at the hotel).

We polished off the last of our drinks, which signaled that play time would soon begin.

"Before we get started, I just want to talk about the condom situation," I asserted. "We probably should have talked about this way before now."

"I'm glad you brought it up," Annie replied. "I know Tom didn't use one last time but I want you to know that he and I are safe. We haven't been with anyone other than you guys."

I felt uneasy that I hadn't told Annie about our past monogamous relationship with Natalie and Steve; however, nothing needed to be said since Kaleb and I had done STI testing several months after it ended and we were both negative. It was agreed upon that the boys didn't need to use condoms in our foursome exchange.

"That's a relief!" Tom exclaimed and Kaleb nodded in agreement.

"Now that's settled, shall we have some fun?" Annie asked.

Kaleb and I subtly gave each other a look, indicating that we weren't happy that we would have to go our separate ways shortly. No foursome exchange ... no sexual arousal watching each other ... and no chance of girl-on-girl play. Tom and I stayed in the family room while Annie stood up and took hold of Kaleb's hand. Feelings of sadness came over me as I watched Kaleb walk out of the room, with her leading him down to the basement spare bedroom. However, this mood quickly changed when Tom took hold of me and caressed my face, kissing me tenderly.

Maybe this separate room arrangement didn't have to be *all* bad, I convinced myself. I tried to focus on the added benefits. Tom was gentle, romantic, and sensual, which differed from Kaleb, who was kinky, wild, and raw in his sexual prowess. With Tom, I could live out my fantasy of being with another man who took pleasure in *pleasing me* instead of me being the pleaser. There was also a different synergy—I was able to focus solely on Tom and what we were bringing to each other in that intimate moment, instead of splitting my attention when the four of us were in the same room. *Kim, this could be a good thing ... give it a try.*

After an hour had passed, Annie and Kaleb emerged from the basement, fully dressed. Kaleb's evening had not gone well, once again, and they walked in on us as we were having sex on the couch for the third time.

"Ahem!" Annie cleared her throat. Tom immediately stopped mid-thrust and pulled out. That was an embarrassing moment. I felt uncomfortable getting caught in the act. We both sat up abruptly, and I quickly threw a nearby blanket around me. Tom grabbed his pants and put them on.

"You guys already done?" Tom asked nonchalantly.

"Yeah," Kaleb replied with a serious tone. I reached down to grab my clothes from the floor and quickly got dressed. I could sense a bit of annoyance and agitation in Kaleb's demeanor, but I had no idea why. Annie also seemed a bit off, which added to my feelings of uneasiness.

"We should get going," Kaleb said firmly.

"Yeah, I guess it's late," I said.

We exchanged quick goodbyes to our hosts, and Kaleb and I walked home briskly in the darkness.

"What's wrong? You seem upset," I asked, as I tried to keep pace with him.

"I don't want to talk about it," he muttered.

"What happened?"

"It's the same old shit. I couldn't get hard again," he replied, exasperated.

I didn't know what to say.

"Why is it so easy with you?" he asked. "Maybe I'm just not into her."

This was not what I wanted to hear. I felt badly for Kaleb ... and also for Annie.

"Sorry babe, I didn't mean to take it out on you," he said apologetically.

"I know you're frustrated. I don't blame you," I said.

"I don't really want to talk about it. So, how was *your* night?" Kaleb asked, trying to change the topic. Should I tell Kaleb the truth—that Tom and I had sex multiple times and he came each time? Normally, we would tell each other every little detail but, right now, I didn't want to say much. It would only make him feel worse.

"It was fine," I said.

"Looked like you two were right into it ... when we came upstairs," Kaleb said. "I assume he came?"

I nodded. Then Kaleb gave me that *look* ... it reminded me of when my father got agitated with me when I was a child. *Was Kaleb blaming me for his inability to pleasure Annie?* I learned as a child that I wasn't supposed to feel happy if others weren't feeling the same. I was raised to be sensitive to people's moods (and non-verbal cues) and to give into their needs, to a fault. I was made to feel guilty, ashamed and embarrassed (all at the same time) if I had done something that my father disapproved of. It was drilled into me that I couldn't be happy if others were not, especially if it pertained to my father. So, if Kaleb wasn't happy in this moment, then why should I be? I felt guilty because I had sex and Kaleb hadn't. His problem became *my* problem. I was desperate to fix Kaleb's situation ... and make him happy (or at least not as upset).

"You need to relax and get more comfortable with her. Maybe give it another try?" I said reassuringly. But despite my encouragement, I had no way of knowing whether things would get better. This could be the end of our foursome fun.

When we got home, we got ready for bed. Kaleb quickly turned off the night lamp and turned over. I guess we weren't going to have sex, like we normally did after a foursome tryst. Lying there in the dark, I replayed in my head the moment when Kaleb and Annie walked in on Tom and I having sex ... my feelings of guilt growing.

13

Even the Score

* * *

Early the next morning, there was a text alert on my phone.

"Morning," Annie messaged.

"Morning," I replied.

"Did you have a good time last night?" she typed with a winking emoji.

"Tom and I had fun," I replied. "What about you guys?"

"Well... I'm not sure if Kaleb had a good time with me," she messaged.

"What do you mean?" I typed, trying to act like I knew nothing.

"Didn't Kaleb tell you?" she typed.

I wished I could be honest with her, but I didn't want to hurt her feelings. My friendship with Annie was making it more awkward and difficult being in this foursome, particularly when she brought up things about her and Kaleb. I was desperately trying to be Annie's best friend *while* she was having sexual relations with my husband and coming to me to talk about their difficulties. My head was spinning, trying to keep these two things separate. Looking back on it now, it was way too complicated to maintain this friendship-foursome. The lines were getting blurred and boundaries were being crossed. Although I wanted to make this work, I was beginning to realize that I was in over my head.

"No," I lied.

"Can I call you? I need to talk," she messaged.

"Sure," I messaged back, taking the phone to the bathroom, since Kaleb was still asleep.

"Are you okay?" I said, once we were able to talk.

"I'm feeling a bit bummed out," she replied.

"Yeah, you didn't seem yourself at the end."

"I wasn't. I don't think Kaleb's into me," she blurted out.

"Why would you say that?" I asked.

13. Even the Score

"It's not that we don't have fun together. Maybe he's just not *attracted* to me."

I knew what Annie was trying to get at, but I didn't want to bring it up.

"He couldn't get hard last night," she continued, "and this wasn't the first time either. I'm starting to wonder if it's me."

My heart was pounding. *Should I be honest with her or cushion the blow?* I went with the latter.

"Kaleb was a bit drunk last night. I know when he drinks too much, he has a harder time," I told her. I knew this was partially a lie. Kaleb was always able to get hard with me, no matter how drunk or late it was.

"It's not that our foreplay was bad. In fact, it's amazing!" she explained. Offering up TMI was not something I needed or wanted to hear. "But when it's *time*, everything goes south."

How backwards was this? My best friend was asking me for reassurance that Kaleb, *my husband*, was sexually attracted to her.

"Of course he's into you!" I replied. *I felt bad lying to her but what was the alternative? Tell her the truth and say that Kaleb didn't feel that she was his ideal type?*

"You just need to give it some time. Once Kaleb feels more comfortable, everything will fall into place," I said, repeating the same spiel that I had given to Kaleb.

"You're right. I'm making this a bigger deal than it has to be," Annie said. "It'll be fine."

"You guys will work it out, I'm sure of it."

Attempting to switch gears, Annie asked, "So how was your night with Tom?"

Was this a test? What did Tom tell her?

"Umm ... yeah, it was nice hanging with him."

"Don't worry, I won't be upset if you tell me. He and I don't share any details. I'm just curious," she explained.

"You guys don't talk about it?" I asked.

"It's sort of like the separate room thing. We prefer to keep things *private*."

"Gotcha."

"I have to ask ... did Tom cum with you?" she asked. I paused. "You can be honest with me."

"Umm ... yeah, he did," I said hesitantly. "Is that okay?"

"No, that's fine."

The way she said things made me feel worse. The guilt meter was rising. I suddenly heard myself say the craziest thing.

"Maybe you and Kaleb should get a hotel room ... by *yourselves.*"

"Huh? What do you mean?" Annie sounded perplexed.

"Maybe it's too much pressure on Kaleb, and all the drinking doesn't help either. You guys can get some alone time to feel more connected. That might help Kaleb to relax and you know, get *ready*," I said.

What was I saying? I was telling my best friend to spend time with my husband and have sex in a hotel room all night long. This was not what I'd envisioned this foursome to be like! My sense of guilt and compassion for their desperate situation far outweighed my visceral gut feeling of how amiss this whole idea was.

"Are you sure?" Annie asked.

"I'm sure. I want you and Kaleb to have another chance."

"Maybe you're right—we need some *alone* time together," she said.

I told Annie that I would talk to Kaleb and figure out where and when this meeting would happen. I couldn't believe that I was going to help set this up! I regretted making this suggestion immediately, but it was too late. Annie was excited and on board with the idea. *What have I done?*

"You told her what?" Kaleb said when I told him about the plan. "So, let me get this straight ... you want me to go to some random hotel room to have sex with her for the night, without you there? Have you lost your mind?" he asked.

"I know it sounds whacked, but maybe you'll be more relaxed if you guys are alone, and there's no time pressure or drinking involved," I said.

"I don't know."

"Listen. I want you guys to catch up, so to speak," I explained. "Maybe this is what you need to get over this hump."

I reassured Kaleb that I was okay with this indecent proposal. Looking back now, it was the most outlandish idea I've ever come up with!

"Fine, I'll do it ... but remember, this is *your* idea, not mine," Kaleb said.

"Okay, good. I'll arrange things and get a hotel."

Annie ended up planning everything. She was the planner after all. She had booked a hotel nearby for that coming Wednesday night. The plan was not to come home until they achieved success.

"Are you sure you're okay with this plan?" Annie asked me again.

I pretended to be nonchalant about it all, like they were going out for a lovely dinner. The reality was I wasn't okay at all. I honestly tried not to think about the sex part; instead, I tried to focus on how this would help strengthen their connection and inevitably reinforce our foursome relationship. There was a method to my madness, so I thought.

As Wednesday approached, I could feel myself getting more anxious and unsettled about what would be unfolding. While Kaleb was getting ready for the evening, I tried to keep myself busy with the kids so I didn't have to think about it.

"I'm heading out now," Kaleb said, as he peered into the kitchen. It was shortly after 8 p.m. "I won't be too late, I promise." He hugged me tightly and gave me a kiss, but I didn't reciprocate. On some level, I felt upset at him that he was going through with it, even though this was my idea. I was now regretting my decision. I didn't want Kaleb to leave.

"You know that I love you, right?" he asked.

"I love you, too."

"Like you said, let's fix this problem so we can all move past this and have fun," he said. I know Kaleb was taking a logical approach to the whole thing; however, my gut instincts were screaming, *Stop this insanity! Why are you allowing her to have your husband?* I watched as Kaleb backed out of the driveway and drove down the street. Now I had to wait for him to return.

A half hour after Kaleb left, I felt an urge to reach out to Tom to see how he was handling this situation.

"Hey! What are you up to tonight?" I texted him. I anxiously waited for his reply, which came in a half hour later.

"Still at the office working on some stuff," he messaged back. How could he even concentrate on work when his wife was banging my husband? He seemed pretty chill about the whole thing.

"Do you want to come over for a drink?" I suggested.

"Sorry, I'll be at the office pretty late tonight," he replied back. Damnit! I let out a big sigh. No distraction to help me through this. I had an overwhelming sense of dread ... my mind was racing all over the place. *What have I done? This was a big mistake.* My intentions were to *help* Kaleb but this wasn't helping me. I felt queasy and my stomach churned.

This private hotel arrangement was not the same as a foursome experience; it was more like an open relationship. It crossed that boundary. Even though we went to separate rooms, we were technically still under one roof, fooling around altogether and *at the same time*. What

Kaleb and Annie were about to do in that hotel room felt separate and secretive ... a love affair of sorts.

I turned on the television, but I couldn't focus on anything. I kept glancing at the clock ... 9 o'clock, 10 o'clock, 11 o'clock...

When would Kaleb be home? How long does it take to have sex, seriously? Was he able to perform and cum? What were they doing now? Were they enjoying themselves? Did I want to know?

Eventually, I heard the whir of the garage door open. It was 12:08 a.m. Although I felt relieved that Kaleb was finally home, I also felt irritated with him. I knew I had no right to be, but I couldn't help it. I felt disconnected and distant from him, like a part of him was no longer mine. I quickly switched off the night lamp so he wouldn't know that I had been waiting up for him.

He walked into the bedroom and quietly headed into the bathroom to shower and get ready for bed. I couldn't bear waiting until morning to talk, so I turned my lamp back on and sat up in bed. As Kaleb emerged from the bathroom, he was startled to see me awake.

"Did I wake you?" Kaleb asked.

"No, I wasn't asleep," I replied.

"Did you have a good night?" he asked.

"It was okay. Watched some of my reality shows."

"That's good." There was a long pause.

"So ... how was *your* night?" I asked.

"It was fine," he replied.

"Did everything go okay?" I asked.

"It's all good."

"So, you guys were able to have sex?" I asked. He nodded. "Did you cum?" He nodded again.

"It was better tonight. You're right, I did feel more relaxed," Kaleb quickly replied.

"I guess Annie was happy," I said.

"She's feeling better."

Thank God, we're even now! Yet, I didn't feel relieved or happy that they fixed their problem; instead, I felt jealous ... she had my husband all to herself tonight. I was filled with mixed emotions. Deep down I knew rationally that Kaleb was my beloved, but that didn't stop me from feeling insecure and wanting reassurance from him. Yet, I didn't communicate my feelings in the best way. It came out more passive-aggressively in my tone.

"So... I guess you're into her *now*?" I asked. Kaleb could sense jealousy in my voice.

13. *Even the Score*

"Listen, I have no more interest in Annie than you have with Tom, if that's what you're implying," he exclaimed. "This was a means to an end, for the sake of our foursome. This was *your* idea, remember?" He sounded exasperated, and I didn't blame him. He was right. He agreed to do this hotel night because of me; I was the one who suggested it, all because I wanted to end the drama and have the four of us get back on track.

"I'm sorry, you're right," I said. "I'm just feeling insecure right now."

"Babe, there's no need to feel insecure. You never lost me," he reassured. Kaleb pulled me in and held me tightly. "I'm glad to be home ... with you."

"I'm glad you're home, too."

Although there was no danger when it came to Tom's intentions in this foursome, my womanly instincts felt differently about Annie. *Was she my friend or did she have other motives?* Tom was pretty obtuse when it came to emotions or feelings. He was too busy with work to want to deal with any drama. This foursome and our sexual hookups were strictly weekend entertainment for him, which is how Kaleb and I saw it as well. For us three, this foursome was meant to be just pure sexy fun. Full stop.

Unbeknownst to us, Annie saw it differently ... and it would soon become clear to us that she had a vested interest in Kaleb. Little did I know then that hotel night was a turning point in my marriage.

14

What About *Us*?

*   *   *

I didn't sleep well that night, tormented by the intrusive thoughts of Annie being in Kaleb's arms. My phone dinged as I was making coffee. Annie's usual morning check-in.

"Morning! What's your plan for today?"

I wasn't in the mood to talk; however, I knew if I didn't respond, she would know that something was off with me.

"Not sure yet. Slow morning for us," I texted back.

"I guess you know by now, everything is good between Kaleb and me," she messaged. Annie seemed more chipper in her tone ... obviously I knew why. I didn't want to let on that I was bothered about their hotel night. I didn't want to admit it to myself that I was having conflicting emotions and feelings. A part of me felt relieved that they got over Kaleb's problem; however, another, huge part of me felt awful and troubled... I *wasn't* okay with them being alone last night, despite me being the one to encourage them in the first place. I had neglected my feelings in the process of satisfying Annie's needs and making her happier. My inner voice whispered *Be careful, you're treading on dangerous ground! Annie's getting too close to Kaleb.* Yet, I chose to suppress this prophetic feeling in order to focus on us four getting back to our fun socials and not having to worry about Kaleb or Annie pulling the plug on it.

"Do you want to meet for coffee this afternoon?" Annie texted.

"I'm not sure if I have time today," I messaged back.

"A quick coffee. Please."

"Okay, 2:00 p.m. Let's meet at our usual spot," I messaged. Even though I didn't want to see her, I couldn't say no to my best friend. I was trained to never ask for anything, never say no to a request, and not be any trouble for others.

As I walked into the coffee shop, I saw that Annie was already there, seated at a table in the back. She smiled and waved at me. She gave me a warm embrace when I reached the table.

"I got you a coffee."

"Thanks."

"You look great!" she said enthusiastically. *Was she trying to get on my good side?* She seemed in better spirits than when we chatted a week ago about her and Kaleb's issues.

"I feel like shit, to be honest," I replied.

"What's wrong?" she asked.

"I didn't get much sleep last night."

"Well ... that's why I wanted to talk to you today. I wanted to apologize about us coming home so late. I hope we didn't keep you up waiting," Annie explained.

"No, not at all," I said, trying to act like I didn't care when Kaleb got home.

"Are you truly okay about last night?" she asked.

I wasn't in the mood to talk about *them* but she wasn't going to let this go.

"I'm fine. Why wouldn't I be?" I said.

"I don't know. I just want to make sure we're still good, you and me," Annie said.

"Listen, I'm happy you guys finally *connected* with each other. We're all good now," I said.

Annie gave a big sigh of relief. "I'm glad, too. I didn't know if Kaleb was into me but now, I know we're good together, sexually."

I felt sick to my stomach hearing these words. My insecurities took over. Why was I jealous? I felt like she and I were competing for Kaleb's attention, like we were in high school. Irrational thoughts swarmed inside my head. *Who was better in bed? Who did he find sexier, me or her? Who did he enjoy being with more?*

"I hope we can move on from this," I said, trying desperately to change the subject and talk about something else ... *anything*. I didn't want to talk about them; there was no Kaleb and Annie. This lack of physical connection between them was exactly that, an obstacle that had to be overcome in order for the four of us to resume our playful fun.

"I think we should all go away together," Annie suggested. "Maybe Vegas?"

Annie and Tom had been there a few times on business conventions, but Kaleb and I had never been.

"That's a thought," I said.

"Let's convince the boys to go, say next month?" Annie said excitedly. "Tom could take Friday off so we can do a long weekend."

"Sure, I'll talk to Kaleb."

"I can check out some hotels and flight costs, and we'll present the idea to the boys on Wednesday. Drinks at our place?" she asked.

"Sure, sounds good," I said. I was happy to be getting back to the fun stuff instead of talking about their night together. Moving on. Next.

Mid-week, we went over to Annie and Tom's place to plan the Vegas trip. The guys were super stoked about the idea and left it up to us gals to plan everything, as usual.

"Tom, we should hire Par Mates while we're down there!" Kaleb suggested. I learned that these were fun, sexy young female caddies for hire at upscale golf courses. Both Tom and Kaleb were avid golfers so they loved this idea of being catered to by hot babes.

"I'm all in!" Tom replied.

"I'm not sure if I like this idea!" Annie interjected.

"Let the guys do their thing and we'll do our own," I said to Annie.

Switching topics, Annie asked, "What about the sleeping arrangement?"

"What do you mean?" I asked.

"It might be more fun to room with our partner for the entire weekend," she suggested.

I didn't see this coming. Neither did Kaleb. We were caught off guard by her suggestion and didn't know how to respond. It was hard for us to process how we felt in the moment, if this was a good idea or not. All we knew was Annie could be extremely persuasive and it was hard to say no to her. She was pushing for this arrangement. Tom being Tom, simply went along with it.

"Listen. If we stay with our partner 24/7 this weekend, it'll be easier that way," Annie voiced. "No need to move our luggage between rooms."

I didn't want to argue and make a big deal about this so I conceded with her suggestion. "If that's what you want, we can try it," I said. Kaleb looked at me in disbelief.

"Wait a minute! So, Kim and I can't even sleep together at night?" he asked.

"Well... I thought it would be nice to spend nights with our partner," Annie stated.

"I don't know about this," Kaleb said to me.

"Don't worry, we'll hammer out the details later," Annie said.

As the evening wore on, we had a few more cocktails before we went our separate ways for play time. I don't remember much of my night with Tom, other than replaying over in my mind what Annie had said—she would be with Kaleb day and night and I wouldn't see him at all. *How crazy was that?*

As we walked home quickly in the early hours of the morning, Kaleb suddenly stopped and turned to me. "Why do you always cave to what she wants?"

"What do you mean?" I asked.

"You always give in to her, and you don't even ask me first if I'm okay with it," he retorted.

"Babe, I don't want to fight with you," I said.

"I don't want to fight either but I'm getting tired of giving in to her. What about what *we* want? First, it was separate rooms during play, then that hotel night with her, and now this 24/7 thing! *What next?*" he exclaimed.

"You saw how adamant she was."

"This foursome is not all about *her*. We need to stand up to her and tell them what *we* want!"

"I know. I'll talk to her, don't worry," I said. Deep down, though, I didn't feel confident she'd change her mind.

That following Monday, I asked Annie out for coffee. I needed to talk to her about this coupling arrangement in Vegas.

"Kaleb and I were talking about this trip. We're excited to go, but this whole separation for the entire weekend is a bit much, don't you think? How about we compromise?"

"Like how?" she asked.

"We could do alternate nights with our husbands?"

"That's not going to work. I don't want to move our stuff back and forth between the rooms," Annie replied. "It's just easier if we stay with our partner all weekend."

"Listen, we've never been away with another couple, let alone get separated from each other. This isn't what we expected ... or want," I explained.

"I'll be completely honest with you. I don't feel comfortable switching between Tom and Kaleb," Annie blurted out. "That's the reason why I always take Kaleb to another room. I don't like orgies or playing with two partners ... it makes me feel cheap."

"Oh..." *I guess that makes me cheap then.* "I didn't realize you felt this way."

"I'm not trying to make it difficult for everyone," she said. "I just want to respect what makes me feel comfortable."

"No, I get it." Obviously, I didn't want Annie to feel cheap or slutty in any way. *How could I argue her point? This was how she felt and I had to respect her feelings, right?* I convinced myself.

"So, can we keep things separate in Vegas?" Annie asked.

"Yeah, sure. I'll explain it to Kaleb so he understands," I said.

"Thank you," she said, giving me a hug.

Kaleb wasn't happy with this arrangement but felt pressured to go along with it, for the sake of the foursome and my friendship with Annie.

The week leading up to our Vegas weekend was a mixed bag of feelings for me. This was our first time away with Annie and Tom. Although I was anxious and nervous about being apart from Kaleb, I was also excited about being in Vegas and how much fun the four of us would have. It was going to be a quick trip, flying out on Friday morning and returning on Sunday morning.

I became increasingly antsy as the date approached to leave. *How would it feel not to reclaim Kaleb sexually right after? Was I okay with not being able to hold and kiss him when I wanted to? Would I miss Kaleb? Would he miss me? Would Tom get on my nerves being with him all that time? Or would we bond even more so?* What had started off as a fun naughty trip now filled me with anxiety.

Were we ready for this?

15

Vegas Weekend

* * *

"We might as well get this party started!" Tom exclaimed, taking a sip of the beer he'd ordered at the airport bar. We'd already checked in and were just killing time now before boarding.

"Exactly! So, why don't we sit with our partner on the flight down? It would be fun!" Annie suggested.

I looked at Kaleb.

"Sure, why not ?" he replied.

On the plane, Tom and I were seated four rows ahead of Annie and Kaleb. When they offered beverage service, Tom suggested champagne to celebrate our first weekend together. With each sip. I became more relaxed. I found myself cuddling into his side; Tom reciprocated by putting his arms around me. I felt excited, being with him, like we'd started dating. I found it strange that I could instantaneously alter my thinking and suddenly transform Tom into a pseudo boyfriend. Tom inched closer to my face, giving me a soft lingering kiss. Kaleb and I never showed any form of PDA, but it felt easy being in Tom's arms and kissing him. I didn't care if passengers seated behind us were judging us—it didn't matter.

I tried not to think about Kaleb and Annie together, and Tom was a good distraction. I was shocked to hear from Kaleb, after the trip, that he and Annie only talked on the flight down, no PDA; they were engrossed in their conversation about life and past relationships. Oops, and here Tom and I were smooching like honeymooners!

Three hours later, we landed in Vegas. Tom and I walked off the plane, hand in hand; Kaleb and Annie were ahead of us. We caught up to them at the baggage area.

"That was a long flight!" Kaleb exclaimed.

"It was quicker than I thought it would be," Tom replied, giving me a wink.

The Swinger in the Mirror

We flagged down a taxi to take us to the Bellagio Hotel. Tom and I checked in together, Kaleb and Annie followed suit. Our rooms were on the 25th floor. When the elevator doors opened, we all got out and stood there momentarily, waiting for someone to say something.

"So ... we're good to pair up for the entire weekend?" Annie asked.

"If that's what you want, then I guess so," I replied. Kaleb nodded in agreement.

"Cool," she said. "It's 5:00 p.m. now, so why don't we meet up for dinner at 8:00?"

"Sounds good!" Tom said. We said our good-byes to our spouses. I didn't know if I was "allowed" to give Kaleb a kiss but I did anyway. Tom followed my lead and gave Annie a quick peck. Then we headed off in opposite directions.

Tom and I held hands as we walked to our room. Before opening our door, he suddenly lifted me up in his arms, with my legs flailing about.

"What are you doing?" I laughed.

"Pretending we're on our honeymoon," he answered, as he carried me into our suite. That was the one thing I loved about Tom—his fun silly side could always make me laugh and smile.

"We have exactly three hours to relax and get acquainted," he said with a devilishly grin. "I couldn't wait to be alone with you!"

Okay, this arrangement might not be all bad...

"I took the liberty of ordering room service. They're bringing up a bottle of champagne and strawberries," Tom called out, while I was freshening up in the bathroom. Despite the excitement of being with Tom, a small knot formed in the pit of my stomach. I wondered what Kaleb was doing at this moment. *No, I'm going to have a great time with Tom and not think about them this weekend,* I convinced myself.

"That's so sweet of you!" I called out.

When I came out, I saw that the goodies had arrived. Tom opened the champagne bottle and we had a toast to us. Then, he took my glass and placed it on the nightstand. He came in closer and held me in his arms, kissing me passionately. Tom was a great kisser and it was hard not to feel attracted to him. He stood six feet tall, with broad shoulders and had a muscular yet athletic built. He'd clearly been going to the gym! He slowly unbuttoned my blouse and slid off my jeans, keeping on my lacy black bra and matching panties. Tom's eyes widened with anticipation of what he wanted to do to me.

He led me to the large glass window by our bed, which overlooked their infamous Bellagio fountains and beautiful pools below. I could see tranquil mountains in the far distance, which contrasted against the bustling street below and flashing billboard signs on the Vegas strip. This was going to be an exciting weekend for us!

I faced the window with Tom edged up behind me, rubbing his body against mine. The palms of my hands pressed firmly against the glass. He swept my hair to one side and began to kiss down my neck, making my entire body tingle. I could feel his fingers slowly slide down inside my panties, attempting to move them to one side. He then positioned himself and quickly thrust inside of me.

"Does that feel good?" he whispered into my ear.

"It feels *so* good," I moaned.

With each thrust, I became more wet and my moans got louder and more intense.

"You feel so good!" I screamed.

"You want more of this?" he teased.

"Fuck *yes*! Give it to me!" I begged him. Tom held my shoulders firmly and kept driving into me, causing me to pant louder. Then, suddenly, he withdrew without warning and began to caress the opening of my ass with the tip of his cock, teasing it back and forth.

I knew what he wanted. It had been a while since I had anal sex with Kaleb; he wasn't particularly fond of doing it. I enjoyed anal more than I had admitted to Kaleb. I felt relaxed and willing to engage with Tom at this moment. I knew he would be gentle and I trusted him.

"Are you OK with this?" he whispered into my ear. I nodded.

"He then gently slid his cock inside. His slow rhythmic in and out motion felt incredible, intensifying pleasure with each insertion. Tom echoed this sentiment with a moan."

"Does she like anal?" I whispered.

"We've never tried," he replied. "She's not into it."

"Oh."

"Do *you* like it?" I asked him.

"Very much," he said breathlessly.

"Me too."

Tom loved that I enjoyed anal sex. He continued to thrust into me with more vigor and then let out a loud groan as he came inside of me. He slowly removed himself. I turned around and gave him a lingering kiss before heading to the bathroom. When I came out, Tom laid on the bed, motioning for me to join him. I nuzzled into him and we fell asleep in each other's arms.

I slowly awoke and focused my eyes ... it was 7:40 p.m.! I didn't realize how exhausted I was.

"Oh no!" I exclaimed. I softly shook Tom to wake him up. "Babe, we have to get up!" I urged him. Tom pretended to be asleep and as I went to whisper in his ear again, he pulled me into him playfully and gave me a lingering kiss.

"Not before we have a quickie!" he said playfully.

"I wish we could but I have got to get ready," I laughed, trying to pry myself away from him.

"Fine, be that way!" he teased.

"You're so cute. Tonight, I promise!" I said, giving him a kiss.

We only had twenty minutes to shower and dress.

I jumped into the shower and did a quick touch up of my make-up. I opened up my luggage and rifled through it. *What was I going to wear tonight?* I needed to look super sexy and make Kaleb pine for me.

"What do you think of this outfit?" I asked Tom. I'd chosen a low-cut body-hugging olive-green dress, with a matching choker and black heels. Kaleb loved this dress ... it'll be hard for him to resist me.

"Wow! You look stunning!" Tom exclaimed, as I stepped out of the bathroom. It felt nice being given a compliment and attention, especially by a man who wasn't my husband.

Tom kissed me on the forehead and said, "I'm glad you and I are spending the weekend together. I've been waiting for this moment."

"Me too." I smiled.

I then looked at my phone—it was already 8:05 p.m.

I quickly messaged Annie, "Sorry, we're running behind. We'll meet you in the lobby in five minutes!"

"No problem. We'll wait for you guys," she quickly messaged back.

It's funny that I automatically texted Annie and not Kaleb; it wasn't that I didn't want to reach out to him, I assumed *her* rules included no contact between spouses the entire weekend.

I missed Kaleb.

Looking back now, I don't know why I didn't break Annie's stupid rules! Maybe I was too afraid and guilt-ridden to go against her. I didn't want to jeopardize our friendship and foursome. Kaleb was aware of how important her friendship was to me ... and Annie knew that as well, and likely capitalized on it.

Ironically, Tom and I ended up waiting for them in the lobby. Kaleb and Annie strolled towards us, holding hands and giving each other playful glances. I felt a lump in my throat. Annie looked sexy in her skin tight black jumpsuit and blingy heels. I saw Kaleb give her a captivated look and smile. I've never felt more invisible and distant from Kaleb than in that moment. My sense of reality became distorted. Kaleb was no longer mine; he was some random guy with Annie. It was a strange feeling I've never felt before. I didn't know how to process all of this in my head.

"Sorry, we got tied up," Annie said, with a coy glance at Kaleb.

"We weren't waiting long," Tom said.

"I made reservations at the hotel steakhouse," Annie told us.

Annie and Kaleb led the way, hand in hand. The hostess sat us at our table. Annie sat next to Kaleb and Tom sat beside me. As we perused the dinner menu, no one brought up details of the three-hour hiatus, as if we were all napping the afternoon away. Right!

"Who needs a drink?" I asked. I wanted to keep the drinks coming so I wouldn't think about them and their afternoon together.

"Yes, let's order a bottle of wine," Tom suggested. That was one thing we always had together—lots of drinks, laughter, and cheeky fun. That's likely why Kaleb and I hung onto this foursome as long as we did; Annie and Tom were a lot of fun to be around.

After a long day of traveling, we all decided to have a low-key evening and head back to the room for a nightcap. Hitting the Vegas strip and club scene would be saved for tomorrow night.

"Come to our room!" Tom suggested after we all got off the elevator. "We have an amazing view!" Tom gave me a side wink.

"Sure, give us five minutes to grab some wine from our room," Annie said.

"We'll leave the door unlocked, just come in," I said.

While we waited, Tom and I got comfortable on the bed and began making out.

"Ahem—are we interrupting you guys?" Annie said, clearing her throat.

Tom and I quickly sat up on the edge of the bed.

Annie remarked with a devilish smile, "Nice bed!"

We all got comfortable on the couch in the living room and put some background music on. As we sat drinking our cocktails, Annie suddenly blurted out, "We should talk about boundaries for this weekend."

"Like what?" I asked, looking surprised.

"I don't know, like what we aren't allowed to do with our partner or our spouse," she explained. "Just so there's no, uh, misunderstandings."

"What were you thinking?" Kaleb asked her.

"Well ... first thing is we shouldn't be texting or talking on the phone with our spouse," she replied. (So, my gut had been right on that one!) "Or any physical touching," she asserted. She felt it would add more to the whole experience of being with our new partner if we weren't in contact with our spouse at all.

"Okay..." I said meekly, glancing over at Kaleb to see his reaction.

"So, *nothing* at all with our spouse?" Kaleb asked.

Annie nodded.

Then came the kicker. She added that anal sex was an absolute no-no. *Oops, you're a tad late with that one,* I thought.

"Come on! Why do we have to impose bedroom rules?" Tom remarked. "It should be spontaneous and anything goes if our partner is okay with it." Kaleb and I gave each other a sideways glance. We didn't expect Tom to stand up to Annie.

"No, I disagree. Anal is off limits," Annie exclaimed. "We shouldn't do anything we haven't already done with each other."

Tom's face had guilt written all over it.

"You had anal already? Seriously?" she asked. Tom's silence confirmed it.

There was awkwardness in the room. Annie did not look pleased but she tried to maintain her composure. "Well, I guess there's no point talking about it now," she said.

"We didn't know it was off-limits," Tom said defensively. "You should have mentioned it before." The tension in the room was palpable. I looked over at Kaleb to see his reaction.

"I know, we should have talked about it first," I said. "Are you mad?"

"I didn't expect to hear *that*," Kaleb replied. "But I'm not upset."

"Well, I'm still bothered by it!" Annie exclaimed, looking in my direction.

"I'm sorry, if I had known, we wouldn't have done it," I explained. I felt this need to rationalize and defend myself, so Annie wouldn't be as pissed. This conversation was going downhill and killing the mood for the night.

"Why aren't you more upset?" Annie asked Kaleb. *Was she trying to rile him up?*

"Why should I be?" he replied.

"Well ... because!" Annie said.

"Look, just because I'm not into anal doesn't mean they can't do it," he explained. "If I had wanted anal with Kim and she said no to me but then did it with Tom, that'd be a different story. Of course, I'd be fucking pissed!" Kaleb expressed.

"Yeah, I guess," she said, appearing calmer. Kaleb's opinions appeared to carry more weight with Annie.

"So, no bedroom rules?" Tom asked.

"Yeah," Annie said. "We can do whatever we want this weekend, no holds barred."

"Good," Tom said.

"Okay, now let's get this party started!" Kaleb suggested, hoping to extend the night. It's almost as if he read my mind—I didn't want him to leave either. If only I could meet him secretly in the bathroom and steal a kiss, that would help to reassure me that everything was good between us, after the anal sex discussion.

"I think we should head out," Annie said to Kaleb.

"But the night's still young!" I added. "What's the hurry?"

"It's been a long day," Annie said, trying to stifle a yawn. "It'll be nice to stretch out on a bed."

I couldn't help feeling sad and disheartened—Kaleb was going to leave *me* to spend the first night with *her*.

"Annie's right. We should get some shut eye," Tom said, as he finished off his drink. "Anyway, we'll see you guys at breakfast."

As we all stood up, there was a moment of uncomfortable silence ... should we not kiss our spouse tonight? I gave myself a shake. *Why should I care what her rules were—Kaleb was my husband!* I gave Kaleb a hug and he kissed me tenderly on the lips. Tom playfully grabbed Annie by the waist, pulling her in to kiss her; however, she coyly turned her head and his kiss landed on her cheek. Annie then grabbed Kaleb's hand and pulled him towards the door.

"Enjoy your night," she said, as the door closed behind them.

I wasn't emotionally prepared to see them go off together.

"Hey, what's wrong?" Tom asked, sensing something was off with me.

"Nothing," I replied.

"Are you sure?"

"I'm fine."

"How about a back massage to make you feel better?" Tom asked, pulling me in closer to him. He began to gently rub my shoulders, which erased any tension I was feeling. I soon forgot about *them*.

"You don't have to do that. You must be exhausted," I said.

"Really, I want to," Tom said, directing me to the bed.

"Don't lose that thought," I said, pulling away from him. "Let me slip into something more comfortable," I said, heading to the bathroom.

Tom laid on the bed, stroking himself; however, he abruptly stopped the moment I walked out in a black lacy satin slip dress.

"Do you like what you see?" I asked. He nodded with a devilish grin. I slowly made my way to the bed and laid beside him. He began to massage my shoulders and kiss my neck gently. I relaxed and tried to embrace this moment with Tom.

"I want to be inside of you all night long," Tom whispered in my ear.

I was grateful to have this distraction.

Let's just say we didn't get much sleep that night. This moment with Tom was different than other times. I felt a deeper emotional connection with him. I was on the brink of breaking **Rule #1** (no intimate feelings towards your sex partner). I didn't know how Tom was feeling (and I never asked him ever) but I could feel myself beginning to develop an emotional bond with him, like he was my boyfriend. I soon forgot about being apart from Kaleb—Tom was a good substitution. He held me closely as I slept in his arms. We managed to grab a few hours of sleep before the alarm went off at 8:00 a.m.

I saw a missed call and message from Annie to meet them at 8:45 a.m. in the hotel restaurant. Tom and I got ready as quickly as we could, in between playful kisses and canoodling.

This time, they were waiting on us. I could feel Kaleb's eyes staring at me as we approached them. He looked especially handsome with his white t-shirt and faded blue jeans. I wanted to reach over and touch him, but I knew I couldn't. I missed Kaleb and it had only been 24 hours!

Luckily, we had a busy day ahead to keep me preoccupied. Annie and I were going shopping and the boys were golfing. We all agreed to meet up for dinner.

"Thanks to Kaleb, we have lovely Par Mates lined up!" Tom said, grinning.

"Why do you even need female caddies?" Annie asked. "You can tee up your own balls!" Although I, too, felt a bit jealous of these young attractive college girls, I knew it was just innocent fun for the boys.

"Let them have their fun and we'll have ours," I told Annie.

16

My BFF

* * *

After breakfast, we went our separate ways. The boys drove to the golf course and Annie and I went shopping on the strip. When it was only the two of us, Annie and I got along like sisters and talked about everything. Since we met, I had shared more with Annie than I had with my own sister. However, lately, I found myself holding back from telling her things, particularly after she had insisted on the weekend trip rules. I didn't understand why Annie was so rigid on keeping everything separate. *Why did she really want to spend so much time with Kaleb—and not with her husband?* I wanted to talk to her about this but how was I going to bring it up without causing a fight? Maybe it was best to leave it alone and focus on having fun this weekend, I thought to myself.

"We should head back to the hotel and get ready for dinner," Annie said.

"What time is it?" I asked.

"It's close to 5:00 p.m." We were supposed to meet the boys at 6:30 p.m.

"Yeah, we need time to glam up for tonight!" I said excitedly. Annie and I made our way back to the hotel.

"Come to my room when you're ready," I suggested.

"Okay, see you soon!" Annie said, giving me a hug before heading to their room. "I'm so glad we spent the day together."

"Me too."

I was excited for our night in Vegas. I wanted to get dressed up extra special—I was hoping to tempt Kaleb into sneaking me a kiss when Annie wasn't looking. I yearned for his touch. This separation was harder than I thought it would be. As I got out of the shower, I heard a knock on my door. I glanced at the clock and saw it was 6:00 p.m. I slipped into my bathrobe and went to the door.

"Who is it?" I asked.

"It's me," Annie replied.

"You're early!" I said.

"Yeah, there's been a change of plans. Kaleb messaged me and said they're running late with their game."

"Oh."

I wish Kaleb had texted me instead of *her*. This non-communicating thing between us was getting to me.

"The boys don't know how much longer they'll be," Annie said. "Kaleb said we should go to dinner by ourselves and they'll join us later for drinks."

My heart sank. I knew in my head I shouldn't be upset because it wasn't their fault that their game was taking longer than expected; however, the emotional side of my brain took over. I was disappointed and upset! I had been waiting all day to see him and he wasn't even making more of an effort to be with me—instead, he was having more fun with those damn Par Mates!

My emotions were all over the place. I was already feeling incredibly jealous that Kaleb spent last night with Annie and now, he was with a Par Mate. *Didn't he miss me?* I felt invisible to Kaleb. I've never felt this way before ... insecure, jealous, and second-guessing his feelings for me. This wasn't what I was normally like—but nothing about this weekend was normal! I didn't know how to process my emotions and thoughts. If only we had spent last night together or, at the very least, had some time to talk to each other today, I wouldn't have felt so upset about the turn of events.

"You and I will have fun at dinner!" Annie said, trying to lift my spirits.

I didn't understand why Annie wasn't as upset as I was; in fact, she didn't seem to be bothered at all that they were ditching us for their golf game and Par Mates. This was strange, given that she wasn't thrilled about getting them in the first place. However, I kept this to myself.

"Okay, I'll finish getting ready," I said.

"Meet me down in the lobby in twenty minutes?" she asked.

"Sure."

As I got off the elevator, I saw Annie sitting at the lobby bar. She was dressed in a hot pink blouse, black leather pants, and heels. I had been excited to get ready for tonight, but that feeling dissipated after learning that the boys had changed plans. Nothing seemed right tonight; no boys at dinner, my make-up looked mediocre, and my black halter dress felt tight and uncomfortable. But I knew deep inside, it wasn't the make-up or my dress ... it was me not feeling right about *everything*. I prayed for the evening to get better.

16. My BFF

"Hey gorgeous!" Annie exclaimed, interrupting my thoughts.

"Sorry to keep you waiting," I said.

"I just got here myself."

"Can't wait to try the restaurant!" I said, trying to pump myself up for a fun evening.

"It's not far from here," she said. "But we should get a move on it."

When we arrived at the Japanese restaurant, we were greeted by a hostess who seated us at a table for four.

"It'll just be for two," I said, giving Annie a side glance.

"Forget about the guys!" Annie exclaimed. "Let's order some drinks!"

"Yes please!" I said.

After quickly polishing off an Old Fashioned, I decided to order another one.

"Could you bring us another round?" I asked our server. I wanted to forget about Kaleb. I could see the restaurant manager casually checking me out, smiling every time I looked his way. I had noticed him on the way to our table.

"Is that guy staring at you?" Annie asked. "He's kind of cute!" He was well-dressed in a blue suit and white collared shirt, looking GQ-ish with his chiseled features and crewcut hairstyle.

"He's okay," I said. The waiter then came to take our order. By this point, I had already downed two stiff drinks.

"Do you think the manager over there would mind bringing us our drinks?" I asked the waiter. *The boys were having fun with their Par Mates so why shouldn't we do the same?*

Several minutes later, the manager came over with two glasses of wine and introduced himself.

"Good evening ladies! I'm Tim, the manager. How's your night going?" he asked.

"Doing better now that you're here," I boldly replied. He gave me a wink and smile.

"Any special occasion you're celebrating?" he asked.

"Nope, just wanna have fun tonight," Annie replied.

"Well, this round is on the house," Tim said, looking directly at me.

"Thank you," I said.

It wasn't busy in the restaurant, so Tim hung around our table throughout the night.

"He seems to be into you," Annie grinned.

"He's just being nice," I said. I knocked back the glass of wine, even though I was pretty tipsy by that point. All I knew was it felt good having any guy's attention—and I didn't want it to end. While Tim was standing next to me, I suddenly heard myself ask, "Are you single?"

Tim grinned and said, "I am." He handed me his business card and whispered in my ears, "You should ring me up some time."

I smiled and quickly placed his card in my purse. Annie was becoming increasingly annoyed with our flirtation, and she subtly gave me a judgmental look.

"We should head back to the hotel," Annie interrupted.

"Why? We haven't ordered dinner yet," I said, in an irritated tone.

"Our wonderful *husbands* are waiting for us!" Annie remarked. "Kaleb just texted me and they're on their way back." Now I was annoyed; he was texting her (instead of me) *and* spoiling my fun evening with Tim.

"Sorry, we have to head out now," I told Tim. "We should get the bill."

"Oh, too bad. I was hoping we could have some fun tonight after I get off work," he grinned.

"Maybe another time," I said.

Tim returned with the bill.

"It was nice meeting you, and thanks for the drinks," I said warmly. Then to my surprise, Annie asked, "Could we take a selfie with you in front of the restaurant?"

"Yeah, sure," he said. Annie got her iPhone ready and had Tim stand in the middle between us. I could feel the warmth of his hand around my waist, pulling me in closer. Was I attracted to him? Absolutely! Did I enjoy his flirtation and attention? Absolutely! But I had no intentions of doing anything more with him. This was all innocent fun and a much-needed distraction for me.

"Now, just the two of you," Annie said. "Come on, get closer."

What are you up to, Annie?

Tim readily agreed, pulling me in and staring into my eyes. Although he was extremely attractive, I felt uneasy. Kaleb would not be happy knowing that this stranger was holding me this close. Just as Annie was about to snap our photo, she suddenly said, "Give her a kiss." Tim didn't hesitate, giving me a peck on the cheek.

"Now, you can do better than that!" Annie insisted. "You know you want to kiss her!"

Tim and I looked at each other, not knowing what to do in this awkward moment. I laughed nervously as he looked to me for permission. I suddenly felt his soft lips on mine. As our kiss lingered, I noticed a flash go off. I pulled away from his embrace.

"I shouldn't be doing this. I'm married," I told Tim.

"No, I understand," he said. "I'm sorry if I overstepped."

"It was nice meeting you," I said. Tim went back into the restaurant and we headed in the direction of the hotel. As we walked quickly, neither Annie nor I spoke. I felt confused, upset at myself that I allowed Tim to hold and kiss me like that yet at the same time, I felt disappointed the moment had ended. Unbeknownst to me, Annie had sent the picture of our kiss to Tom when they were back at the hotel getting changed. And, of course, he immediately showed it to Kaleb.

Just as we reached the hotel, I heard a text alert on my phone. It was Kaleb. Why was he texting me? He knew Annie's rules.

"Who's this guy? And why the fuck are you kissing him?" Kaleb accused. I didn't know how to respond. I couldn't believe Annie sent this photo to them. *Did she want me to get in trouble?* My head was spinning. Everything was happening so fast. One minute, I'm in LaLa land smooching with some guy and the next minute, my husband is pissed-off, and rightfully so.

"Why did you share that picture of me and Tim?" I asked angrily.

"I didn't think it was a big deal," Annie replied.

"What do you mean? Kaleb's upset at me right now, thanks to you!" I exclaimed.

"I only sent it to Tom," Annie tried to explain. "I didn't know he was going to show it to Kaleb."

"Well, he did!" I exclaimed. How would I explain this to Kaleb?

"Don't worry, I'll talk to Kaleb. Everything will be fine," Annie reassured. "It was my idea for you guys to kiss." I didn't have a good feeling; my stomach was in knots.

Annie and I went straight to her and Kaleb's room. The boys were seated on the couch when we walked in. Kaleb folded his arms and glared at me, waiting for me to say something.

"Do you want to talk outside?" I asked. He stood up, not saying a word. Annie and Tom smiled awkwardly at each other. We went into the hallway. At last, Kaleb and I were finally alone but I didn't want it like this.

"What the fuck were you thinking?" he shouted at me.

Although I knew Kaleb had every reason to be mad, in some perverse way, I felt justified doing what I did. I rationalized in my head that he got to do whatever he wanted to do today—flirting (and Gods knows what else) with his Par Mate, and I got to do what I wanted—so an innocent kiss with a cute guy seemed fair. As juvenile as it sounds, I admit I wanted to get back at Kaleb for not giving me any attention. I wanted him to feel jealous.

Although I knew in my head that I was in the wrong, Kaleb's irate reaction fueled my anger and prompted me to lash back.

"What's the big deal?" I remarked.

"You don't think what you did was wrong?" he countered.

"It was a stupid innocent kiss. I didn't mean anything by it."

"Are you kidding me?" he yelled.

"What about you? You were flirting with your fucking Par Mate all day!" I hollered back.

Instead of apologizing for my inappropriate behavior, I reacted defensively to his anger and tone, which incensed Kaleb further. He was beyond angry and we were getting nowhere with this conversation. We were purely reacting instead of listening to one another. **Rule #2** (communicate openly and honestly) quickly went down the drain.

Kaleb shook his head and stormed back to his and Annie's room, leaving me standing in the hallway. I'm not sure what I wanted in that moment other than simply to go home. I felt more distant from Kaleb than ever, the exact opposite of what I had wanted. Ironically, I missed him yet I was pushing him further away. I walked back to my room with tears streaming down my face. *What have I done?*

17

Red Flags

Back in our room, I sat on the couch and looked out the window. *How did everything go so wrong with Kaleb?* I replayed the scene in the hallway in my mind, feeling sad and dejected at the way we had left it. Tom suddenly opened the door. Feeling self-conscious, I quickly wiped away my tears.

"Are you okay?" he asked, taking me into his arms before I could answer. His embrace felt both comforting and like a knife to my heart—*this* was what I had needed from Kaleb in the hallway.

"I'm fine," I lied. "Kaleb's annoyed with me, that's all."

"Everything will be okay," Tom said reassuringly. "Once we're having fun, he'll forget all about it." I gave a weak smile, trying to make myself believe his words.

"I'm going to freshen up a bit," I said as I headed into the bathroom. I wanted to be by myself and just breathe. I stared into the mirror and saw an unhappy girl looking back. I was a complete mess and felt out of control—nothing was going right. I vacillated between feeling sad and disappointed that we were fighting, irritated with Annie for suggesting this stupid separation idea in the first place, and angry at myself for going along with it.

How did I allow myself to agree to this ludicrous weekend arrangement? Why couldn't Kaleb understand how frustrated I felt that we couldn't communicate or physically touch each other? I transferred the sadness I felt into anger, acting out like a two-year-old throwing a tantrum because I wasn't getting my way.

I stepped out of the bathroom, and saw that Tom was sitting on the bed.

"Come sit by me," he said. He pulled me into his comforting arms. "Don't let this spoil our evening, okay?"

I nodded.

"And by the way, did I tell you that you look incredible tonight?" Tom smiled, gazing into my eyes.

"You know exactly how to make a girl feel better," I said with a big grin. He gave me a deep lingering kiss.

Tom looked so handsome, dressed in his beige khakis and white crisp long-sleeved shirt, which contrasted against his tanned face from being out in the sun all day.

"Let's have some fun tonight," Tom suggested.

I appreciated him trying to make me feel better. If only Kaleb was holding me instead—I desperately wanted him to tell me how much he loved and missed me. That would have changed everything. I had a lot of regrets that night, especially kissing Tim.

Suddenly, I heard a message alert on my phone. Could it be Kaleb? I quickly searched my purse ... it was Annie. My heart sunk. "Are you up to going out? Kaleb and I want to hit the clubs," she messaged. She's making it sound like they're a couple or something!

"We'll be down shortly," I hesitantly replied back. Annie was getting on my last nerve—why did she send that damn picture? I needed to talk to her but now was not the time. I needed to smooth things out with my husband, first and foremost.

On the elevator ride down, I was nervous about seeing Kaleb. *Had he calmed down or was he still mad?* Annie and Kaleb were waiting in the lobby. I looked to Kaleb for some reassurance but he said nothing and looked away.

"Are we all ready to rock-and-roll?" Tom quickly asked, sensing the tension in the air.

"Definitely! It's our last night, so let's party!" Annie said. "We should grab a cab."

As we walked to the front doors, I tried to extend an olive branch to Kaleb.

"You look nice," I told him. Kaleb didn't respond. My heart sank. *I guess that answers that: he's still mad.*

"Are you ready?" Annie grinned, taking hold of Kaleb's hand.

"Yeah let's get this party started!" Kaleb was more exuberant in his response to Annie. He was giving me the cold shoulder to get back at me.

The four of us went through the revolving doors and approached a waiting minivan taxi. Kaleb opened the right passenger door and jumped in, extending his hand to Annie to lead her to the back. Tom went to the other side and slid open the door to allow me in first. Tom and I sat in the row in front. I could see Kaleb deliberately being overt with his flirtation and attention on Annie—it was nauseating (and hurtful) to see him behave this way.

Okay, so that's how you want to play it, I fumed. *Two can play at this game.* I leaned over and gave Tom a long, passionate kiss.

"Mm ... you taste sweet," Tom said.

"I can't wait to do more with you tonight," I said loudly.

I heard Kaleb and Annie giggling and smooching in the back.

"Stop it! You're making me ticklish," Annie said.

Luckily, the cab ride was less than five minutes, ending this over-the-top performance.

When we arrived at the nightclub, Tom opened the cab door and jumped out, taking my hand to help me out and Kaleb did the same with Annie. Fortunately, we'd made reservations and were able to bypass the long line out front. The hostess showed us to our table. The club was in full swing with loud electronic dance music playing and a jam-packed dance floor.

"Who needs a drink?" Tom asked. "I'm buying!" I certainly didn't need more alcohol in me, but I wanted to drown my sorrows any way I could. Passed the point of sensibility, I continued to order one cocktail, then another, and another.

"Let's dance, Tom!" I shouted, grabbing his hand before he had a chance to say no. We pushed through the crowded dance floor to an opening. I wanted to get away from Kaleb and Annie but they were right behind us. The four of us were pressed tightly together; I could feel the warmth of Kaleb's body near my backside. Annie wrapped her arms tightly around Kaleb's neck, pulling him close to her. They gazed into each other's eyes, smiling and kissing, oblivious to anyone around them.

Did Annie not care about my feelings, knowing full well that Kaleb and I weren't getting along and all thanks to her? I guess she didn't care. She was enamored with Kaleb and he was enjoying her attention. Then there was Tom in his own world; he was clearly in the mood to have fun, dancing away with a drink in hand. He was flirting with several young ladies beside him, offering to buy them drinks. Everyone was having fun ... except me.

I turned to Kaleb and shouted in his ear, "I want to go back to the hotel!"

"Now?" he asked.

"I don't want to stay."

"We just got here," he said with annoyance.

"Then stay! I'll go back myself." I was drunk and not thinking straight. I needed to get away ... from the club, from the loud music, from the three of them. I saw Kaleb whispering into Annie's ear.

"Come on! Don't be a party pooper!" Annie told me.

Now my blood was boiling! I really had to get out of here fast—before I made a scene. I turned to leave, but Kaleb grabbed my hand, giving me the look to stay. The alcohol was talking now. I yanked my hand away from him.

"Leave me alone!" I yelled. Everything from today was bubbling inside and Kaleb had no clue how upset I was.

I rushed out of the club and hailed a cab. I jumped in, with tears streaming down my face. I could see the cab driver glancing back at me in his rearview mirror, but he said nothing. Ironically, after fighting so hard to get away, I now felt disappointed that no one came after me.

I got back to my hotel room and climbed into bed with my clothes on. I pulled the covers over my head. *Why was I acting this way? This was our last night, and I was throwing a tantrum.* I wasn't usually the emotional type, but I couldn't stop crying. This wasn't how I imagined the trip going. The person enjoying this weekend the most was Annie—she had Kaleb all to herself and now he and I were fighting, all thanks to her! At that moment, I loathed her.

About a half hour later, there was a loud knock on our door.

"Open the door," Kaleb said firmly. I didn't answer.

"I *said* open the door," he repeated louder. I hesitantly got out of bed and opened the door. I could see the anger and worry in his eyes.

"Why did you take off like that?" he demanded.

"I don't know," I said, holding back tears. "I was upset ... at you."

"Upset with *me*?" he exclaimed. "I should be the one who's pissed off, not you!"

He was right; I was the one who messed up, not him.

"You're right, I shouldn't have kissed that guy," I said apologetically. "That was wrong."

Kaleb's eyes softened; his anger now turned to hurt and disappointment.

"When Tom showed me that picture, I couldn't believe you would do that to me," he said.

"I'm sorry, I didn't mean to hurt you," I said.

"Well, you did," he said softly.

"I know it was stupid but I was angry that you didn't come for dinner."

"And that gives you the right to go off and kiss some guy?" he demanded.

"No, of course not."

"Then why did you do it?"

"I've been feeling invisible, ever since we got to Vegas. This weekend has not been going the way I wanted and I acted out ... badly," I said.

"Yeah, you sure did!"

I looked down, avoiding his stern eyes. "I shouldn't have behaved the way I did tonight."

"It's not that we didn't want to meet you guys for dinner. Things ran way later than we had expected."

"I know it wasn't your fault. I was just upset—with *everything*."

"What do you mean?"

"Well ... you and I haven't spent one minute alone since we got here. It's been hard for me to watch you and her together, like a couple. I felt like you didn't want me anymore," I said.

"Babe, you know that's not true. This weekend was how Annie wanted it, not how I wanted."

"I guess I was feeling jealous. I hated feeling last, vying for your attention... Annie was first, then your Par Mate, and then me."

I hadn't felt this insecure since my twenties when I was dating. I had always felt secure with Kaleb and knew exactly how he felt about me; he had always been my unwavering rock. But this weekend, I was questioning all that.

I was having a hard time processing my feelings. I had so many emotions running through my head that I couldn't make sense of it all, let alone relay these feelings to Kaleb in a coherent way. This weekend was triggering; it reminded me of my relationship with my father and his lack of attention/love towards me as a child. I never knew what it felt like to have unconditional love from my father. It left me growing up always in search of reassurance, comfort, and constant validation from people—that I was lovable enough, that I mattered, and that they would never abandon me in times of need. Kaleb was the one person I could turn to and trust implicitly. He would never hurt or disappoint me, so I confidently thought. However, our forced separation stirred up old feelings of insecurity and played havoc on my emotions.

"This trip has been pretty shitty!" I blurted out.

"I know, I feel the same. Aside from the Par Mates, I mean..." Kaleb teased. I playfully hit him on the arm. "Come here, you." He took me into his arms and held me tightly. I started to cry ... again. *This* was all I wanted, him and me alone together.

"I've missed you so much," I said, tears streaming down my face.

"You don't know how much I've hated being apart from you," he said.

Why couldn't we have said this to each other sooner? That's all we needed to hear from each other, instead of reacting defensively and lashing out. I held onto Kaleb tightly, not wanting him to ever let me go.

"Can we be *together* tonight? I need to hold you and feel your touch," I pleaded. If there was ever a time I needed to reconnect with Kaleb, it was now.

"I want that too babe," he said, holding me close to him. "But what about Annie?"

"I don't care. This is not about her, it's about us!" I told him.

"I know but we're flying out early tomorrow morning and my stuff is still up in the room. I'd have to pack up now and move everything down here. It's going be drama with her! I honestly don't have the energy to deal with it tonight."

I let out a heavy sigh. I knew Kaleb was right; it was too last-minute and Annie wouldn't take this change up very well, especially being the last night. Plus, I felt badly about walking out on the three of them at the club with my outburst, ruining the evening for everyone. Maybe I should give everyone their last night together, as planned.

"You're right. You should be with her tonight. I don't want to cause any more trouble," I said.

Once again, we deferred to what was good for Annie instead of looking after our own needs. This was becoming a broken record...

"We'll be home tomorrow," Kaleb said reassuringly. "And we'll be together then."

Kaleb kissed me and held me close.

"I'm sorry about tonight," I apologized.

"I'm glad we talked it out. I hate it when we fight," he said.

"Me too."

Kaleb kissed me on my forehead. "I love you, babe."

"I love you, too," I told him. I desperately wanted Kaleb to stay with me all night; however, I knew he had to go back to *their* room. This was the crazy part—sending him off when he should have been with me.

"I'll see you in the morning, okay?" he told me. "Try to get some rest."

Kaleb gave me another kiss and walked out, the door closing behind him. I felt sadness sweep over me, desperately wanting to run after him and tell him to come back ... but I didn't. When the door opened a minute later, my heart fluttered. *Had Kaleb changed his mind?*

I was disappointed when I saw Tom standing in the doorway.

"Are you okay?" he asked.

I nodded. "I'm sorry about my behavior at the club," I said. "I shouldn't have left like that."

He gave me a kiss and told me, "Don't worry about it; we all have our days."

"It's late, and our flight is early. We should get some sleep," I said. We got ready for bed. Even though it was our last night together, I wasn't in the mood to have sex.

"Is it okay if you just hold me tonight?" I asked. Tom nodded and he held me as we drifted off to sleep.

The alarm went off at 7:00 a.m., and we got up and quickly packed our bags. Finally, we could go home. I couldn't wait to sit with Kaleb on the plane and go back to our normal life. Kaleb, Annie, and I were on the same flight; Tom had a business meeting in Miami and was booked on an afternoon flight. We all said our goodbyes in the lobby and Tom gave me a big hug and kiss.

"Thanks for an amazing weekend," Tom whispered into my ear.

"I enjoyed spending time with you too," I replied.

Then the three of us boarded a taxi while Tom stayed behind. There was an awkward silence during the 20-minute ride to the airport with Kaleb sitting in between Annie and me.

At the airport, Kaleb and I checked in together and got our seats assigned next to each other. Annie stood in line behind us. Despite my agitation with Annie about this weekend, I felt badly that she was sitting by herself.

"I should probably sit with Annie," I whispered to Kaleb.

"Sure, you guys sit together. I'm going to take a nap anyway."

While waiting for our boarding call, the three of us sat together, with Kaleb, yet again, seated in the middle. As I leafed through my magazine, the events of the weekend flashed through my mind. So many *why* questions were swirling in my head. *Why did Annie insist on this separate arrangement between spouses? Why did she only want to be with Kaleb and not with her husband? Why did she encourage Tim to kiss me? Why did she send that photo to Tom? Did she feel bad about creating problems between Kaleb and me?* At the heart of it, I was beginning to question Annie's motives. *What did she want with Kaleb? Did she suggest this weekend arrangement so she could have him all to herself?* Deep down, I knew the answers to all of these questions. My inner self could sense some potential problems brewing between the three of us; however, I chose to ignore these *bad* feelings, just as I had always done as a child. Stuff it down, way, way down and hopefully, it would go away. This mistrust and uneasy feeling in the pit of my stomach were at odds with how I *wanted* to feel and what I wanted to *believe* about Annie. Like the saying goes, you see what you want to see; you believe what you want to believe. Annie was my best friend and I wanted to believe the best in her. And so, I squashed these gnawing doubts about her.

Although I tried my best to hide my feelings, Annie was perceptive enough to sense the tension between us. She tried to lighten the mood by saying something funny or showing me pictures from her magazine. I tried to act normal and not let on that I was upset. We didn't talk much on the plane either, focusing instead on our in-flight movies. When we arrived at Annie's place, Kaleb got out of the driver's side to help her with her luggage. I got out, too.

"Thanks for the ride," Annie said, giving Kaleb a hug and a quick kiss on the lips. "I had a great time with you."

She then turned towards me. "Are you okay?" she asked.

"Yeah, why?" I replied.

"You were really quiet in the car."

"I'm just tired, that's all," I said.

"Okay, I'll talk to you tomorrow," she said, giving me a big hug.

Kaleb and I drove home and brought our luggage inside. I was glad to be home and have my husband back.

18

Give an Inch, Take a Mile

* * *

"Watch me, Mom!" Samantha shouted, beaming with pride as she threw the ball right into the center of Kaleb's glove. This was the best part of the mornings, all of us hanging out together before the bus came.

"Mom, come throw the ball with us! Please?" Lucas begged.

"Hon, you take over for me," Kaleb said. "I need to check my phone." I assumed it was work related, as usual.

As we threw the ball around, I took a quick glance over at Kaleb and noticed him texting.

"The bus is here!" Lucas shouted, dropping his glove on the grass.

"Don't forget your backpacks," Kaleb said, handing them to them. We gave the kids quick hugs and kisses before they raced off towards the bus. "Love you!" we both shouted in unison.

Kaleb looked back down again at his phone as we strolled back to the house.

"Is it work?" I asked him.

"No, it's Annie *again*," he replied with a scowl on his face.

"What's wrong?" I asked tentatively.

"Texting her is getting to be a chore. She wants to chat *every day* and about nothing. You know how much I hate texting!" Kaleb replied.

It had been two weeks since the Vegas trip and I'd been noticing Annie texting Kaleb more and more, sending lengthy messages throughout the day. It was apparent that Annie was becoming enamored with Kaleb and texting was her way of feeling connected to him. Her former, once-in-a-blue-moon "hey" texts were steadily becoming a part of her morning routine, sent off while her kids and ours waited for the same school bus. Tom was in his office by 7:00 a.m., leaving Annie on her own to get their kids ready for school. The difference between her life and ours was that Kaleb and I were always together, with work, grocery shopping, getting the kids off to school, or taking them to their extra-curricular activities. Annie, on the other hand, was the primary caregiver of their household and received little help or input from Tom. It's possible Annie and Tom might have been attracted to this foursome scenario because it was a distraction from their routine life but it also allowed them to do something together, even if it was only on weekends.

"Aren't you sick of being together 24/7?" Annie once asked me. "I couldn't imagine being with Tom *all the time*—he would drive me insane!" I realized she was jealous of our relationship and the amount of time that Kaleb and I spent together—this was something she lacked in her marriage.

"You guys are certainly strange birds," she added.

"We don't mind. It works for us," I chuckled. My response likely only added to her irritation and envy.

"She's probably bored being at home," I told Kaleb.

"I guess she needs something to keep her busy," he said.

"Yeah, like texting you," I teased.

"Well, I wish she would focus on texting you, and less with me."

Kaleb viewed his relationship with Annie as strictly a weekend deal; now that it was bleeding into his weekdays, it was becoming more of a chore and *expectation*.

"You don't have to message Tom every day! Why do I have to do it with her?" he voiced with irritation.

"Be nice," I reminded him. "She wants to feel connected to you, remember? Feeling cheap and all, if she didn't."

"I know but this whole texting thing is stupid! Do you know what I've been doing all this week? Copy and pasting the same message and she doesn't even notice!"

"Honestly, I can't believe you did that!" I exclaimed.

"Heck, I don't even text you, why would I want to text her? Plus, she sends me messages that I can't even give one-word answers to!" Kaleb continued to complain. "What are your plans for today? What do you want to do this weekend? What are you going to do to me when you see me ... wink wink?" she would text him.

"Look, Annie needs to feel that you're into her ... and texting makes her feel *better* about these weekend romps," I explained.

"But that's exactly what we're doing! Having pure, unadulterated sex! No more, no less!" Kaleb exclaimed. "Didn't she get the memo?"

"I know, but she doesn't want to feel cheap," I reiterated.

"This is starting to feel like work," he complained.

18. Give an Inch, Take a Mile

"I know."

"Look, if it doesn't get easier and more fun, I don't know if I want to continue with this foursome. It's not worth it."

Unfortunately, Annie's need for Kaleb's attention and texting didn't wane; in fact, it got worse and continued this way until the very end. With my urging, Kaleb eventually stopped complaining about Annie's overbearing ways; he knew this was what *we* had to do to maintain the friendship/foursome. I even talked myself into believing our text messages to our partners were helpful in solidifying the foursome dynamic. Luckily for Tom, I had no expectations for us to text daily—it was simply a cute sidebar to our flirtation. He was too busy with work to text, responding only if he was free or maybe not at all. Sure, I felt slightly disappointed when he didn't reply, but at the same time, I was well aware that Tom was *not* my husband. With us, we knew exactly what our relationship entailed—it was fun weekends of acting out our sexual fantasies and nothing more. Our pairing worked perfectly because neither Tom nor I expected much from each other. He was my weekend lover and this worked perfectly for our schedules.

In the beginning of my relationship with Annie, I didn't see this manipulative side to her ... or maybe I did but I didn't want to admit it and ruin my perception of her as the perfect friend. Looking back, I now see Annie was adept at knowing how to push our boundaries and get what she wanted from us. Annie cast the reel and Kaleb and I took the bait hook, line, and sinker. Despite my growing concerns about Annie and her increasing demands on Kaleb, I chose to ignore my intuition; instead, I focused on continuing to foster a close friendship with her. I hadn't had a BFF since grade school, and I felt lucky to have a girlfriend living so close that I could share things with. Kaleb knew how much I valued my friendship with Annie—I constantly talked about her. We did *everything* together—she became an integral part of my life during this two-year period. Our lives became intertwined with Annie's and Tom's, spending literally every weekend with them. An important part of making this foursome work for us was the trust. It never crossed my mind that I couldn't trust her, Tom or Kaleb. Over time, Kaleb and I realized that Annie was the more clingy and needy type; someone who craved Kaleb's attention more and more since she wasn't getting it from Tom. If I had honestly felt (and admitted to myself) or known there was more to Annie's underlying intentions, I would have ended the foursome much sooner. But I had no idea *who* I was dealing with ... and neither did Kaleb. How naïve we both were.

The Swinger in the Mirror

As Annie's demands for Kaleb's attention increased, even encroaching into our family life, I could see cracks forming in our foursome dynamic. Not only did she want to text Kaleb daily, but Annie also suggested more weekend get-aways to garner more dedicated alone time with Kaleb. *Did we like how things were going?* No. But we gave in. In Kaleb's mind, it was easier to take the "path of least resistance," so he didn't have to deal with the hassle or drama of saying no to her. And I gave in to preserve the friendship we had.

Instead of addressing it with Annie, which is what I should have done, I unconsciously transferred my frustration and resentment onto Tom. During our social nights out, I would find some reason to become irritated with Tom and throw shade at him.

"You can be pretty inconsiderate sometimes!" I told him, one night after having sex.

"Huh?"

"Is it so hard for you to send me a quick text back when I message you?" I asked him.

"Well... I didn't realize you wanted me to text immediately. Wasn't it a *whenever I could—I would* kind of deal?" he asked. I pulled away from Tom. He could tell that I didn't like his answer.

"When I send you a text, it would be *nice* to get a response right away ... not hours or days later!" I told him in an irritated tone.

It didn't help that Tom had a low emotional IQ to begin with. He didn't pick up on social non-verbal cues and was emotionally unavailable to both Annie and me. Tom didn't have a clue what he was supposed to do to make things better with me ... and I didn't make it easier for him either.

"Okay, not sure why you're making a big deal about it," he said sarcastically.

"I'm not making a big deal. It'd be nice if you showed me you cared by messaging back, like Kaleb does with Annie. Isn't our relationship more than just sex?" I asked.

What was I saying? Of course, it was *only* about the sex! Somehow, Annie's expectations of Kaleb attending to her emotional needs had clouded my judgment and perception of my situation with Tom. Everything Annie wanted of Kaleb, she got. I only wanted what was fair for me when it came to Tom's time and attention, too.

"No, it's not only about the sex. I enjoy being with you," he reassured me. "I promise, I'll text you more, if you want me to." I shrugged. I felt exasperated. I didn't know what I wanted ... from Tom or this foursome situation. All I knew was that it was getting *complicated*.

18. Give an Inch, Take a Mile

"Do you think Kaleb would mind helping me look for a new car?" Annie asked me, about two months after our Vegas trip. She knew Kaleb loved vehicle shopping and negotiating deals.

"I don't think he would mind," I said.

"I hate going to the dealership by myself! I don't know what these salesmen are saying half the time," she chuckled. "And Tom isn't much help! He doesn't know much about cars and he's always busy at work."

Over the next few weeks, Annie texted Kaleb about cars, asking which ones she should look at. She scheduled *dates* for them to go out to different dealerships for the afternoon. Kaleb didn't mind; he enjoyed looking at cars and Annie enjoyed having him all to herself. It was a win-win situation for them.

"Do you want to come with us?" Annie texted me one morning.

"You guys go by yourselves. I have things I need to do."

But gradually, their car shopping afternoons started to bother me. One morning in particular, I was in the basement running on the treadmill when Kaleb popped down to say Annie was on her way over to pick him up. It was weird that I hadn't gotten a text from Annie all morning.

"She said she'll come down to say hi before we go,"

"Okay," I said, out of breath.

"Are you sure you don't want to come with us?" Kaleb asked.

"No thank you! I'd rather watch paint dry," I teased.

The doorbell rang and Kaleb quickly ran upstairs. I heard their muffled voices. I waited for Annie to come down to the basement, but she never did. Then I heard the front door close and their car drive off. I had a funny feeling in the pit of my stomach. *It was weird she hadn't come down to see me.* I was also surprised that Kaleb didn't shout out a good-bye, like he normally would.

I felt left out, like I didn't exist. *Had Annie purposely not wanted to see me because she felt guilty?*

145

19

Second Vegas Trip

* * *

Over the next while, Anne continued to push boundaries, and Kaleb and I kept going along with her. Were we simply stupid, too nice or too naïve? Check, check, check. All of the above. Three months after we'd returned from Vegas, Annie brought up the idea of going back. After all the drama that unfolded that first time, I didn't think anyone wanted to redo Vegas, especially me. I wanted to forget about that trip—it was a complete disaster!

"I don't know," Kaleb told Annie. "Last time didn't exactly go smoothly."

"Come on, it'll be more fun this time around ... we'll take in a few shows, go shopping, golfing for the guys again, and eat at a few restaurants I'm dying to try," she said persuasively.

"Would it be the same arrangement as before?" I interrupted.

"What do you mean?" Annie asked.

"Are we doing the same splitting up for the entire weekend?"

"Well ... yeah. I thought it worked pretty well last time," she replied.

No, it worked well only for you! a voice inside my head screamed. Kaleb and I didn't have any time to reconnect with each other and that messed with my head, making me question our relationship. I wasn't going through that again! As I was about to say something, Kaleb piped in, "Sorry, I didn't like that arrangement *at all*."

"Oh. Okay ... what would you prefer?" Annie asked him.

"The only way I would do this long weekend is if Kim and I got to spend the nights together," he voiced.

"I'm okay with that," Tom added. Annie shot him a look. "What? I don't see any problem with that!" he said.

"That sounds like a reasonable plan. We still get to be with our partner for most of the time," I said.

"Nope! I don't like that idea at all," Annie exclaimed.

Kaleb looked irritated. Tom didn't say another word; he knew how stubborn Annie could be once she set her mind on something.

"What's up with you not wanting us to hang with our own spouse?" Kaleb demanded.

"It's not that I'm against it," she said, exasperated. She paused. "You guys just don't understand."

"Well then, explain it to us," Kaleb stated.

Tears welled up in her eyes. "I find it hard to go back and forth between ... partners," she stammered. "I'm not comfortable like you guys are with swapping. I need more time to get used to it." *How much time does she need?* I thought to myself. We had been in this foursome for over six months by this point.

Neither Kaleb nor I expected Annie to become emotional in that moment—we felt bad. We didn't know how to respond. We didn't want to upset Annie or make her feel like a *slut*, as she phrased it, jumping from one bed to another. I never felt guilty or bad being with Tom one moment and then being with Kaleb the next but that was me. Annie was different. Maybe she was right—we had more experience with swapping and she just needed more time to feel comfortable.

"We don't want to make you feel uneasy," I told her. "Right, Kaleb?"

"No, of course not," he replied.

"It's fine. We can keep the same arrangement as before," I heard myself saying.

Oh no! I can't believe I just said that... Here we were, once again, sacrificing what we wanted to do in order to make Annie happier. *What was wrong with me? Why couldn't I stand up to her and say what I wanted?* I too began to adopt Kaleb's path of least resistance stance—it was easier. Kaleb and I were similar that way; if we made a suggestion and the other person pushed back, then we leaned towards what they wanted because we didn't want to kick up a fuss. Annie knew that about me—*I hated conflict.*

Walking back home that night, I stopped and turned to Kaleb.

"Are you really okay doing another trip back?"

"I do enjoy Vegas but honestly, why does she always have to get her way?" Kaleb complained.

"I don't like being apart from you either, but like she said, she's not comfortable doing it any other way."

"How long does she need, for God sakes?" Kaleb demanded.

I shook my head, and said, "I don't know."

"Okay, fine! If we do this trip, we're going to take back some control."

"What do you mean? How?" I asked.

"We will see each other on this trip, one way or another."

"She's not going to let that happen," I said.

"Well, then, we'll find a way to do it behind her back. What she doesn't know won't hurt her, right?"

"How? She's always with you!" I exclaimed.

"Don't worry, I'll figure something out. This will be a better trip … *for us,*" Kaleb said confidently.

The second trip to Vegas went much better, just like Kaleb had promised. We checked into a different hotel and had more things planned … but no Par Mates this time! Although the sleeping arrangements remained the same, going into this trip was way different for me. This time, Kaleb and I communicated beforehand, and I knew we were on the same page; we had plans to secretly meet up at certain points during the trip to feel *connected* to one another. This made being apart more tolerable for me.

The day after we arrived in Vegas, Kaleb broke Annie's rule and sent me a text from their bathroom. Meet me right now? My eyes lit up when I saw his name on my phone.

"Okay! But what do we say to them?" I messaged back. "Sorry, it's work," I told Tom so he wouldn't suspect it was Kaleb.

"I'll tell her we have to discuss a new work contract and it can't wait."

"Okay, meet you soon. I love you," I texted back. I had butterflies in my stomach, feeling excited to see him, like it was our first date.

"It shouldn't take more than an hour," he told Annie.

"Where are you guys meeting up?" she asked.

"Down in the hotel cafe."

"Okay, but don't take too long. Remember, you're mine for the weekend," she teased.

"I'll text you the moment we're done," Kaleb said.

"Okay, Tom and I will walk around the strip." Annie gave Kaleb a lingering kiss and smiled as she headed out.

The moment Annie left the room, Kaleb sent me a message to come over to their room. I peered out my door to make sure the coast was clear, and then I raced down the hall. Before I had a chance to knock on the door, Kaleb opened it and quickly pulled me inside, like it was a covert operation. He gave me a big hug and we both laughed like two teenagers playing hooky from school.

"We don't have much time!" he said, looking at the alarm clock on the nightstand, which read 1:48 p.m. "I told her we'd be done in about an hour." Kaleb embraced me and unbuttoned my blouse and bra.

I quickly undid his shirt buttons and unbuckled his belt. We continued to kiss and grope each other as we fell onto their bed. I flashed back to my seventeen-year-old self, fooling around with my then-boyfriend on my parents' bed before they came home. *Guilty pleasure.*

"If she only knew what we were doing!" I giggled.

"She would *not* be happy." It felt so good to be lying in Kaleb's arms, no matter how little time we had together. I missed him, and it had only been one night. After we made love, Kaleb held me close, kissing my lips over and over again.

"I wish I could spend the night with you," he said.

"Me too. When can I see you again?" I asked. The time was ticking to returning to our partners but I didn't want to leave Kaleb's side.

"I'll figure something out," he said. We both knew this whole situation was messed up, having to meet in secret. Kaleb and I had two more rendezvous during this trip ... thanks to some "emergency staffing issues." Annie never did find out.

20

Blurred Boundaries

* * *

Our Vegas secret meet-up was one of several moments that called into question why we continued being in this fucked-up friendship/ foursome dynamic. Although Kaleb and I tried to be understanding and accommodating of Annie's needs, we felt increasingly more boxed in by her controlling behavior. Our sexual fantasy swap was becoming less about *us* as a couple and more about Annie's dependency and connection with Kaleb.

"I feel like I'm always putting out fires with her!" Kaleb complained about a month after the second Vegas trip. "I'm getting tired of bending over backwards for her."

Several months after the trip, Kaleb and I began planning a trip down south by ourselves. It worked out that Annie and Tom couldn't join us since Tom had a work conference. Mutual friends of ours coincidentally were going to the same resort as us. Annie was not pleased with that news and she was very clear on how Kaleb and I should and shouldn't behave on this trip. Although she would never admit it, she was jealous and suspicious that we (or more so Kaleb) might hook up with these friends while we were there. Annie wanted to keep us (or more so Kaleb) all to herself. She jokingly mentioned how they might be swingers as well and that we should watch out for them. Before going on our trip, she reminded us that she wanted to keep our foursome as it was and had no interest in inviting other couples into our circle.

Although Kaleb and I had no intentions of playing with these friends, we did not appreciate Annie telling us what we could or couldn't do. It seemed we had replaced our monogamous relationship with Steve and Natalie with a more restrictive foursome in Annie and Tom. Kaleb and I found we couldn't truly express ourselves and explore the Lifestyle in the way we wanted. For instance, we weren't *allowed* to go to a downtown LS club or initiate relationships with other couples we might have had an interest in. This foursome was beginning to feel much like the oppressive household I grew up in, controlled by one dominant figure. The only way I could get my wants/needs met was to go underground and lie about it, which summed up my adolescent years living under my parents' roof.

It was getting to be routine for Kaleb and me to hide things from Annie in order to keep the peace and still get to do what we wanted. I remember one weekend when Annie and Tom were away, Kaleb and I decided to go downtown and check out a new sex club; this was our first time in a legal establishment, so we were excited to see how things had changed since 2003. We had no intention of telling Annie and Tom because we knew exactly how Annie would react. Although we didn't play with any couples at the club, we felt like we were cheating on them by being there without them knowing.

About nine months into our foursome, while we were watching our son in a semi-final soccer tournament game, I heard a "ping" on Kaleb's phone.

"Who's that?" I asked curiously. He checked his phone.

"It's Annie," he said surprisingly. *Why she was contacting Kaleb now?* She knew the rules of engagement—no contacting your partner during family time ... that was an absolute NO.

"What does she want?" I asked in an annoyed tone.

"She wanted to reach out and say hello," Kaleb replied. Knowing that added to my irritation ... did she think I wouldn't find out she was texting him? Kaleb messaged back with a short text, trying to end the conversation; however, the pings kept coming.

"Tell her you have to go!" I said, irritated.

"I did, but she keeps texting," he replied.

"Just ignore her!"

"Look at her texts, she expects a response!" Kaleb said with exasperation. He handed me his phone.

"Why aren't you replying? Don't you miss me? I need to feel you inside of me. What's wrong? Are you mad at me? Did I do something? I need to see you! When can I see you? Talk to me!" she incessantly texted.

Her text messages came in one after the other, each more desperate than the next. There was anguish in her tone. She *needed* him to respond to her. She had no clue I was reading her messages. Kaleb took back his phone and sent her one final message.

Stop texting me. I'm with my kids.

No further ping sounds. Annie stopped.

151

I was beyond pissed! Annie was playing by her own rules, doing whatever and whenever she wanted with no regard for me. *How could Annie be my friend if she could do this to me? Did she not care about my feelings?* I felt hurt and disappointed that my best friend would disrespect the rules and, more importantly, disrespect me. Despite how I felt, I didn't know if I had the courage to bring this up to her... I was afraid it would end our friendship if she couldn't see it from my side and apologize for her actions.

I flipped-flopped between feelings of anger and sympathy. But because I was much better at rationalizing people's behaviors than confronting them, I chose to make excuses for Annie and her constant need to reach out to Kaleb. Maybe she was feeling lonely? Maybe she was having a bad day? Instead of calling Annie out, right there and then, and sending her a nasty text, I displaced my anger at Kaleb and indirectly blamed him for her actions. *Had Kaleb done something to invite and elicit this behavior from her? What did he say to her during their private intimate moments that would make her feel this close to him, telling him she missed him?* This seemed all too familiar; Natalie was needy as well, reaching out to Kaleb behind my back because she was lonely. *Was there more to this with Kaleb?* He seemed to be the common denominator here...

"Why would Annie send you text messages like that? Missing her? Being inside of her?" I asked him in an accusatory tone.

"I don't know! Why don't you ask your *best friend*?" he retorted with agitation.

"I'm asking you! What have you been telling her in private?" I yelled.

"I haven't said anything! She's the one who keeps initiating this drama," he exclaimed.

"Well, someone's saying and doing *something*," I voiced.

"That's it, I'm done with this fucking foursome! Look, it's making us fight with each other!" Kaleb exclaimed. "It's not worth it." He turned away from me but I quickly grabbed his hand.

"I don't want to fight, I'm sorry."

"This is getting to be too much," he said. "Honestly. When will it all stop?"

"I know I shouldn't be taking it out on you. I'm just hurt and angry she would do this to me," I said apologetically.

"Listen, I don't want to be in this if it's going to affect *us*," Kaleb voiced.

20. Blurred Boundaries

"But if we end the foursome, then what about me and Annie?" I asked.

"I don't know. You guys figure it out. Maybe it won't change things," he said.

"No, it'll change *everything*! I know it."

"So, what do we do?"

"I don't know. Maybe things will get better … and she'll come to her senses."

Those words would come back to haunt me. Things didn't get better; instead, they got worse and more complicated. Tom, Kaleb, and I knew not to cross the boundaries outside of the foursome socials/weekends and then there was Annie on her own island; she did *whatever* she wanted, *whenever* she wanted. I hoped and prayed Annie would realize what she was doing wrong and make things better for everyone involved so we could continue with our foursome (and friendship). Boy, was I a fool!

21

Surprise Birthday Party

* * *

After the soccer tournament incident, I let things slide with Annie once again. I never did bring it up to her about how hurt I felt by her actions. The four of us resumed our weekend social fun, and so all the hurt feelings were pushed to the side.

About a month before my 40th birthday, Annie asked me if I had plans to mark this milestone. I was dreading this birthday and wanted it to pass quickly and quietly. However, Kaleb and Annie had different plans. Unbeknownst to me, Annie had enlisted Kaleb's help to plan a surprise party for me. She had convinced him that I deserved something special for my birthday, and he went along with her.

As part of her plan, Annie wanted me to think she would be away during my birthday, so she told me she and Tom and the kids were going to her parents' cottage that May 24 weekend.

"How do you want to celebrate?" Kaleb asked me one morning at breakfast.

"I don't know—I'm fine with spending it with you and the kids," I replied. Birthdays were never a big deal for me, and after all the recent drama, being with my family seemed perfect. We didn't have to worry about hurting Annie and Tom's feelings because they would be out of town.

"Okay, dinner and a birthday cake it is!" Kaleb said. "Easy peasy!"

With Kaleb's help, Annie planned this surprise party with 40 of my closest friends. Did I mention she loved to plan things? This was right up her alley. Kaleb's only job was to take me out to a fancy restaurant as a decoy.

"Let's try that new fancy Italian place on Main Street. We can get a babysitter for the night," Kaleb suggested.

"Samantha and Lucas aren't coming with us?" I asked.

"I wanted a romantic dinner, just the two of us. Then we could do cake with the kids after."

"Okay, that sounds good," I said.

"You should wear something nice for our evening out," Kaleb suggested.

"It's only dinner," I said.

"Well ... it's nice to dress up every once in a while," he replied.

"All right, why not?" I replied.

I decided to put on a black shimmery one-shoulder dress my mom had sewn for my birthday gift (she was in on the surprise!). I felt extra special. Kaleb was right, it was nice to get all dolled up for an evening out. He looked handsome in his light blue blazer, a white long-sleeved shirt, and his beige khaki pants. As we sat in the restaurant, we held hands and sipped on champagne, which Kaleb had ordered for this special occasion. But this romantic mood was suddenly interrupted by a text alert on Kaleb's phone as we were eating. Kaleb seemed concerned and distracted by this message.

"What's wrong? Are the kids okay?" I asked.

"No, they're fine. It's nothing," he replied.

I noticed him continuing to check his phone every few minutes.

"Why do you keep looking at your phone?" I asked, annoyed.

"I'm sorry. It's the guy from the car dealership," he explained. "He needs an answer tonight or Annie's deal will fall through."

"Oh."

Over the past month, car quotes and dealership visits had been ramping up and taking up most of Kaleb's time. I wanted tonight to be about me and us, not about Annie and her stupid car deals.

We ate our dinner and finished off the bottle of champagne. Annie continued to text Kaleb all through dinner, but it wasn't about cars.

"When are you guys heading back?" she messaged.

"15 mins max.," he quickly typed back.

"No, you need to stall her. Not everyone is here yet. Have another glass of wine or something," she instructed.

"Sorry, babe, with all the car stuff lately," Kaleb said, turning to me.

"It's all right. I know you're trying to help her out as much as you can," I replied.

"Let's have another glass of champagne and toast to Annie's car deal and more importantly, the end of vehicle shopping!" he said, giving me a kiss on my lips.

"Cheers to that!" I replied with delight.

Annie had it all planned out—guest list, invitations, birthday cake, decorations, music, and food. She even considered the littlest details ... asking everyone to park their cars at her place or down the street so I wouldn't become suspicious.

Ping! "Everyone's here now!" Annie texted.

"Ready to go, babe?" Kaleb asked. "The kids have a surprise for you when we get home."

"I can't wait!" I said, taking my last sip. When we got back home and drove into the garage, Kaleb grabbed my hand as I was about to get out of the car.

"Listen, before you can get your surprise, you need to put this blindfold on," Kaleb instructed said.

"What?" I chuckled.

"Yes, the kids' orders." He placed a black silk scarf over my eyes, kissing me gently as he tied it.

"Promise, you'll do as I say," he said.

"What are you and the kids up to?" I laughed.

"Shhh ... just trust me," he whispered. Kaleb held my hand as he slowly guided me out of the car and up the steps into the house.

"Where are we going?" I asked.

"Hold onto the rail, we're going to the basement," he directed. I envisioned the kids downstairs, waiting with birthday candles all lit and ready to scream "Happy birthday, Mommy!" I didn't want to ruin their surprise, so I went along with it.

When Kaleb took off my blindfold, I slowly opened my eyes and heard, "SURPRISE!!" My eyes quickly scanned the room—all of my closest friends gathered around in the basement ... *for me*. I was speechless. I felt overjoyed with emotion at this sight. This was the first time in my life I'd ever been surprised like this.

And there they were, standing off to the side—Annie and Tom, wearing the biggest smiles on their faces.

"What are you guys doing *here*?" I exclaimed in disbelief.

"And miss your birthday? Not a chance!" Annie replied. I gave them both a big hug.

"I can't believe you did this for me," I said, tears welling up.

"You deserve this!" Kaleb said.

"I love you," I whispered in his ear and kissed him tenderly.

"I love you *more*," he replied.

"Wow! How did you pull this off?" I asked.

"It wasn't me. Annie planned this whole surprise ... and yes, she was texting me at the restaurant," Kaleb confessed.

21. Surprise Birthday Party

I felt badly that I was pissed off at her during dinner and now to find out she had done this for me only made me feel like shit. Despite my disappointment in our friendship over the past few months, especially after that Kaleb texting incident, this birthday surprise renewed my faith in Annie and getting our friendship back on track. This party was not only a celebration for my 40th, it also commemorated our foursome relationship lasting more than a year. It meant so much to me that Annie and Tom were a part of this important night and went out of their way to make me feel special. That night was magical; the four of us danced, drank and had so much fun, like old times...

I was 40, and at the peak of my life. I had everything I ever needed or wanted. My kids were healthy and amazing. My relationship with Kaleb couldn't be stronger. We had a great network of friends, including Annie and Tom who provided extra *benefits*. I couldn't have been happier. But that was all about to change.

22

Sex and Lies

* * *

Three days after my surprise party, I boarded a plane to Thailand to spend two weeks with my twin sister. It had been over a year since I last saw Katelyn, so Kaleb decided to buy me a plane ticket for my birthday. I was excited to get a chance to spend undivided time with my sister. My trip was lovely, and it felt so good to see Katelyn again, but by the end of the two weeks, I was anxious to come home to Kaleb; I missed his touch. It was no surprise we had incredible nonstop sex my first night back. I couldn't get enough.

"I've missed you so much!" Kaleb told me as he embraced me in his arms. "Promise me you'll never be away for that long again!"

"Next time, I'll take you with me," I teased. "It feels so good to be with you. How did we go that long without sex?"

"How about we make up for lost time?" he suggested with a big grin.

"What do you mean?" I grinned.

"Well ... we could try having sex *every day* for as long as we can," he suggested.

"Really?"

"Sure, why not? It'd be a fun to see how long we can last," Kaleb said.

"Okay! Let the games begin!" I smiled, caressing his face and kissing him passionately.

Whether we were in the mood or not, through sickness, stress, or exhaustion, saying no to sex was not an option during our experiment. Kaleb and I plowed through and managed to stay the course for three whole weeks ... coming to an end only when Samantha got sick, and I ended up sleeping with her throughout the night.

"Guess what Kaleb and I are trying right now?" I giggled, while out on a girls' night during Week Two with Annie and two other friends.

"What?" Annie asked curiously.

"Some kind of cleanse or fad diet?" Reanna asked jokingly.

"Well ... no."

"Then, what?" Katie piped in.

"We've been having sex *every single day* since I got back from my trip. It's been two weeks so far ... and we're still going strong!" The girls gasped and exploded into laughter, with the exception of Annie.

"You're kidding," Annie said

"No, for real," I replied.

"Good for you guys!" Reanna exclaimed.

"Yeah, I wished I could say the same for Paul and me!" Katie responded with envy. "We're lucky if we have it once a month."

"Tell me about it," Reanna echoed.

"You guys haven't missed even *one day*?" Annie asked.

"Nope!" I said proudly.

We all had a good chuckle that I had the stamina to be able to follow through for this length of time.

"Not bad for a forty-year-old!" Reanna exclaimed.

I noticed Annie was unusually quiet during the rest of the dinner.

"Is something wrong?" I asked Annie as she drove me home.

"No," she replied guardedly.

"You didn't seem like yourself tonight."

There was silence. Annie seemed apprehensive about sharing her thoughts. At a traffic light, she looked over at me and said, "To be honest with you, I was bothered when you said that you guys were having sex every day for the past two weeks."

Huh? I didn't understand why this would make her upset.

"You're upset at me for having sex with my husband?" I asked in disbelief.

"No, that's not what I mean."

"Then what?" I asked tersely.

"I didn't need to hear you announce you've been doing it non-stop for two weeks, that's all."

"Okay, so I shared too much," I said facetiously. I didn't notice the other girls getting upset with my story, so I didn't understand why Annie was acting this way. We drove the rest of the way in silence. When she drove into my driveway, we exchanged quick good-byes as I jumped out.

The next day, I didn't get the usual bubbly morning text from Annie, which was odd. The last thing I wanted to do was upset her or get in a fight. I needed to make things better between us, even though I didn't feel I had done anything wrong. At my urging, Kaleb sent Annie a quick text to check in on her. To my surprise, she promptly replied back, asking *him* to come over to talk instead of having this conversation with me. I guess she was still upset about last night.

Kaleb told me later that she met him in her driveway and seemed normal when she greeted him, as if nothing was wrong.

"You doing okay?" Kaleb asked.

"Yeah, I'm fine," Annie replied.

"Heard what happened last night ... that you were upset," Kaleb said.

"What do you mean?" she asked.

"About Kim and I having sex ... and all."

"Well, to be honest with you, I was bothered hearing about it," she said.

"So, you're upset that I'm having sex with *my wife*?" he asked.

"No, that's not it."

"Then what?" he asked.

"It makes me feel like you enjoy being with her more than with me, like I'm disposable," she tried to explain. "We were together two nights ago ... and then you had sex with her *right after*?"

"Why wouldn't I? She is my wife!" Kaleb exclaimed.

"How do you think that makes me feel? Going from my bed to hers?" she asked.

"If I want to have sex with Kim, right after I'm with you, then that's my prerogative!" Kaleb yelled, losing his patience.

"Don't be angry with me. I'm just having a hard time hearing about you and her when we're *not* together," she tried to explain.

"What you and I share sexually is separate from my real life. It's two different things," he exclaimed. "It's none of your business what I do with Kim after we go home. I don't care what you do with Tom."

"You're right, I'm sorry. I guess I'm being silly and overthinking things," she said, reaching out to touch his arm.

"I don't think you should do that. The neighbors will see us," Kaleb said, pulling his arm away.

"Okay, let's just forget about this? Pretend we never had this conversation," Annie said.

"I agree," Kaleb said. "I have to go now. Kim's waiting for me."

Annie watched Kaleb walk away, down the street.

Despite all the warning signs, Kaleb and I chose to remain in the foursome, trying to *make it work.* We sounded like a broken record, constantly rationalizing to each other the benefits (despite the mounting costs) of staying in this relationship; we took turns championing the cause. Overall, Kaleb was most vocal about ending it but I always managed to talk him down off the ledge; I reminded him that breaking off this foursome would ultimately end my friendship with Annie, and he didn't want to feel responsible for that. That's probably the main reason why Kaleb relented more times than he should have ... because of *me* and how much I valued this friendship. Unfortunately, I chose to turn a blind eye to the continuous drama that Annie was creating in our lives for another year. I was fighting for something that I wasn't even sure about anymore.

23

The Breakup

* * *

After two years of trying to maintain our foursome relationship with Annie and Tom, Kaleb and I finally decided we wanted off this wild roller coaster ride. The only challenge was, we didn't know when or how to get off ... until a situation presented itself that we could no longer overlook.

The proverbial straw that broke the camel's back was when Annie crossed the line by interfering with how we parented our children. It was Good Friday, ironically enough, and Annie was throwing a dinner party at their place. The plan was for all of us to have supper together, and then all the kids would sleep over at our place, with Annie's nanny accompanying them for the night.

The night of the dinner party arrived, and, in typical Annie fashion, the meal was spectacular and the table looked like something out of a home magazine. After dinner, everyone retired to the living room to have drinks. Anne slumped on the couch beside Kaleb, cuddling into his arms.

"Whew! I'm exhausted!" Annie said.

"You outdid yourself! Everything was delicious!" Kaleb praised Annie, giving her a big squeeze.

"I'm so glad you liked it," she replied. "You're worth all the effort!"

"Yes, it was absolutely delicious!" Tom added.

Tom poured himself another drink and then sat next to me on the other couch. We continued to drink and chat for the next hour, catching up on the past week. Then there was a lull in the conversation.

"Okay, folks, are we going to talk all night?" Kaleb chuckled, as he stood up and began to unzip his pants. "I think we should get the *real* party started!"

Oh gosh! Kaleb never seems to surprise me anymore with his antics. "You're too much!" I blushed.

23. The Breakup

Just as we were getting cozy and clothes were starting to come off, Kaleb's phone rang. He sat up to answer it. *Who could it be at this time of night?*

"It's Lucas," Kaleb said. I could hear our son in the background, asking when we would be home.

"We'll be home in a little bit," Kaleb reassured him. Hoping that our son would eventually drift off to sleep, we resumed our play. Half an hour later, Lucas called back again, this time sounding more desperate in his plea for us to come home. This was unlike him to keep calling, so we knew that he needed us, *now.*

"Okay, we're coming home," he told our son. "Sorry, guys, but we have to go."

"I guess he really needs us," I said in a concerned voice. Kaleb and I got dressed.

"No, do you really have to go?" Annie moaned. She looked disappointed and agitated by this interruption. "Stay a bit longer ... please."

"We should go and check on him," I told Annie. "He doesn't sound like himself."

"He's a big boy; he'll be fine," Annie remarked. "You guys really cater too much to your kids."

Kaleb and I looked at each other, surprised and upset by her remarks. "Let's go!" Kaleb said firmly and we headed out.

Our son needed us and nothing Annie could say could persuade us otherwise. Annie was used to always having her way so this spurn threw her for a loop. When we got home, we ran upstairs and found Lucas asleep in his bed, holding onto his pillow. We laid on either side of him and cuddled all together. Kaleb and I looked at each other, feeling the same way ... guilty.

Over the past two years, Kaleb and I had been indulging in our foursome fantasies and whims, often cutting into the time we should have been spending with Lucas and Samantha. This was a wake-up call. We realized that we had gotten caught up in this foursome relationship, selfishly tending to our adult needs instead of focusing on the kids—they still needed us as parents. Kaleb and I quietly left Lucas' room. As we were getting ready for bed, I heard a text message alert on Kaleb's phone.

"It's Annie," he moaned. Then Kaleb's look of irritation quickly turned to anger.

"What's wrong?" I asked.

"She asked me if it's *over* between me and her," he remarked incredulously.

"What? Why would she ask that?" I questioned.

"I don't know, and I don't care! I'm done with her and this whole fucking relationship!" Kaleb exclaimed.

Why was Annie creating undue drama over us going home to comfort our son? Was she having a tantrum because she was losing out on her alone time with Kaleb? This was all about her, and no one else mattered.

Although there would be clear consequences of breaking up with them, I knew in my heart it was the right thing to do. We had had enough of Annie's antics. We both knew that we had to end it. We couldn't keep going like this. I was now finally ready to let go of my friendship with Annie if it meant protecting my family and my marriage. This was the wake-up call I needed.

"I know babe. I agree with you. It's gone too far," I concurred.

"I know this might ruin your friendship, but I don't care anymore. I'm done!" Kaleb stated. I knew he was fed up and, for once, we both were on the same page. I, too, was at my breaking point and wanted out of this relationship. There was no more rationalizing and hoping that things would get better. Annie was showing her true colors and acting irrationally and selfishly. She wanted too much of us (or so I thought—the real story, unbeknownst to me at the time, was that it wasn't me and my friendship that she wanted ... it was only Kaleb).

The next morning, Kaleb and I woke up when we heard the kids watching TV and laughing. We laid in bed and held each other. It felt nice to be home with the kids ... a sense of comfort and normalcy.

"How are you feeling this morning?" I asked.

"The same as last night, maybe even stronger," he replied.

"Me too."

"Since she texted me that crap about us breaking up, I'll deal with her myself and do it in person," Kaleb declared.

I didn't see it then, but, looking back, it was odd that only Kaleb and Annie would meet, instead of all four of us, to dissolve this foursome relationship. I should have been there, as her best friend, to talk to her since it was going to affect our friendship as well. But at the time, I didn't question it. I was relieved that Kaleb would handle what was likely going to be an emotional situation. Plus, I didn't want to confront her—I was afraid of her reaction.

"If you think it's best to meet her in person, then I guess so," I told him.

"She's not going to take it well but maybe doing it this way will be easier on her," he explained.

23. The Breakup

Kaleb responded to Annie's text and told her to meet him that afternoon. Annie was quick to answer back, assuming that he merely wanted to be with her. They agreed to meet at the nearby park at 2:00 p.m. While he was gone, I found myself feeling uneasy and distracted, wondering how the conversation was going. *How was Annie taking the news? Would she understand? Or would she be mad? Did it even matter how she felt?* We had made up our minds.

When I heard the garage door lift, about a half hour later, I rushed down from the bedroom. I was anxious to hear how it went.

"It's done. She knows it's over," Kaleb announced as he came in the back door.

"How did she take it?" I asked.

"Not well," Kaleb replied. "I don't think she saw it coming, honestly."

"Oh," I said meekly, unsure how to respond.

"She started crying and promising to change, to make things *fun* again, but we both know she can't change."

"Did she mention me at all?" I asked.

"Not really. I told her your friendship didn't have to change, that we just wanted the foursome part to end." Kaleb shrugged.

"Although I was relieved that Annie knew it was over, I was worried about how she might be feeling at that moment. Many things ran through my mind. *Did she tell Tom, and how was he taking it? Was there still a friendship between us to salvage?*"

It was strange how I hadn't reached out to Annie during this emotional and tense scene; I left it up to Kaleb to handle the breakup, to do the dirty work. I wanted to avoid conflict, at all cost. Tom and I sat back and watched this drama unfold between Annie and Kaleb, as if we didn't even exist in this foursome or have any say in the matter. This plot twist revolved around two main characters... Annie and Kaleb. I had a supporting role as the third wheel in this threesome while Tom played a cameo role. To this day, I'm not sure how Tom truly felt about the breakup, whether he was okay with it ending or would he have fought for it. I'll likely never know the answer.

Even though I knew ending this foursome was the right thing for us to do, I felt guilty that Annie had gotten so upset over it. What I didn't foresee was the contempt and rage that she would unleash at me. Fifteen minutes after Kaleb came home, I received a text message from Annie.

"You bitch! You say that you're my friend but then why didn't you

165

talk him out of it?" she messaged. I was stunned. How dare she turn this around and make it my fault that this foursome was over?

"Talk him out of what? This was both our decision!" I quickly typed back.

"How could you do this to me?" she replied.

"Why can't you understand that this was getting out of hand? Look at your behavior last night!"

"How can you be so selfish? You were never my friend! You should have had my back, if you were!" she typed.

What the hell was she talking about? I'd only ever thought of her and her needs throughout this messed-up saga, even at the expense of my relationship with Kaleb. *What more did she want from me?* I was beyond irate.

"Had your back? Just like you had my back?" I retorted.

At that point, I was so done with Annie, our so-called friendship, and this stupid foursome.

* * *

The next morning, I received another text from Annie. This time, she was calmer.

"Do you want to meet?" she messaged. I didn't respond.

"I need to talk to you," she went on.

"Talk about what? I have nothing more to say," I typed back.

"Just give me 15 minutes, please" she typed.

I turned off my phone... I didn't want to engage with her. I'd had enough of all the drama she'd brought into our lives. I'd bent over backwards to keep the peace and smooth things over so this foursome could continue, despite Kaleb's growing angst about staying in it. I tried to be a good friend to her over the past two years and everything fell apart.

There was one thing I knew about myself; it took a lot to get me angry but when someone pushed me over the edge, watch out! This was the lesson I learned from my father. Once anyone disrespected or offended him, he would cut you out of his life without a second thought, including his own children (each kid had been disowned at one time or another). I wasn't as extreme as my father but I, too, have been guilty of ghosting a person if I couldn't forgive or forget what they had done to me. I had a hard time letting go of the hurt.

In my heart, I knew there was no recovering from this with Annie. I couldn't pretend to myself that I was okay with the way she treated me with her nasty text, full of blame, anger, and name calling and go back to the way we were as friends. This wasn't someone I wanted in my life. I kept giving and giving, and Annie only kept taking and taking, thinking only of herself. When she couldn't convince Kaleb to stay in the foursome, she threw a hissy fit and spewed venom at me instead. I wanted nothing to do with her *ever again* (so I thought).

*   *   *

As the days turned into weeks and months of not talking to Annie, I became sadder and more disheartened. I had lost my best friend. Over that summer, I reflected on the breakup and what had gone awry. But something was not adding up ... it didn't make sense to me why Annie displayed such over-the-top rage at me when it was Kaleb who broke the news to her—he was the one who wanted out the most! Sure, it was sad that our relationship had suddenly ended but neither Kaleb nor I (nor Tom as far as I knew) felt this upset. None of us used nasty names and put blame on the other for the failure of this relationship. The foursome simply didn't work out. *So why was Annie so angry with me? Was I missing something?*

24

I Was a Fool

* * *

Over that summer, Annie tried desperately to reach out to me through texts and even a handwritten letter. I ignored them all. Even though I was trying to block the whole foursome situation from my mind, the sadness of losing my friendship with her would creep back in from time to time. If I was honest, I did miss our friendship. I grieved the loss of it and found myself often going to Kaleb for comfort and talking to him about the sadness and disappointment I felt.

Then, one day in late August, I realized it was Annie's birthday. I wavered and decided to send her a birthday greeting. She was taken aback by my sudden message but was appreciative nonetheless. After having time to process everything, I was now open to talking to her. I didn't expect us to become friends again; I just needed to have closure about why the end of the foursome had caused such friction and the subsequent demise of our friendship four months earlier. I wanted to understand from her point of view and put everything into perspective. There were issues that still gnawed at me, and maybe Annie could shed some light on it.

"Would you be up to meeting for coffee?" I asked her.

We agreed to meet the following Friday at a local coffee shop. It was a sunny afternoon in early September, and Annie was seated at a table, looking at her phone. I was feeling anxious about seeing her after all these months. I didn't know how I would feel or what I would say exactly. However, I was willing to keep an open mind and an open heart. I didn't want it to be another cat fight. I took a deep breath before I approached her. It was awkward when she looked up and our eyes met. She smiled at me. I sat across from her and, before I could say anything, Annie apologized.

"I'm sorry ... how we ended things," she said. "It was pretty messed up."

"Yeah, it was," I said.

"How have you been?" she asked. "I've missed talking to you."

"This summer has been different ... that's for sure," I said.

Annie went on to express her regret over how badly she'd handled the situation when our foursome ended. "I shouldn't have said those things that I said to you. I was upset but that's no excuse."

"I accept your apology," I told her.

"Do you think we could start over?" Annie asked hesitantly.

"I'm not sure if I'm ready."

"No, I get it," she acknowledged.

"How about we take it one day at a time and see where things go?"

"Okay, understood. We'll go at your pace," Annie agreed.

I felt surprised and relieved that she had taken ownership of her behavior, unlike four months earlier. I was willing to give Annie another chance at friendship, but I was scared. This time I would proceed with caution but I was hopeful that she had changed, based on this meeting.

Over the next several weeks, Annie initiated brief text messages to me, asking how my day was going. It was hard at first to trust her and let my guard down fully, but I found myself gradually opening up. I could tell Annie was trying to make things better between us, and deep down, I wanted that too.

* * *

Then my worst fears came true. I remember the date perfectly: September 30, a month after I had let Annie slide back into my life. I was searching on Kaleb's laptop for business contact information when I inadvertently came upon a recent email he'd received from Annie. *What?! She was communicating with him?* Without thinking, I opened the email and proceeded to read what appeared to be a personal email from Annie to my husband. In it, she asked Kaleb how he was doing and then proceeded to share what she had been up to over the summer and how she had started to connect with me again.

All the emotions from a few months ago came flooding back: anger, disappointment, and hurt. Our "friendship" wasn't even on solid footing yet, and now she had the audacity to reach out to Kaleb. *Was our friendship important to her or was reconnecting with Kaleb what she wanted all along? Was she just using me again? What did she want from him?*

When I confronted Kaleb about this email, he told me that he never replied to her.

"But you never brought it up to me either!" I yelled.

"I didn't think it was important. I just forgot, okay?" he remarked defensively.

As far as I knew, he hadn't talked to Annie since the breakup. I wanted to believe and trust Kaleb that he would have told me otherwise. My anger was aimed at Annie for initiating contact with him but I also felt angry at myself for letting my guard down and giving her the benefit of the doubt ... yet again. I should have known better!

I immediately sent Annie a text to confront her about it.

"Why did you send Kaleb an email?" I questioned her. "Was our reconnection a way to get back into his life?" I asked. She didn't respond.

Was there something going on between the two of them? I found Kaleb in the backyard patio, working at his computer.

"Tell me again why you didn't tell me that she had emailed you," I demanded.

"I told you already, I had forgotten about it," he said, his eyes fixed to his computer.

I could feel my blood pressure rising. "You don't get it, do you?" I yelled. Kaleb looked up from his screen.

"Calm down."

"No, I'm not going to calm down! You knew about Annie getting back into my life, and then she sends you this bloody email behind my back and you don't think it's important to tell me?" I questioned.

"I just thought she was trying to be nice by reaching out to me, now that you guys were talking again," Kaleb rationalized. "Anyway, I didn't respond to her, okay?"

"It's not okay! I've been telling you how hard it's been to trust Annie and how scared I felt about being friends with her again. You knew that!" I yelled.

"What difference would it have made if I told you last week?" he asked, getting annoyed.

"If you had told me about this email, then I would have seen her true colors sooner. There would have been no way in hell that I'd continue to communicate with her! You knew what I've been going through all summer, questioning if it was right to be friends again."

"Look! I didn't think her stupid email was going to be a big deal!" Kaleb reiterated.

"Why can't you understand?" I shouted. I was so pissed at Kaleb. I needed him to be there for me, but he let me down. I ran inside the house, fuming. There was no point trying to convince Kaleb why he should have told me about her email. He just didn't get it.

The next day, I tried again to talk to Kaleb. I couldn't put my finger on it, but there was something nagging me about the whole situation. I didn't trust Annie.

"Babe, I don't want to fight. I just want to know why you think Annie sent you that email?" I asked over breakfast.

"We're starting up with this again?" Kaleb replied, not looking up from his newspaper.

"She hadn't communicated with you all summer and then she *suddenly,* out of the blue, decides to email you," I pressed. "It doesn't make any sense."

"I don't know, maybe she was bored," he replied.

"Still, she had no reason to reach out to you. Our foursome was dead. Why reach out to you now? It's never crossed my mind to contact Tom, so why would she engage with you?"

Kaleb kept silent.

"Is there something you're not telling me?"

He didn't respond.

Minutes passed. Neither of us said a word. Then, suddenly, he placed his hands over his face and bowed his head.

"I'm sorry," he whispered as a tear rolled down his cheek. I froze and looked at him, confused and afraid of what he was going to say next. I've never seen him emotional like this. Kaleb averted his gaze downwards and continued to be silent, building up his courage to say something. His chin trembled, and then he blurted it out.

"I cheated on you while you were in Thailand ... *with Annie.*"

25

The Affair

* * *

"What?" I stared at Kaleb in disbelief.

I couldn't have heard that correctly ... could I? The room began to spin as I tried to digest the news. So many thoughts swirled through my head, but mostly I felt confused. Affairs happened to *other* people; it wasn't supposed to happen to *us*.

"I don't understand," I stammered.

"I'm sorry, I didn't mean to hurt you."

My legs buckled under me and I fell to my knees, burying my face in my hands.

"How could you do this to me?" I sobbed. Tears streamed down my cheeks. Kaleb tried to reach out to embrace me, but I pulled away.

"No, don't touch me!" I uttered; my jaw clenched.

"Please. Let me explain," he pleaded.

As more tears came, more thoughts whirled through my head. Kaleb (and Annie) had been lying to me this whole time? My trip was over a year ago. Even though they had had sex multiple times over the past two years, Kaleb's confession was gut-wrenching. It wasn't about the sex so much as it was this secret that he could keep from me.

"How could you make a fool of me like this? Don't I deserve better?" I cried.

"Honestly, I didn't mean to hurt you," Kaleb repeated. "Can we talk about this ... please?"

So many different emotions jockeying for position, alternating between shock, *anger*, denial, *anger*, pain, *anger*, hurt, *anger*, disappointment, *anger* ... and then broken-heartedness.

Suddenly, I needed to know *everything*, right from the beginning ... the *how*, *when*, and most importantly, *why*. I took a deep breath, trying to ready myself for the wave of emotions to unravel.

"How did this happen?" I demanded.

"I'll tell you everything, anything you want to know," Kaleb agreed.

"When did it start?"

"When you went to Thailand."

"After I got on the plane that morning?" I asked.

"Yes. Annie had texted me and asked if she could come over ... while the kids were in school," he explained. "I thought she was bored and just wanted to chat."

"Then what?"

"She came over in the afternoon, and we sat on the patio and had a glass of wine," he went on. "Babe, honestly, I didn't think anything beyond having a drink was going to happen! Please believe me."

"Who made the first move?" I asked, ignoring his commentary. *His* feelings didn't matter to me in that moment; I needed answers.

"She sat on my lap and we kissed ... then one thing led to another."

"Did you have sex in *our bedroom*?"

"No, we were in the basement."

"Was this the only time?" I could tell from his shamefaced expression that it wasn't. "It was more than once?"

"Twice more," he admitted.

I felt the anger building.

It then occurred to me about their vehicle shopping together ... had they been seeing each other then?

"Did you see each other *before* my trip?" I questioned.

Kaleb hesitated. Without looking at me, he said in a low voice, "Yes."

His answer stung. We had a foursome going on and all this time, these two were meeting on their own. Kaleb been lying to me this whole time, and I couldn't even be sure that what he was saying now was the truth. In the span of 10 minutes, I had learned that my husband had been having an affair with my best friend, that it had started when I was in Thailand, but—no—actually, it had started *before* my trip. What the fuck?

Anger flooded through me and I couldn't stand to be in the same room with him anymore. I walked out of the kitchen, feeling so out of control. Nothing made sense. What had happened? I thought Kaleb and I were solid. How could I have been so wrong?

"Please let me explain everything," Kaleb pleaded. His voice startled me. I hadn't realized he had followed me into the living room.

I took a deep breath, swallowing my anger and frustration. "Be honest with me. I deserve that much," I said.

Kaleb admitted that the secrecy all started when he began helping Annie search for her new vehicle. They regularly met for coffee and spent the afternoon together. I guess she wanted to spend any time she could with Kaleb, and car shopping was her ruse. Annie was smart about it, too. She would check with me first thing in the morning to see what my day was like; if I told her that I was busy with work, that was her opportunity to send Kaleb a text to "check out vehicles."

"Did you even go to dealerships?" I asked.

"We did ... but not every time I said we were going."

"Did you have sex during those afternoons?"

"Never. I swear. We only talked," Kaleb exclaimed.

"Then why couldn't you tell me you were going for coffee, if it was just innocent chatting?" I questioned. "We always told each other everything."

"I wanted to, but Annie convinced me it wasn't a good idea. She said it was easier to not say anything."

"Oh, did she? Easier for who?" I countered. "And why did you listen to her, anyway?"

"She said you would be upset and jealous, since she was already taking up so much of my time with the car shopping," Kaleb explained.

"Swear to me that you didn't have sex!" I demanded.

"I swear to you. That only happened while you were away in Thailand."

"Oh, that's right. Three times to be exact," I retorted sarcastically. Kaleb avoided eye contact and was quiet.

"So, I guess she *made* you promise not to say anything about that part either?" I asked. Kaleb nodded.

"I know it's not a good enough excuse but she said that if I told you, you would tell Tom, and it would be over for them. I didn't want to be responsible for ruining your friendship or their marriage. She convinced me that it was better not to say anything."

"Here we go again, doing everything Annie wants! What about doing what's right for *me* ... for *us*, Goddamnit!" I yelled.

"I knew it was wrong not to tell you. There were so many times I wanted to, but I was caught up in her stupid drama and excuses. She persuaded me that talking would just mess things up for everyone," Kaleb explained.

"I can't believe you didn't tell me! If you really loved me, then you should have told me and protected *me*. I should have known what kind of person she was. Instead of having my back, you were more concerned about what *she* needed to protect herself!" I shouted.

"I knew how much she meant to you, and I didn't want to ruin your friendship with her," Kaleb explained, trying to defend himself.

"Who needs enemies when you can have a friend like that?" I muttered.

Kaleb sat there with his hands over his face. "I'm so sorry. I know now how wrong it all was ... *everything*," he said.

I looked at him with disgust. "Now, you know?" I cried, shaking my head. "How could you do this to me?" I didn't know who this person sitting in front of me was anymore. This was not the man that I loved. Tears welled up in my eyes. I felt numb and dejected.

"I'm so sorry," Kaleb repeated.

Our foursome relationship flashed before my eyes, all the highs and lows and the endless drama Annie had crafted. It finally dawned on me ... this falling out between Annie and I had nothing to do me or her or our friendship. This was all about Kaleb! She had fallen in love with him. *Why didn't I see this before?* No wonder Annie took it so hard when Kaleb ended the foursome. She wasn't upset about our foursome ending. In her mind, Kaleb was breaking up with her, as if they were in a *real* committed relationship. Annie had been trying to win Kaleb's heart all this time, right beneath my nose, trying to convince him that *she* was the woman of his dreams ... instead of me.

It was all making sense now. I'd made the foolish assumption that Annie valued our friendship as much as me; in reality, she coveted her relationship with Kaleb far more. Our friendship was simply a coverup. Kaleb should have told me the truth sooner; then I would have known what kind of person she was. And it's not like there weren't opportunities! In April, when the foursome ended ... over the summer when I poured my heart out to him about missing Annie and wanting her back in my life ... or when I decided to reach out to her in late August to rekindle our friendship. Kaleb could have stopped me at any of these moments, but he chose not to. Instead, he buried *their* secret deep inside, hoping it would simply vanish.

Raw anger shot through me. I was sick of Annie and all her lies! It was time she knew exactly what I thought of her. I grabbed my car keys from the kitchen counter.

"Where are you going?" Kaleb asked.

"To confront that bitch!" I snarled. I jumped into my car, in a fit of rage. Her new SUV was parked in their driveway.

Racing to her front door, I pounded the knuckles of my fist against it, over and over again.

"How could you betray me!" I screamed at the door, tears streaming down my face. "I trusted you!" The house was quiet.

"I know you're in there!" I yelled. I continued banging on the door, louder and harder until my hands went numb and red, but she wouldn't open the door. She didn't have the nerve to face me.

Breathless with anger, I kicked the rear passenger door of her vehicle, leaving a sizable dent.

"Hope you like your new car!" I shouted.

I reversed out of their driveway and sped off. I was relieved that Kaleb had gone upstairs to the bedroom—I didn't want to see his face. I sat in the family room. Thankfully, the kids were still in school and were spared this melodramatic crap. Anger then shifted to sadness when I thought of Lucas and Samantha. What would happen to us ... our family? I felt physically sick to my stomach. *What would we tell them?*

My life was falling apart and there was nothing I could do about it ... all thanks to Annie and Kaleb. I was consumed with such rage picturing her face. Annie was not going to get away with this, I vowed. Tom had to be told the truth about his wife—he deserved that much. I quickly dialed his number, but it went straight to voicemail. I dialed incessantly. *Why won't he pick up?* I decided to send a text:

Tom, it's important, I need to talk to you. It's about Annie. But no response.

Tom never did return my calls or texts; I never heard from him again. Annie must have gotten to him first.

I dialed Annie's number. Finally, on the sixth ring, she picked up but didn't say a word. I could hear her breathing on the other line, waiting for me to say something.

"You couldn't have the decency to face me?" I exclaimed.

"Please calm down," she told me.

Taking a deep and controlled breath, I said, "Don't worry, I am calm."

"Give me a chance to explain," Annie pleaded.

"No. For once, you have no say, which I know will be hard for you," I said. "Kaleb already admitted everything. I know the truth. I don't want to hear any of your bullshit lies or excuses!"

Annie was silent. She knew the jig was up.

During our foursome relationship, I didn't stand up to Annie. I didn't express what I wanted, like I should have. I felt powerless, silenced and afraid to voice my true feelings, much like I had felt as a child under my father's roof. *No more. N*ow it was my turn to say my truths.

"You were in love with him all along, weren't you?"

Silence.

"You pretended to be my friend so you could get to him."

More silence.

"You lied about going to car dealerships so you could spend time with him."

Annie remained quiet.

"You went out of your way to plan an amazing surprise party for me, only to then reward yourself with my husband while I was away."

There continued to be only silence on the other end of the phone, so I barreled ahead.

"At what point did you think it might be wrong to fuck my husband while I was away? The first time? Second time? Or third time's a charm?"

I kept spewing out all truths that she could no longer deny. It didn't matter that she wasn't speaking—I didn't even give her much of a chance to say a word, and I probably wouldn't have believed her anyway.

Choking back tears, I said "I loved you like a sister … how could you do that to me?"

"I'm sorry," Annie said in a low voice.

"Don't *ever* contact me again!" I screamed, hanging up my phone. I stood there, crying uncontrollably. I heard a noise and looked up to see Kaleb standing in the doorway. I didn't know how long he'd been there or how much he heard. He came in and tried to offer comfort by putting his arms around me. I didn't pull away this time. Although I felt angry at him, I needed his comfort more than ever. As he held me tightly, tears rolled down my cheeks. I didn't know what to do next or what to say anymore. I felt beaten and emotionally drained.

"Do you want to be alone?" Kaleb asked.

"I'm going to stay in the spare bedroom tonight," I said. "The kids will be home soon."

"I'll take care of them," he said. I nodded.

I slowly made my way to the spare bedroom and crawled into bed. I pulled the covers over my head, hoping that I would wake up from this nightmare. I cried myself to sleep, my heart broken into a million pieces.

26

Fight or Flight?

* * *

Endless thoughts bombarded my mind as the room grew darker, colder, and lonelier. I snuggled deep under the covers ... protecting myself with a layer of blankets. My life had exploded before me, and I felt utterly lost. I'd never felt pain like this before—betrayed by my husband *and* my best friend. How could this have happened to me? How could the man who (supposedly) loves me betray me in such a hurtful way? Could we overcome this titanic obstacle together? Or was I fooling myself to believe there was still a chance between us? And if we miraculously did, would I be able to trust him again? Or was the damage irreparable?

Although I didn't know the answers to these questions, I knew that this moment had forever changed me. It had also changed my relationship with Kaleb. Through my anger and hurt, there was also a deep sadness. I wanted to feel Kaleb's touch and comfort, as if it were yesterday when everything was fine. Today, I cursed him and wanted nothing to do with him. I wished *today* had never come.

I kept hearing Kaleb's words in my head over and over again.

I cheated on you while you were in Thailand ... with Annie.

I felt stupid not having known earlier, not having even the slightest idea. I started replaying every interaction we had with Annie in my mind, as if these were scenes from a movie, looking for clues. That time when Annie asked Kaleb to come quickly and meet her at the dealership so he could help her negotiate a deal. Those trips to Vegas so Annie could have Kaleb all to herself. Or all the times they went out on the porch to have a cigarette ... was there more to that?

My detective work was interrupted when I heard voices coming from the family room; Kaleb was helping Lucas and Samantha with their homework. I felt guilty that I didn't greet the kids when they came off the bus, but I knew I couldn't. I felt depleted and had nothing left to give as a mom. I'd barricaded myself in this room to protect myself and to shield them from seeing their mother in this fragile state. I didn't trust myself to be with Kaleb in front of the kids; I didn't know which emotion would suddenly come out, and that wasn't fair to Samantha and Lucas. They shouldn't have to witness our adult debacle.

Although I directed more of my anger towards Annie, I knew that Kaleb was not innocent in all of this. Annie didn't put a gun to his head and force him to have sex with her. He chose to have sex with her and *then* he chose to keep his mouth shut. He had choices all along, but he messed up each time.

Did Annie have any feelings of remorse, or had she known exactly what she was doing? Even though the four of us entered into this swinging relationship, there was no justification for lies, secrecy, and betrayal. This was not the Lifestyle I had envisioned when we started. This foursome was supposed to bring excitement and sexual fulfillment into my relationship with Kaleb, not detract and destroy it. Tom and I were in this foursome too and we didn't deceive or lie to our partners. We too could have gone behind Annie and Kaleb's backs … but we didn't. I wondered if Tom was hurting as much as I was right now. Or if he even knew the truth yet. Did Tom really know his wife? Had he suspected anything between Kaleb and Annie? *Did he even care?* They didn't seem to have the solid connection that Kaleb and I have … or had, rather.

My emotions kept cycling between disbelief, sadness, hurt, anger, anguish, and grief. I had always believed in my heart that Kaleb was the love of my life, and I trusted him implicitly. I would have staked my life on it that he would have never cheated on me. We always had a strong connection and respect for one another, to the envy of most of our friends. Nothing could ever break our bond, so I thought. Everything that I once believed in was now gone … just like that. What do we have left if we have no trust? Could I feel the same way towards Kaleb again? He fucked up and I honestly didn't know if I had it in me to forgive him or even care if we patched up our relationship. Where do we go from here? What about our beautiful family? How would our separation affect the kids? I had endless questions but no definitive answers. I felt numb and exhausted.

I didn't sleep much at all that night. I couldn't get my mind to turn off, and when it eventually did, my subconscious gifted me a nightmare.

Annie is swimming alone in the ocean. It's getting dark. Suddenly, she starts gasping and struggling to keep her head above water. She's drowning, her arms flailing fervently. She's not able to hold on for much longer…

She cries out, "Help me please, help me!"

Hearing her cries, I quickly jump into the water and swim towards her as fast as I can. I have to save her! Annie waves her arms to signal to me.

"I'm coming, hang on!" I shout. When I reach her almost lifeless body, I see she's barely conscious. I grab hold of her, struggling to keep us both afloat as I swim towards shore, which drifts further and further away.

I try desperately to hold onto Annie's body, but I slowly lose my grip. I hardly have enough strength to keep swimming. I know I have to make a choice—let go of her and save myself or try to save us, risking drowning us both. I manage to find the strength to hold onto Annie and keep swimming.

Suddenly, Annie regains consciousness, and she violently gasps for air. Without warning, she grabs onto my shoulders, pushing me under the water. I try frantically to push her off of me, but I can't. My head sinks under water with every one of Annie's pushes, only bobbing back to the surface with a lot of effort on my part.

The next time I breach the surface, I scream at Annie to let go of me but she continues to press down, once again sinking my head below the water. Her survival instinct kicks in. She then uses my submerged body to keep herself afloat. I slowly stop struggling under the water, and my body goes limp.

As Annie swims back towards shore, she turns back to watch my body sink below the surface. I watch from above, my body descending lower into the dark depths of the ocean.

I woke up in a sweat, gasping for air, disoriented. *Where was I?* When the room stopped spinning, I realized I was alone in the spare bedroom. I had slept here all night and still had my clothes on. Kaleb wasn't lying next to me.

What time was it? I must have overslept. Reaching for my phone, I saw that it was 8:15 a.m. The kids would be getting ready for school. I could hear Kaleb's voice, which sounded familiar, yet it *wasn't*. It was a regular school day ... but nothing seemed normal about it.

I quickly jumped out of bed and went to the bathroom to freshen up, hoping to catch the kids before they boarded the bus in ten minutes. Kaleb looked at me as I came into the mud room. We didn't say a word. The kids were putting on their jackets.

"Mama, are you feeling better?" Samantha asked, giving me the biggest hug.

"We were worried about you," Lucas said. "Dad said you were sick." I looked at Kaleb and then back to the kids.

"Yes, I wasn't feeling well yesterday, but I'm much better today," I told them. "Have a good day at school, and I'll see you when you get home."

26. Fight or Flight?

We kissed the kids good-bye and they raced off to the waiting school bus. I felt relieved that it wasn't the weekend and the kids were at school; I didn't want them to witness the pending explosion.

Kaleb headed off to the kitchen to make some breakfast. I didn't feel hungry, so I climbed back into bed. Yesterday replayed in my mind, looping over and over. A fresh swell of rage rose in me. I didn't know if I could talk to Kaleb without screaming and hurling insults at him. *What could he say that would make things better?* Maybe I needed more time away from him to calm down. I didn't know what I *should* be doing.

I stayed in bed all day long, trying to avoid him. I was dreading the talk that would confirm our marriage was officially over. I had so many emotions within me. I still loved this man, but I didn't know if I could forgive what he had done to me.

A knock at the door interrupted my thoughts. "Can I come in?" Kaleb asked, not waiting for an answer to enter. He sat on the edge of the bed and looked at me with red remorseful eyes, like he had been crying. He looked exhausted; he likely didn't get much sleep either.

"Can we talk?" he asked.

"Go ahead, talk," I said flippantly.

"I'm sorry, babe," he told me. "I never meant to hurt you."

"Then why did you lie?" I snapped.

"I know it was wrong to lie to you," he said with remorse. "But it was complicated."

"It's not complicated ... you don't keep secrets from the person you love. Period." I retorted.

"I know but there were a lot of factors here."

"Oh, so Annie *made* you do this!" I accused.

"Well ... no. I was confused by *everything*," he explained. "I've never hidden anything from you before."

Like yesterday, Kaleb was making excuses and putting the blame on everyone else except himself. According to his logic, it was Annie's fault (and mine as well) that propelled him to keep this secret so that our friendship and respective marriages could stay intact.

"I'm sick of hearing your excuses! It doesn't change the fact that you lied to me. You had sex with her behind my back ... repeatedly!" I snapped.

"Let me explain..." Kaleb pleaded.

"You don't get it, do you? Take fucking responsibility for your actions! Don't tell me how you were forced to lie to me! I don't want to

181

hear it!" I yelled. His explanation was not helping to restore my faith and trust in him. He could tell me *sorry* a million times over, but it wouldn't change the fact that he was dishonest with me. The damage was already done. All along, Annie had been hurting me and now she was hurting our family ... and Kaleb let this happen.

Kaleb bowed his head, saying nothing. He put his hands over his head, shaking it. This conversation was going nowhere. I was more upset than when we started.

"You're not hearing me! I can't even have a calm conversation with you!" he said angrily.

"I don't know if there's any point in talking," I asserted.

"Fine," he said. "I'll sleep upstairs."

"That's the smartest thing you've said so far," I said offhandedly.

Kaleb stormed out of the room.

This sleeping arrangement went on for a couple of weeks, and there was tension in the house. All I remember from that time was feeling incredibly lonely and sad. We both were. We tried to act as "normal" as possible in front of the kids, but it was getting harder to hide the friction and strain in our marriage. I knew the kids could sense something was wrong, but they never asked about it. Fortunately, they were going on a week-long school trip, and so Kaleb and I would get a chance to be alone and have another go at talking.

"Do you think we should go somewhere while Lucas and Samantha are away?" Kaleb suggested one morning after the kids left for school. "We could stay at that resort up north."

Maybe a change of scenery would be good for us. At that point, I wasn't sure what would help me to heal but I was desperate enough to try anything. I knew that what we had been doing—tip-toeing around each other while the kids were home, avoiding each other when they weren't—wasn't working. Why hadn't we tried marriage counseling? The thought did cross our minds but Kaleb and I were cocky enough to think we could fix things by ourselves, without external intervention. We were professionals in the mental health field, after all. We could put our marriage back on track by talking it out, like we've done in the past, from business disagreements to petty fights. However, I had to admit to myself that this time felt *different* ... more dire. I wasn't confident that we could make things better by going away to some resort. I knew that it would take much more than that, but this was a start. Kaleb and I weren't ready to give up on our marriage yet—we needed to *try* and that was a promising sign.

"Maybe," I said.

26. Fight or Flight?

* * *

And so, two weeks after I had found out about the affair, Kaleb and I drove an hour and a half up north to this resort. We were both quiet in the car. The more I thought of Annie, the angrier I got. It cycled between her and Kaleb. They both were at the root of my anguish, and I hated them equally. And since Annie wasn't a part of my life anymore, that meant my anger was all directed at the person who was right there in the car with me.

Kaleb decided to stop along the way to pick up some lunch for us. I knew he was trying but I wasn't ready to make nice with him yet.

"Where do you want to stop for lunch?" he asked.

"I'm not hungry," I stated.

Kaleb could sense my anger and irritation with him. He kept his frustration in check and didn't say anything. He stopped at the gas station and picked up a sandwich for himself and ate in the car ride. Everything about him irritated me, even the way he chewed his food.

We continued driving in silence, until Kaleb sighed loudly. "Are you going to be like this the entire trip?" he asked.

How dare he! If I want to be mad for hours, days, weeks, or years, I bloody hell had the right! "I'm not the asshole who cheated! If I want to be mad, then that's my prerogative," I spat.

I knew I wasn't communicating effectively. But in that moment, I wasn't a therapist. I was a human being in tremendous pain. I didn't know how to sort through my feelings and release my anger. Instead of being empathetic to how I was feeling, Kaleb reacted with irritation and drove faster, which he knew would make me madder.

"Why the hell are you driving so fast?" I yelled at him.

He responded by slamming on the brakes, causing them to squeal, and abruptly pulling off onto the shoulder. He glared at me. "What do you want from me? I've said I'm sorry a million times!" he exclaimed.

I stared straight ahead.

"You want to go home? Is that what you want? Then, let's go! I can't do this anymore," he screamed at me. I looked out my window, averting my eyes.

"If this is how it's going to be, you punishing me with your anger, then I want out! I can't live like this!" he said.

We were both quiet. I knew he was right; we couldn't give this marriage a fair shake if I was going to keep on with my hurtful jabs at him. It wasn't helping to make things better between us; it was only dividing us farther. I took a deep breath and looked at Kaleb.

"Okay, I'm sorry," I said. "Let's talk … calmly."

"I *know* I want to work on our marriage. I need to know if you want the same thing, too," he said.

I sat quietly, thinking of what I truly wanted. I did want to work on us, but I didn't know how to begin to forgive him and move past my hurt and pain. My eyes filled with tears. I knew I didn't want to fight with him anymore. I wanted to fix *us*.

"I do want to give us another try," I told him. *I'm not ready to give up on us yet,* I admitted to myself.

Kaleb started the car, and we continued driving, both lost in our thoughts. We arrived at the resort and checked in. Would we be able to resolve our issues? Was there anything left in our relationship worth fighting for? I needed to know *how* I could trust Kaleb, that he could make me feel safe and secure again. I needed to know that he understood how deeply hurt I felt by his betrayal and what he would be willing to do to make our relationship better so this would never happen again. I needed to feel his love for me was genuine.

For the next three days, morning through night, we locked ourselves in our hotel room and hashed everything out. We were not going to leave until we both felt that we had said everything that we needed to say and came out feeling that we each felt truly understood by the other person. We ordered in food so we didn't need to leave, but my portion was left mostly uneaten. We went from moments of calm and synergy, even connectedness at times, to knock-out screaming matches and back again. We were honest and raw with our emotions and feelings. It was the most mentally and emotionally draining experience that Kaleb and I have put ourselves through—even more so than when we started our business together. But this was different. Our marriage depended on it.

"I need to feel safe with you again," I told him, on day three of our self-imposed quarantine. "Right now, I don't."

"I know," he said in a low voice. "It'll take time but I promise we will get there again."

"It's important for me to hear you say that you truly understand how much you hurt me," I stated.

"You're right, what I did was wrong and very hurtful. I should never have kept anything from you, no matter what the circumstances," he said.

I kept silent, trying to process and accept his words.

"I'm sorry that I hurt you by what I did and what I didn't do. I know that I can't blame anyone else but me. I take full responsibility for my actions," he continued.

This time, Kaleb didn't put the blame on Annie or the situation he was put in. He acknowledged that he should not have abided by Annie's wish to unequivocal secrecy, which was against his better judgment.

"I should have and could have done more to protect you ... and I didn't," he said, breaking down with emotion. "I should have been a better husband."

That was the defining moment when my anger began to fade. This was what I needed to hear from him. An acknowledgment of his own actions and an expression of remorse. I believed him. In my heart, I still believed in our marriage and I wanted both of us to fight for it, for the sake of our family and for the love we still had for each other.

"Please forgive me. I'm truly sorry."

"I loved you ... and I still love you," I whispered to him.

Kaleb embraced me, and I didn't want him to let me go. We laid in each other's arms that night, holding onto each other tightly.

In the past when we had our fights, we'd end the night with passionate make-up sex. This would not be one of those nights. Even if Kaleb had wanted to be intimate, I couldn't... I wasn't emotionally there yet. My walls were still partially up. I needed time to heal and rebuild my trust in him. For me, actions spoke louder than words. I also needed his patience, understanding, and compassion to give me the time and space to restore faith in our relationship.

We both knew we had a long road ahead but we were both willing to give it another try.

27

The Aftermath

*　*　*

The following six months were pretty rough for me and Kaleb. I had a lot to work through emotionally, not only dealing with the betrayal of my husband, but also by my best friend. I didn't know if and when I could get past it *completely*. My world, as I had known it, had collapsed all around me, burying me alive; I was trying to slowly dig myself out, not knowing if I could do it.

Although Kaleb and I tried to connect as a couple and find happy moments together, it was wrought with emotional insecurities, as I tried to work through the feelings of betrayal and trust issues I had. It felt like I'd take one step forward but then two steps back.

I was also grieving the loss of a friendship and the loss of our four-some adventure. I'd be lying if I said those past fun hedonistic moments with Annie and Tom didn't crop up in my mind, from time to time. Did Tom miss our time together? Did Kaleb miss those nights with Annie?

Feeling utterly frustrated and out of control with my emotions, I often took it out on Kaleb and we'd have arguments that seemed to come out of nowhere, which made me feel less positive about our relationship. I wanted to get past it all and become my old self again, but it wasn't that easy.

It didn't help that I was constantly reminded of my anguish and pain every time I laid eyes on Annie at school, or when Samantha and Lucas asked why they couldn't play with Annie and Tom's kids on the weekends like they had before. I didn't have a good answer other than "they're busy." Whether it was seeing Annie out walking her dog past our house or driving by their house while she and her kids played in their front yard, it rattled me each time. It never got easier. Just when my wound was beginning to heal and scab over, the sight of her or hearing her name would rip off the band-aid and expose my deep cut. I couldn't escape.

27. The Aftermath

At Lucas' eighth grade graduation ceremony, about nine months post-affair reveal, I was taken aback when I saw Annie seated two rows ahead of us. She occasionally looked back to try to catch my eye and engage with me. I felt sick to my stomach that she was this close to us. *Was she looking at me or at Kaleb?* Probably the latter. I avoided eye contact with her, looking stoic and straight ahead. It was an odd feeling that this now-stranger was such an important part of my life less than a year ago. As hard as I tried to not let Annie's presence affect me or ruin this special day for our family, I found myself being pulled back to that fateful day when Kaleb confessed. Tears welled up in my eyes. *Keep it together*, I told myself. *Don't let her affect you like this!*

Seeing Tom next to Annie was also jarring. Neither Kaleb nor I had seen or spoken to Tom since the foursome breakup. He never did call or text me back—he simply disengaged, keeping his distance from the entire drama. I'll never know if Annie told Tom the truth about her affair. Interestingly enough, a year and a half after the affair came to light, Lucas told me about a rumor going around school that the Jennings couple had separated.

During that time, Kaleb and I took countless walks together, and I admit I made it a point to walk past Annie and Tom's house, so they knew we were still together. We talked daily about Annie in one way or another. I didn't hold back my feelings. Anything that was on my mind, I'd bring up and we'd talk about it, almost to the point of nauseum. I wanted us to be transparent and not hide anything from each other— this was important to me in rebuilding the trust. And it worked. Over time, and slowly, I started to reconnect with Kaleb and feel safer. This incessant communication is what saved our marriage, honestly.

Despite making some progress in our relationship, I was still struggling internally with my emotions. I went into a dark place, feeling vulnerable and lacking control over my life. I couldn't understand how two of the closest people to me could wound me like that. If they could hurt me, what's to say that other people (who weren't as close) couldn't do the same? I no longer trusted anyone. I ended up cocooning myself into a protective ball, keeping my distance from everyone, including family and close friends. I felt I had to put up walls to protect myself. I wanted to stay safe inside the house, surrounded by the kids and our dogs. I wouldn't let anyone inside my close-knit circle for the next six months.

Kaleb noticed that I was becoming more depressed and withdrawing from everyone and he was rightfully concerned. I knew that I wasn't the same person I was before all of this. I admitted to myself and to

Kaleb that I needed help from a professional to sort through my feelings. This time, I couldn't do it alone. I knew that I had to work through issues of betrayal, mistrust and anger with a therapist or my relationship with Kaleb would not get better.

Finding out about Kaleb's affair tapped into the same emotional rawness and hurt that I experienced in my relationship with my father. I realized now that I had transferred a lot of my daddy issues to Kaleb and how it significantly played a role in our marriage and the way we communicated with each other; I would often look to Kaleb as though he *were* my father, especially during heated moments of conflict and arguments. My father never had my back, and more times than not, he looked after his own needs first before giving any thought to the people he supposedly loved, like my mother and us kids. In hindsight, I had always been attracted to strong male dominant figures when I was dating.

When I met Kaleb, I liked the fact that he was similar to my father in that he was strong, vocal, and opinionated in character. However, the key difference between them was that, unlike my father, Kaleb provided unconditional love, which I've been missing and yearning for all of my life. The affair brought me to my knees because I felt abandoned by Kaleb, just as I had felt with my father. Kaleb wasn't there to love and protect me like he had promised. His affair hurled me right back to my wounded inner child (Kneisl 1991). I felt scared, insecure and vulnerable again. I couldn't stop feeling hurt and I didn't know how to get rid of these awful feelings, despite Kaleb's constant reassurance that he would never hurt me again.

I made an appointment later that week to see Dr. C, a psychologist. Oddly enough, Dr. C reminded me of my father; he was in his early seventies with wavy gray hair, a moustache, and silver-rimmed glasses. Despite the resemblance, I felt comfortable talking to him. He possessed a gentle, empathetic, and kind soul. I was relieved that he knew nothing about me—no past history, expectations or preconceived notions. We were starting from scratch.

"What brings you here today?" Dr. C asked me during my first session.

"Where do I begin?" I asked with a nervous laugh.

"Anywhere you want to," he replied.

I talked about my childhood and growing up in a strict Korean family. Dr. C listened attentively, occasionally nodding his head and scribbling down notes. The 50 minutes went by quickly with me doing most of the talking. I agreed to come back the following week.

27. The Aftermath

I continued to see Dr. C every week for the next six months. During our sessions, we progressed from talking about my childhood and family dynamics to my relationship with Kaleb. I was in a safe space to say everything and anything to him. It was like going to confession. I could expel my "emotional garbage" and this was exactly what I needed—to be heard, to have a voice, and to have my thoughts and feelings validated.

Despite feeling safe and comfortable with Dr. C, I was hesitant to bring up the Lifestyle. I didn't know if he would judge me or think less of who I was as a person. I soon realized, though, that I couldn't leave the foursome if I wanted to get to the root of my trust issues with Kaleb. With each week, I became more comfortable with Dr. C and was ready to share my alternative lifestyle choice and how that impacted my marriage.

"Kaleb and I are in the Lifestyle," I admitted, bracing myself for Dr. C's reaction.

"How long have you and Kaleb been swingers?" he asked, his voice and expression neutral. I felt no judgment from him.

"We've been in two monogamous foursome relationships in the past seven years," I stated.

"Tell me more about these relationships," Dr. C replied.

And so I did. Dr. C didn't seem to be one bit fazed. A true professional. I also assumed he'd probably heard stories far more sensational than mine.

We talked about why the relationships ended ("secrecy," I stated) and the drama that became part of our lives when Annie came on the scene. I then told Dr. C about the affair and how Annie had fallen in love with Kaleb.

"So, both of these relationships ended because Kaleb and the female partner overstepped boundaries, correct?" Dr. C queried, after listening to the whole story.

"I guess you're right," I replied. "I never thought about it that way."

"It seemed both women, Natalie and Annie, fell for Kaleb."

"Yeah, you're right. They did."

"Kaleb must be very charismatic."

"I've thought about that," I admitted, noting my own uncertainty over whether Kaleb might have led them on in some way.

"How does that make you feel?"

"Not good. I'm questioning whether Kaleb is telling me everything. Was he to blame for those situations happening?"

Dr. C nodded. "Possibly."

"I don't know. Part of me doesn't want to believe that."

"When Annie made demands that you didn't agree with, why didn't you and Kaleb stand up to her and say 'no'?" Dr. C questioned.

"I really don't know," I replied, shaking my head in disbelief.

"It seems that Annie was persuasive with you both," Dr. C stated.

Looking back now, we went along with Annie's demands because we didn't want to make a big deal out of it. I avoided conflict and Kaleb steered clear of drama at all costs. Annie picked up on that and knew how to work it to her advantage. What I then thought of as us accommodating her, I was starting to realize was her manipulating and controlling us. Annie was unhappy in her marriage with Tom and saw an out with Kaleb. Kaleb was everything she fantasized about in a partner. By swapping husbands in this foursome, she got the opportunity to spend more time with Kaleb. And by gaining Kaleb's attention and affection, Annie surmised that she must be better than I was. The more Kaleb gave into her requests for more compliments and alone time together, the more she demanded of him; it was never enough for her. She was on a high when it came to getting attention from Kaleb. Tom, on the other hand, was emotionally unavailable to her.

Dr. C and I spent a lot of time exploring how Kaleb's decision to keep the affair a secret made me feel.

"Kaleb told me that Annie made him feel guilty about saying anything because it would affect my friendship with her and also break up her marriage," I said. "At least, that's what he told me."

"Do you believe him?" Dr. C asked.

"I *want* to believe him. I want to believe that Annie was the villain and that he was pulled into her web of lies."

"How does it make you feel when he gives you this excuse?" Dr. C queried.

"Very angry."

"Towards Annie or Kaleb?" he asked.

"Both."

"Do you believe Kaleb when he says he's sorry?" Dr. C asked.

"I do," I said. Kaleb had admitted to me that he was naïve in thinking that he could *handle* Annie in his own way. He had never met anyone like her who was so passive-aggressive and manipulative.

Dr. C helped me to process and navigate through my emotions. Verbalizing my thoughts in our sessions was far different and more beneficial than talking to Kaleb or having these thoughts ruminate inside my head. When I heard myself expressing what I was feeling, it empowered me and made things more real and clearer in my mind. It was powerful because I felt validated that someone was listening to how I felt. Dr. C gave me the space to talk openly about my hurt and pain, which allowed me to move forward and not dwell on the past.

I stopped asking "Why did this happened to me?" Instead, I was able to process and understand why the foursome situation unfolded as it did and the choices that Kaleb made when it came to Annie. I came to understand that there were two sides to a coin. Humans are complex and complicated beings who make mistakes. This helped me to start my process of forgiving Kaleb.

"Is it possible for Kaleb to get caught up in another foursome situation and lie to you again?" Dr. C asked.

I paused. We hadn't participated in any Lifestyle activities since the affair had come to light. I hadn't really spent too much time focusing on whether we would return to the Lifestyle; I'd been too focused on our marriage.

"I'd like to say no ... but I'm not sure," I admitted.

Kaleb and I had stopped talking about the Lifestyle. It had simply disappeared from our lives, like it never existed. I came to associate LS with negativity and drama. So far, our track record of two failed foursome relationships made me think this was not the best option for us. Kaleb and I had reached a point in our relationship where we didn't want any more drama in our lives. We'd rather deal with routine and monotony than risk everything we had.

So, we returned to our vanilla way of life and kept to ourselves. We spent more time with the kids, took them to their soccer games, their dance and swim lessons. Lusty weekends of debauchery were a distant memory. It wasn't hard to leave it behind. Kaleb and I were emotionally spent; we had nothing left to give after the whole Annie ordeal. I didn't even have the energy or interest to reach out to our vanilla friends. I cocooned myself and avoided any type of social gatherings. I wanted to protect the fragile parts of me. Kaleb and I still had a lot of work to do to rebuild our relationship, so that was our focal point.

We lived like this for four years.

Eventually, though, I came to realize that I couldn't blame the affair on the Lifestyle. Foursome or no foursome, our relationship would have been tested at some point. It was a wake-up call for us. Kaleb and I needed to address the underlying problems in our relationship, what went wrong between us and how this major misstep even happened. I was arrogant to assume that nothing could ever go wrong with my marriage, even if we were tempting fate by engaging in the Lifestyle. Swinging was not the problem; the problem was our communication (or rather, lack thereof). The foursome circumstance only brought to light the cracks in our relationship and showed how little we actually communicated with each other.

28

A Fresh Start

* * *

"I can't do this anymore!" I told Kaleb one morning at breakfast.

"You can't do what?" Kaleb replied.

"I can't continue to live near *them*," I said tearily. "It's been over four years now but I still get triggered every time I see her or Tom around."

It seemed that everywhere I went, Annie was there. Although she had moved out of the family home two years earlier (when she and Tom separated), she often drove through the neighborhood when she picked up and dropped off the kids. She drove past our house every single day, even if it was a longer route to her condo; she and her kids walked their dog up and down my street; and I would see her sitting in her car in the school parking lot, waiting to pick up her kids. Anxiety shot through me at the mere sight of her. I wanted to forget about her ... forget about *everything*. Every time I was ready to move on with my life, it'd all come flooding back the moment I laid eyes on her. *How could I ever heal when I couldn't escape her ominous presence?*

"I know it's been hard for you to see her around but what can we do?" Kaleb asked.

"Maybe we could move from here ... and go downtown?" I suggested. "We could downsize to a condo since Samantha is going to be at college, too, come September."

"Maybe a change would be good for all of us ... a fresh start," he acknowledged.

We took the plunge and listed the house, two weeks after I had brought it up. It must have come as a complete shock to Annie when she saw the *For Sale* sign on our lawn; however, she never reached out. It didn't take long to get a buyer, and that summer, we packed up and moved down by the city's waterfront. We had a huge garage sale and sold off everything; it was such a cleansing and cathartic feeling to purge my old life. This move was exactly the change we all needed. No longer little kids, Lucas and Samantha looked forward to having their home base downtown where all the action was, to the envy of all of their friends.

Now that both Samantha and Lucas were living away from home, Kaleb and I suddenly found ourselves empty nesters. Even though we were in a much smaller space, the condo felt empty and lonely without the kids around. Over the past four years, Kaleb and I had refocused on the kids and appreciated the quality time we spent as a family. We hadn't realized how much of our lives had been taken up by Annie and Tom and all their shenanigans.

Several months after moving downtown, I felt more myself. *Out of sight, out of mind* was a good thing for my mental health. Kaleb and I also felt more settled; we got to know our neighbors on our floor and explored the local restaurant scene. Despite the welcomed change of scenery, however, the novelty and excitement of living downtown was starting to wear off. I started to feel bored, being in a tighter condo space and going through the motion of work, day in and day out. Weekdays moved slowly, as we counted down the hours to Friday when we could turn off our computers and phones. It felt like we had nothing to look forward to. Days and every weekends seemed to blend from one to next. This feeling of monotony and dissatisfaction with life was exactly what landed us in trouble in the first place, when we jumped headfirst into each foursome.

As memories of Annie and Tom slowly faded and my connection with Kaleb began to rebuild, I found myself in a better place, emotionally and mentally. I wanted to move forward and forget about the tumultuous relationship that had consumed our lives—two years to be exact. But if I was being honest with myself, not all moments of our foursome were bad; I did miss the sexual spontaneity, the freedom and excitement of being with another lover—it was exhilarating. While I was tempted to ask Kaleb if he had ever thought of getting back into swinging, I didn't dare bring it up, mainly because we were still working on our marriage and I didn't want this to be a distraction. I contemplated the pros and cons of getting back into the Lifestyle. Would it be good for us to re-engage? After all, our relationship took a big hit after the whole Annie affair. *How could I even think of going down the rabbit hole again?*

But, despite my trying to forget and bury it, I felt an undeniable pull and connection towards the Lifestyle. I didn't know why it was a recurring thought. Our foursome experiences had undoubtedly caused so much pain and unwanted drama in our lives, so much so that I should have had serious reservations about getting back into it but I was *reconsidering*. Although we were having sex fairly regularly, the intensity of our physical connection was waning. I remembered the times when we couldn't get home fast enough to be with each other after our sexual play with Annie and Tom. But now, our sex life was becoming routine *again*. I was afraid to bring this up with Kaleb; I didn't want him to think that there was something wrong with *us*. Not that I wasn't happy with him... I was. I just wanted to feel *sexually* happier.

This change of heart reminded me of how I felt after giving birth to Lucas. I had gone through a difficult labor, lasting 28 hours and an episiotomy to boot. The exhaustion of endless breastfeeding and sleepless nights should have solidified my decision that Lucas would be our first and only child. I swore that I would *never* put myself through that unbearable experience ever again, so I thought. Then, less than a year later, I became pregnant again; my body seemingly had forgotten what trauma it had gone through. Luckily, with self-induced memory loss, I embraced this childbirth journey again, praying to the divine gods to grant me an easier experience the second time around. I guess I was hoping the same would happen with the Lifestyle.

After a four-year hiatus, was it time to scratch that itch again?

Would Kaleb want to explore it again? Was he as bored of the sexual monotony in our bedroom as I was? How would we do things differently if we got back in? Although I didn't have the answers to these questions, I knew that I was ready to start a new chapter in my life.

Would Kaleb be as ready as I was?

* * *

"It's been a while since we've gone out, just you and I," I said to Kaleb, one December morning.

"Did you want to go out for a cocktail tonight?"

I hadn't mentioned to Kaleb that I'd been secretly checking out downtown LS clubs on the internet. There was one website in particular that caught my eye: *Young Swingers—Wednesday Nights at Club Fantasia*. I wasn't sure if Kaleb would be up to going to this sex club, but at least we would have the night to ourselves.

And, so, that evening Kaleb and I made our way to the local pub and ordered drinks at the bar. I decided I needed to go for it and ask Kaleb how he was feeling.

"Do you miss having sex with other women?"

Kaleb seemed shocked by my question. With his eyebrows raised, he asked, "Why are you asking me this?" He took another sip of his Old Fashioned, trying to avert his gaze.

"I'm just curious," I said.

"Not really."

Why didn't I believe him? I knew he missed having sex with someone other than me because I've been feeling the same way, and we're a lot alike in our preferences. *Did Kaleb ever fantasize about another woman when we were making love? Was he bored with our routine Friday night monogamous sex?* I couldn't believe four years had passed since we swapped with Annie and Tom. Neither of us wanted to bring up our foursomes or swinging, shutting it out like it never happened. But maybe it was time to talk about it.

"Would you like another round?" the bartender asked, interrupting my thoughts. Both Kaleb and I nodded.

As we continued to sip on our drinks, I suddenly heard myself ask Kaleb directly, "Do you want to get back into swinging?" There I said it. I felt relieved, finally bringing it up. I was hopeful that Kaleb would be as excited as I was to start back into it again; however, this quickly changed to feelings of anxiety and regret when Kaleb didn't immediately respond. The look of shock on Kaleb's face said it all.

I shouldn't have said anything.

"Never mind. It's nothing," I said, quickly trying to change the subject.

"No, tell me where this is coming from," he said. His eyes softened and he looked concerned.

"Lately, I haven't felt like we've been connecting ... sexually. I'm just scared about losing *us* again."

"I didn't realize you felt this way."

"I think we just need a reboot, that's all. Remember the amazing sex we used to have after we got home ... *reclaiming each other*? I miss that," I said.

Kaleb couldn't deny that our sex life had become too comfortable and predictable. We both agreed that we missed the spontaneous, spicy, and sexy couple we used to be when we were with our other partners.

Kaleb took my hand and held it tightly in his. "I'm glad you brought this up. I've been feeling the same way but I wasn't sure if you wanted anything to do with swinging ever again," he said.

"So you miss it, too? *Really?*" I asked. He nodded.

I sighed a breath of relief. "Okay, this time, we'll do it differently," I said, firmly. "We'll put *us* first."

Kaleb gently took my face in his hands and asked, "Are you sure you're ready to jump back in? Are *we* ready?"

"I think it would be good for us."

"Okay, I'm going to follow your lead," Kaleb said.

"Good! There's this place called Club Fantasia not too far from here," I suggested.

"What? You want to go right *now*?"

"Sure, why not? It just so happens that tonight is *Young Swingers* night," I said excitedly.

"You've already checked this out?"

I grinned and nodded yes. It was obvious by Kaleb's expression that he had no idea I had been researching clubs for well over a month.

"I'm shocked but I'm glad that you did," he smiled. "If you're sure about it, then what are we waiting for?" he exclaimed.

"I'm sure."

Annie and Tom were never interested in going to an LS club; they wanted to keep us to themselves. I was excited that we could do what *we* wanted for once, instead of worrying about what other people wanted us to do. We grabbed the bill and quickly threw on our coats before we had a chance to change our minds. I felt like we were teenagers again, sneaking out of the house on a school night, and doing something we shouldn't be doing. Kaleb grabbed my hand as we left the bar, giving it a squeeze.

"Where to?" the cab driver asked, once we'd hailed a taxi and climbed in.

"Club Fantasia."

29

Lifestyle 2.0

*   *   *

Standing on our balcony with Kaleb holding me from behind, I took a deep breath of the cold crisp air and listened excitedly to the bustling sounds of the city street below with rowdy revelers. We anxiously awaited the countdown to the beginning of the new year. This was the first time I felt at peace in a long time. Kaleb and I were at a much better place in our relationship; I'd let go of a lot of the pain from the past, and I was now ready to embrace a fresh start.

"Here's to exciting new adventures downtown," Kaleb whispered into my ear, as if reading my thoughts.

Excitement. Yes, we were starting to see glimpses of that in our lives again. My mind flashed back to our recent experience at Club Fantasia. The towel-only dress code, having sex with another couple in front of a bunch of people, and, yes, even walking around barefoot (shudder) all added up to an eye-opening experience. The club's edgy, uninhibited, high sexual energy was invigorating and enticing. The unadulterated sexual hookup with no strings attached, no drama, and no jealousy contrasted with the past drama-filled experiences with Natalie/Steve and Annie/Tom. We could have amazing sexual encounters with as many couples as we desired! And we now knew what did—and what did not—work for us. No more monogamous foursomes ... only fun, sexual play. We both agreed that we were ready to jump back into the Lifestyle. But were LS clubs the only place we could hook up with other couples for casual sex?

One afternoon, while Kaleb was watching Sunday football on the couch, I decided to do some research. I Googled *swingers + lifestyle*. Different sites came up, including "Best Swingers Sites," "Exploring Swinging: Tips for Beginners," and "Lifestyle Swingers—Local Swing Site." I had no idea how much information there was and right at my fingertips. I clicked on one site that seemed pretty innocuous, *ABC Lifestyle**. It said it was created for Lifestyle couples looking to meet other like-minded couples in a safe, private and discreet way. *That's exactly what we were looking for!*

I decided to sign us up for a trial account version. I typed in a fake name and came up with a fun handle for us, *Drama-free Couple*. I should have checked with Kaleb first, but I wanted to do up a draft version with all profile information filled out before I let Kaleb in on this.

This website's questionnaire was far more personal and detailed than I had expected, asking me to state my and Kaleb's sexual orientation: *straight, bi-curious, bi-comfortable, or bisexual*. I quickly checked off *straight* for Kaleb, no question about it. Now, what about me? Hmmm ... this was the first time that I have ever been asked to categorize my sexual preferences. My knee-gut reaction was to check off the *straight* box; I had been happily married to a man for 23 years and it was a safe answer to choose.

But was I really straight?

Despite my two past experiences with Natalie and Annie, I wasn't quite comfortable or ready to come out as anything other than a heterosexual woman. *I'm just experimenting*, my little inner voice reminded me. Although my view of my sexuality had shifted after my experiences, especially with Annie, I still wasn't 100 percent there yet. It was a slow process of coming out to myself, let alone to other people in my life. I didn't even admit it to Kaleb at the start of our LS journey. I'm not sure why that was, but I wasn't ready to label myself as bisexual.

(This would eventually change. After a few years of dating in the Lifestyle and meeting other bisexual women, I gradually changed my profile from straight to *bi-curious*, and then to *bi-comfortable*, not certain of what the difference was in definition between the two. These two terms were the easiest way to be non-committal—it allowed me to dip my toes in the pool, instead of jumping in headfirst. While I admitted to myself that I did enjoy playing with women, I still continued to hide behind the wall of denial, telling myself that it was only during foursome exchanges and how infrequent my female sexual experiences were in comparison to other bisexual women in the dating pod. Sometimes I engaged with the female partner and other times, I didn't. It depended on the foursome ... specifically, if the female partner initiated playing with me.)

But back to that Sunday afternoon, where I decided to check off the straight box. *For now*, I told myself.

I moved to the next section, which was easy and automatic to type in—our age, hair color, eye color, and ethnicity. Then it asked us to rate our appearances, which caused me to pause. Not wanting to sound middle age (and boring), I decided to check off the "Hot & Spicy" box, which was beneath the "Next Top Model" box. That should get people in through the door, I chuckled to myself. I moved on to education level, smoking, and drinking habits. I checked off the "social drinker" box, which I knew was stretching the truth. "Binge drinker during socials" would have been a better descriptor for us. We pretty much had a glass of wine every night and definitely more on the weekends, but I didn't want us to come off as lushes.

Now moving on to Lifestyle experiences. Hmmm … how would I classify us? Beginner, some experience, or experienced? I guess we could consider ourselves *experienced*, given our two long-term foursome relationships over the past 10 years.

Next up came adding some sort of bio on us as a couple and our "wish list" for the type of couples we wanted to meet on the site. Although we were new to this dating scenario, Kaleb and I had a clear idea of what personality traits we were looking for in a couple and what were our deal breakers. As I'm sure most people do, I embellished some aspects of ourselves in our bio. I wanted to showcase us as a super sexy, flirtatious, and carefree couple, which would ideally attract the type of couples we were looking for—good-looking, sensual, high energy, and adventurous in the bedroom.

> We're a professional biracial couple looking for "friends with benefits." We've been happily married for over 20 years and are new to online dating. We are looking for other like-minded couples to travel with us to amazing destinations. We believe in quality over quantity. Looks are great but personality and a great sense of humor go a long way!
> We're looking for full swap but will entertain the possibility of soft swap. We are very sensual and love giving and receiving oral. We enjoy voyeurism, light bondage, oral sex, high heels, lingerie, foursomes, and same room play. Watching each other be pleasured by another partner is sexually appealing. Traits we dislike are arrogance, jealousy, insecurities and poor communication between partners. Let's grab a drink at a bar or LS club to see if there is a four-way connection.

There was a section where photos could be uploaded and placed in the following three categories: White (any member could view), Gray (only validated members could view), and Black (private and locked photos, which required permission). I decided to leave this photo upload section for later.

I was now ready to share what I was up to with Kaleb.

"Guess what I've been doing for the past hour?" I said excitedly.

"Online shopping?" Kaleb smirked.

"Very funny. I actually found an LS website," I said.

"There are websites for that?"

"Yeah, I know! Not one but there are a number of them," I stated. "I found one that looks pretty easy to join and I already went ahead and filled in the questions."

I handed Kaleb my laptop, and he slowly read through *our* responses.

"Looks good. Sign us up!" Kaleb exclaimed with enthusiasm.

"That was easy!" I grinned.

I took a deep breath in and exhaled out, as I readied myself to press the SUBMIT button. I felt anxious, yet excited about embarking on this new journey with Kaleb. Would this adventure pan out better than our past foursome relationships? Would joining this LS website give us opportunities to meet engaging and sexy couples? And more importantly, would this LS experience deepen our relationship or do the opposite?

I parked my thoughts aside and turned my attention to our blank profile picture. I realized we needed something there to attract attention. Like any dating site, the profile pictures had to be selected carefully to ensure we marketed ourselves in the best possible light. I perused other couples' profiles, opening the public photos to get a sense of what type of pictures they were sharing. Some were dressed up formally in suits and cocktail dresses, while others showcased themselves in sexy club or beach wear. I was surprised to see some public photos exposing the couple's face entirely; the majority of couples obscured their faces with digital markup to conceal their identities. Then there were the outliers: some couples who didn't give a damn and posted face and provocative nude public pictures, while others chose not to post any photos at all.

Okay … what type of pictures should we take for our public photos: tame or provocative? Maybe in between? We decided that we wouldn't provide face pictures publicly; we'd determine who would have access to our faces on a case-by-case basis.

"Kaleb, I can't find any pictures of us together!" I exclaimed, shocked.

"Then, let's take a few," he replied. "But the focus will be on you, not me, since it's mostly about the ladies."

"You know I hate posing for pictures! It feels so unnatural," I said with a sigh.

"It's up to you. We don't have to upload any pictures if you don't feel comfortable," Kaleb reassured me.

"It's not my thing, but everyone seems to upload photos. I guess I'll do it," I said.

"Don't worry... I'll be gentle," Kaleb smirked.

I looked through my closet and eventually settled on a deep V-neck red lacy dress that seemed appropriate; it was sexy enough to wear at a club but not too slutty that I couldn't walk into a restaurant with it on. I took my time with my hair and make-up to look just right for my LS online debut.

"How does this look?" I asked Kaleb, as I strutted into the bedroom.

"You look amazing!" Kaleb exclaimed. "Is that new?"

"No, I just haven't had a reason to wear it," I replied.

"It's picture-perfect," Kaleb winked.

"All right then, let's get this over with!" I exclaimed.

"Okay, stand by the window and strike a pose, like this," Kaleb instructed, placing his hand on his hip.

"I'm not posing like that! You look ridiculous!" I laughed. Modeling was so *not* me, but I knew I had to step out of my comfort zone if we were going to do this exploration. The flash went off, slowly at first and then continuously as Kaleb photographed me in different poses.

"Smile and pretend like you're enjoying this!" he laughed, which made me relax and loosen up.

"I am smiling!" I chuckled.

"Okay, now tilt your chin up. A bit more. Yeah, like that!" he suggested, getting right into his photographer persona. "Love it, love it!" he called out.

"Are we done yet?"

"Yup, I got the perfect picture of you!" Kaleb said excitedly. "Now, for the next outfit change."

"What? More pictures?" I moaned.

"We need shots for the private viewing, don't we?" he reminded me.

"Fine, what should I try on? Lingerie or a bikini?" I asked, but Kaleb didn't hear anything past *lingerie*.

"I'd go with the lingerie!" he exclaimed.

I changed and hesitantly came out of the bathroom, dressed in a lacy navy-blue one-piece intimate and black stilettos. Kaleb's mouth fell open.

29. Lifestyle 2.0

"Wow!" he exclaimed. "Where have you been hiding that?"

"Glad you like it," I grinned.

I felt more comfortable and self-assured as the afternoon progressed, even having a bit of fun with the poses. We put the phone on a timer and took several pictures of us together. I spent the next hour selecting and editing photos to upload onto our profile. By the end of the afternoon, we were officially the newest couple on *ABC Lifestyle** website.

This website kept track of how many people visited our profile every month and even broke it down to daily views. During the first month of membership, Kaleb and I logged on incessantly, at least 4–5 times per day to check out different couples and also how many views we received. Given that we were *fresh meat* on this website, we got hundreds of daily hits from curious members. It blew my mind that we got 234 visits and 47 flashing messages. I guess it didn't matter to them what we looked like (our face pics were blurred out), as long as we were breathing, live, new bodies! Most of the messages were greetings to welcome us to the website. Then there were others who were down to business and wanted to meet up for a quick bang or orgy. I was shocked by their candor, sexting with complete strangers. I guess there's anonymity to hide behind a screen and type whatever you want. They had nothing to lose and could only gain by asking.

I soon became fixated with the daily posted view count. Sad but true, the posted number, on occasion, affected my mood; a high count boosted my ego and a lower count brought me down. I could see how this could affect people's mindset, in building up your confidence, especially if you've never had attention like this before, or equally in tearing it down. I soon noticed an *inverse correlation* between the number of days under membership and the number of views couples received—the higher the number of days, the lower the daily views. Older members got pushed down in queue among the newly added thirty thousand plus members. There were ways to get "noticed" or into the spotlight—get on the Booty Call list (casual sex that night) or send out a ton of messages to the masses, skyrocketing your daily view count!

Given that physique and attractiveness play an important role in the dating world (LS or non–LS), it got us motivated to get back into shape. The thought of being naked with another couple (especially an attractive one) was enough to get our butts in the gym and working out five days a week. Maintaining our fitness regime was positively reinforced by the compliments and invitations for hookups. As I became more fit and toned, I felt more comfortable about Kaleb taking seductive and racy photos.

After a couple of months on the LS website, Kaleb and I became more familiar with the ins and outs of communicating with other couples. Most members did not converse on the website beyond the first intro greeting message or to request permission to view a couple's face pics; many felt that privacy might be compromised on the website and therefore any further communication was usually done through a free instant messaging mobile app, which did not disclose personal cell phone numbers. Kaleb and I decided to divvy up responsibilities; he would vet potential couples on the website, and I would then continue to communicate with certain couples on the messaging mobile app. Photos were exchanged to determine mutual physical compatibility. If I found the couple had no interest in communicating other than to send crude and inappropriate porn-like pics, I abruptly ended the conversation. If a couple was able to carry on a decent conversation, then I would suggest a meet-and-greet date.

Although we didn't know much of the general lifestyle out there when we started, one thing's for certain: Kaleb and I wanted to engage in swinging way differently than we had with the monogamous foursomes in our past. We were done with *restrictions* imposed by other couples. Kaleb and I would explore the Lifestyle on our terms and make it all about *us*, and no one else.

It wasn't easy for us to find our ideal couples in the Lifestyle—in fact, it was a lot harder than we thought it would be.

"What about them?" Kaleb asked, pointing out one profile.

"She's cute! But him, no way!" I replied.

"Why not?"

"He looks like my ex-boyfriend!" I exclaimed.

Kaleb and I scrolled through countless profiles and pictures, dismissing most of them because either we weren't on the same page in terms of physical attraction, or their profile description didn't feel like a good match. I (more so than Kaleb) scrutinized their bio, taking serious notes of their profile description. If the couple wrote little, then it was a pass for me. I didn't need them to write a novel, but it had to be more than a few words strung together... Next! If they only bothered to make sexualized comments or send nude frontal pictures, this wasn't the couple for me. Kaleb, on the other hand, placed more importance on physical appearance. Forget about their novel writing ability; if the female partner was attractive, the couple was short-listed! Often, many of our attempts to message potential couples ended up nowhere. A lot of talking and back-and-forth messaging with occasional flirting, but it usually stopped there.

* * *

Then, one day, a message came in from SEXYC&H (Clifford and Harriet), a couple who lived an hour away from us, asking if we'd like to get better acquainted. Kaleb and I checked out their photos and carefully read over their profile. They were in their early fifties, a bit older than what we were looking for but they seemed nice and relatively harmless. Their profile described them as easy-going, drama free, and avid travelers—perfect! However, they only uploaded one private profile photo and even that was difficult to make out their faces.

"I can't make out what they look like!" Kaleb stated.

"Maybe they need to be discreet for work."

"What do you think? Shall we give them a try?" Kaleb asked.

This would be our first date on the website.

"Sure, why not?" I replied. "We can find out more about them when we meet up."

We messaged them back and suggested that Friday for drinks. To our surprise, they responded immediately, saying they were free.

"Where should meet them?" I asked.

"Let them choose a place," Kaleb said. Clifford wrote back, suggesting we meet up half way at a franchise rotisserie chicken restaurant, right off the highway.

"At that chicken place?" I asked.

"Yeah, I know! Weird."

"Why can't we meet at a bar or lounge?" I asked.

"I don't know, but let's go with what they want."

We messaged back, agreeing to meet them at that location. That Friday evening, both Kaleb and I dressed casually in jeans. As we drove there, Kaleb sensed my nervousness and grabbed my hand.

"You okay?" he asked.

"Sort of. Just anxious," I said.

"It'll be fun, don't worry," he said. "As long as you don't go asking too many questions," he teased. Yes, I hadn't forgotten about my Spanish Inquisition of the couple at that underground sex club over a decade ago.

I smirked at Kaleb.

We walked into the restaurant, hand-in-hand, scanning where they might be seated. Then a wave came from the back.

"I guess that's them," I whispered as we made our way to them.

The Swinger in the Mirror

Clifford and Harriet were sitting opposite one another, indicating that they wanted us to pair up with the partner. They both stood up and greeted us with a hug. This was the moment when this date went downhill for me. Harriet wore a body hugging short black glittery dress and Clifford had on a brown suit with a wide tie. We couldn't have been more mismatched in our appearance. I knew I shouldn't be judging, but my first impression of them was not a good one. *Strike one!*

Kaleb sat down next to Harriet, compelling me to sit next to Clifford. Luckily, I sat to his left side and I didn't immediately notice his lazy right eye. (Kaleb later admitted on the car ride home that it was difficult for him to know if Clifford was looking at *him* or at Harriet when he was talking—his right eye looked in all directions.) I didn't know how Kaleb felt about Harriet but I was not attracted to Clifford, not one bit. I felt more of a physical connection with Harriet. But I didn't want to give up on this date so quickly so I convinced myself to try and keep an open mind … maybe his personality would win me over. After we placed our order, I noticed a family with young children sitting at the table directly behind us. This wasn't ideal. *What if they heard us talking? Would the parents know that this was a foursome date?* I tried to keep my voice low, hoping the others would follow suit. But Clifford and Harriet didn't pick up on my cue to use their inside voices; our conversations got louder and more animated with more wine. A few heads turned our way.

Clifford and Harriet were an interesting couple; they loved to travel and spend time with their friends with benefits. They'd only been with one couple in the past and were looking to pursue another monogamous foursome. *Strike two!* There was no way we would ever go back to that again!

We ended up chatting for more than two hours, sharing our horror monogamous foursome stories. When the waitress came with our bill, she made small talk and asked if we were from around here. Clifford proceeded to tell her that we weren't and that we had just met tonight. I cringed. The waitress likely assumed that we were hooking up. We ended the night with a hug and politely thanked them for meeting with us. I was pretty sure they were more interested in us than we were in them.

"What do you think?" Kaleb asked on the drive home.

"You have to ask?" I exclaimed. They were a lovely couple, but there was no attraction whatsoever. I can't be intimate with a couple if there's no chemistry.

"Did you see his lazy eye?" Kaleb chuckled.

"Don't get me started."

The next morning, we saw a flashing message on our profile board.

29. Lifestyle 2.0

It was from SEXYC&H. Clifford expressed how much he and Harriet enjoyed chatting with us and wanted to know if we could meet up again. *Oh no! How do I turn them down gently?* I crafted my message carefully, telling them that we enjoyed their company, but it wasn't a good match for us given their preference in pursuing a monogamous relationship. I assumed that would be the end of it, but, to my surprise, Clifford did a switch-a-roo; they would be willing to forgo the monogamy part and hook up with us. Yikes!

Thank you for considering us but we don't want to sway you from what you're looking for. We wish you guys all the best in finding the right couple! I messaged. We never heard from Clifford and Harriet again.

Although it didn't work out with SEXYC&H, it was a good first experience. Our next few meet-and-greets didn't fare any better. It was getting to be an expensive venture, going out on countless dates in search of the *perfect* couple. Initially, Kaleb and I were enthusiastic about these meet-and-greet dates and went on as many as possible, but as time wore on, it got to be more cumbersome. If there was any chance of getting close to finding the "ideal couple," one of us would kibosh it. More often than not, Kaleb was the harder one to please. I was feeling discouraged with the whole business of foursome dating.

"Why can't you be more lenient?" I challenged Kaleb after yet another failed connection.

"What do you mean?" he replied defensively.

"You're so picky!"

"Well, I can't fake an erection like women can fake an orgasm!"

He explained that he needed to be sexually attracted to the woman if anything was going to happen down there. This foursome dating was more challenging than I imagined. Not only did I have to be attracted to my new partners and equally like their personalities, Kaleb had to be attracted to the female partner to make this foursome doable. There were lots of times I felt attracted to both the male and female on the meet-and-greet dates; however, Kaleb didn't feel the same way and our prospects went south pretty quickly.

The reverse situation happened too—where the other couple were only attracted to one of us. Knowing what we know now, a perfect four-way match is next to impossible—it's like finding a needle in a haystack. Unless either Kaleb or I were willing to *take one for the team*, a potential hook up was never going to be in the cards.

30

Communication 101

Kaleb and I learned through our LS mishaps that we weren't as good at communicating as we thought we were and this almost cost us our marriage. We should have checked in on each other more to see how the other was feeling and that we were on the same page in terms of what we needed from each other. And when I say we should have communicated *more*, I mean *a lot more*. What holds true one moment may not apply in another moment, these check-ins should never be taken for granted. Kaleb and I should have talked to each other *before, during* and *after* each LS hookup—to make sure we were both okay with what had transpired and to clear up any misunderstandings.

We didn't want to repeat the same mistake on our latest venture into the LS world. Instead, we took the time to talk about our individual expectations—what we were each hoping to get out of our LS experiences—and also where our boundaries were. Our non-negotiables. We had failed to do this with our previous foursomes, and the fallout was huge. If we were going to do this again, we vowed to do things *differently*!

I thought, given my professional background and experience, that I was an above-average communicator. Boy, was I wrong! I made the mistake of thinking one conversation covered us, when, really, we needed to have continued and regular check-ins. Given how long we've been in the Lifestyle (and weathering through two failed monogamous foursomes), Kaleb and I assumed that we had hammered out all possible scenarios of what was acceptable/unacceptable, but we were mistaken. It's impossible to decide how to act in every single situation. You don't always know what you'll encounter and it's difficult to plan for those new experiences. There have been many times a dilemma occurred where we weren't able to talk to each other in the moment or we'd come across a situation that we've never encountered before and the other party made assumptions, giving rise to a few tense car rides going home. We tried our best to set out clear boundaries when it came to a hookup with a couple; however, we couldn't anticipate all emotions we might feel in the moment or right after.

* * *

A few months after signing up with *ABC Lifestyle** website, while at a club, Kaleb and I took a seat on a white leather couch, leaving enough space to the right for another couple to potentially join us. A couple approached and to my surprise, the female cozied up to Kaleb's right, while I was on his left. Her partner proceeded to sit next to her, looking like a lost puppy following her lead. It was obvious that this woman was attracted to Kaleb and wanted to engage with him, oblivious to my presence. Her partner seemed under her spell and took his cues from her. Likely they were a newbie couple, who had not communicated with each other about their expectations. This woman started canoodling and whispering into Kaleb's ear. No introductions or conversation amongst the four of us occurred. It was her and Kaleb, as if her partner and I didn't exist. He sat there, feeling confused but didn't have the nerve to say or do anything. And at that moment, neither did I.

As Kaleb and this woman were rudely engrossed in their conversation, I became increasingly more irritated. Seeing him enjoying her undivided attention incensed me further. Then, suddenly, she gave Kaleb a kiss on the lips and they started making out. Awkwardly, this chap and I sat there, watching them engage. I felt sorry for him. He looked like a deer in the headlights and didn't know what to do. I was fuming! *How could Kaleb be so insensitive?* He knew the rules, yet he didn't bother to ask me first if it was okay before revving things up with this woman. Instead, he was being selfish and his ego took over, relishing in *his* moment of pleasure. Out of spite, I decided to get up and sit in next to her man to initiate something. But, to my dismay, he was focused on winning back his partner's affections, not on giving me any attention. Now, not only was I pissed at Kaleb, but I was also feeling rejected by this guy whom I wasn't even attracted to. What the fuck?! I slunk back to my side of the couch, hoping this episode would end.

Not even five minutes later, the man suddenly stood in front of me and smiled. He had changed his tune. "We might as well have fun too, right?" he smirked.

Before I had a chance to respond, he squeezed in next to me. He suddenly made a bold move and kissed me without asking for permission (which is an LS no-no) or at least receiving a green light proceed ahead look from me. I was taken aback by this but I knew exactly what he was doing—he was trying to make his partner jealous and using me as bait. Although I knew it wasn't right, I had the same retaliatory objective with Kaleb. We kissed passionately, as he embraced my body.

Have you ever felt like you were watching a train wreck about to happen? Here I was making out with this guy, only to make Kaleb jealous. I wasn't going to sit idly by and watch my husband grope another woman. Jealousy and insecurities came out. *Two can play at this game!*

This was not exactly what I envisioned our night to be like... Kaleb and I were supposed to have a fun foursome experience. Instead, the night ended in a big blowup on the car ride home. Kaleb was baffled that I was upset with him, which irritated and incensed me more.

"I didn't start anything—she did!" he exclaimed.

"But you didn't stop her either!" I shouted.

Normally, I hate fighting but I wasn't going to give in this time. He was in the wrong and he didn't want to admit it. Kaleb knew the rules—nothing happens with a couple unless we both agreed to proceed.

The next morning, Kaleb apologized.

"You're right. I should have asked you before I did anything," he said. "She took me by surprise and I didn't have a chance to talk with you."

"Admit it, you liked the attention. And you wanted her too," I said. "That's why you didn't want to stop."

"Well yeah, I got carried away with the moment and that was wrong," Kaleb apologized. "It wasn't right to put you in that situation and I'm sorry."

Because we'd gotten into trouble when things progressed beyond one of our comfort zones and we felt we didn't have a chance to communicate with each other, we realized we needed to create an opportunity to press *pause*—one might not just suddenly appear for us. Physically removing ourselves from the situation would give us a moment alone to check in and talk things over. We also made a pact that if one of us wasn't physically attracted to our potential partner, then it was an automatic no hookup scenario ... no matter how gorgeous the spouse was! There was no need to take one for the team!

One Saturday night, we'd decided to go to a meet-and-greet with a couple at the club. They had messaged us on the LS website and seemed nice. Before heading out, Kaleb and I had *the chat* about our rules and how to deal with a situation if we weren't feeling a four-way connection.

"What sign are you going to give me if it's a no-go ... a wink, a kick under the table or a cue word?" I asked.

30. Communication 101

"I'll say we got a call from our daughter," Kaleb said.

"Okay, perfect! We'll excuse ourselves and say we need to make a phone call to make sure she's okay," I continued.

Now, that sounded simple enough, but it didn't execute as planned that night. Although we didn't feel a sexual connection with this couple, we didn't call a *time-out* to communicate this fact to each other—something we found difficult to do at first, as is often the case with new habits. Also, it didn't help that neither of us were comfortable being direct with a couple and telling them that we weren't attracted to them. We didn't want to hurt or offend them. So, we kept engaging with them, when really, we should have walked away. We ended up having sex with the couple—now that's taking one for the *other* team! I'd like to say that this unfortunate situation only happened once, but that'd be a lie.

Let's just say we didn't learn from our mistakes as quickly as we should have. It would take a few more trial and errors to see how dangerously close we were to putting our relationship in jeopardy when we didn't put *us* first. The consequences of not communicating far outweighed the arousing pleasure in the moment.

* * *

About six months after our latest re-entry into the LS world, we were at a club when we spied this hot Latino couple. They looked to be in their early thirties. Kaleb and I stood at the bar, discreetly smiling at each other to signal that we were *both* attracted to him *and* her. So far, so good!

We walked over to introduce ourselves and Kaleb did most of the talking to confirm the mutual interest. We learned their names were Dean and Esther, they were Columbian, and had been in the LS for about seven years. They knew a lot of the regulars at the club. I was very attracted to both of them. Dean was tanned, had an athletic build and, dark hair and light brown eyes. Esther was petite with long, straight brown hair and had curves in all the right places.

Dean took Kaleb aside and explained that they were interested in us; however, his wife was shy and they didn't typically play with a couple until she felt comfortable. So, nothing happened that night, but we did stay in touch with them. After a month of Dean and Kaleb texting back and forth, we decided to meet up with them at the club one Saturday night. We got there at 10:00 p.m. and they had a table reserved for us. After having a few cocktails, the four of us made our way to the dance floor. I was dancing with Esther and then Dean made his move, dancing sensually in between us. Dean started grinding up against me. I looked over to Kaleb to see his reaction; he didn't seem to mind so we continued. Then Dean's hands began to wander, touching my body all over. I didn't stop him and soon, we were making out on the dance floor, forgetting about everyone around us. Suddenly, I snapped back to reality and realized we were the only two dancing; Esther was nowhere to be seen and Kaleb was standing by our table with a beer in his hand. He didn't look happy. I quickly broke away from Dean's embrace.

"I should get back to Kaleb," I said abruptly.

Dean looked surprised. "Okay," he said.

"We're going to head to the back room," I told him, hoping he would get the hint for them to join us.

"We'll catch you later," Dean said.

Kaleb seemed distant when I walked back to the table. *Was he angry that I was dancing with Dean?* I had a sick feeling in the pit of my stomach. I automatically assumed that it was something I did that got Kaleb upset and I needed to make things right and *fast*.

I decided to test my assumption. "Are you having fun?" I asked Kaleb.

"Yep, what about you?" he asked. I nodded.

Phew! He wasn't mad.

"Do you want to head to the back and play?" he suggested.

"Sure."

Kaleb took hold of my hand, leading me through the dance floor and into the back area. We found a private room and laid on the bed. I needed this physical connection to convince myself that Kaleb was truly not upset with me.

We left the door half open in case Dean and Esther decided to come looking for us but they never showed up. After we made love, Kaleb and I decided to head home as it was getting late. As we emerged from the back area, we were surprised to see Dean and Esther on the dance floor.

"Hope you had a good night!" I told Esther, giving her a hug.

"I'll get our coats and call a taxi," Kaleb told me.

"I'll join you," Esther said to Kaleb. "We should be going too."

The two of them went off to fetch our coats, and I smiled at Dean.

"Did you have fun in the back?" he asked.

"Yeah, it was good," I replied.

"I wanted to come back there but Esther wasn't in the mood," Dean explained. Then, leaning in, he whispered in my ear. "I can't wait to be inside of you."

To my surprise, he then pulled my body close to his and gave me a deep lingering kiss. I knew Kaleb wouldn't take kindly to Dean overstepping, so I pulled away. It was one thing for us to be kissing on the dance floor with Kaleb there watching us (and assuming he was giving consent), it was another thing to be putting the moves on me while Kaleb wasn't around. That went against LS code of conduct—disrespecting someone's partner. Dean persisted with his playful antics, trying to pull me back in for more kisses.

At that moment, Kaleb walked in with my coat. "Ahem."

Dean released from our embrace.

"The taxi's here," Kaleb said tersely and walked away.

Now he was clearly mad. I could see the look on his face and sense the agitation in his voice.

I quickly put on my coat and walked to the front of the club. Kaleb was waiting by the doors, looking outside. No taxi in sight. I stood there in silence, replaying the scene with Dean in my head. Then, all of a sudden, Kaleb turned around and lashed out, "Why the fuck were you kissing him?" I felt anxious. My kiss in Vegas with Tim, the restaurant manager, flashed before me.

"I didn't kiss him ... *he kissed me*," I tried to explain, but that only fueled his agitation further.

"You didn't look like you were resisting!" Kaleb accused. I knew it was better to say nothing and let him calm down. Kaleb gave me the silent treatment all the way home. When we got into bed, he turned over to me.

"I don't understand why you were kissing him," he said. I could sense the jealousy in his voice. This was one of the pitfalls of LS. To be in the Lifestyle, you need to be secure within yourself *and* secure in your relationship. If these two parts don't hold true, then jealousy can slowly eat away at your relationship. This ugly side surfaced more than a few times when it came to me seeing Annie and Kaleb together.

"I didn't expect him to kiss me, especially while you were getting our coats," I explained. I didn't want to make the situation worse by telling Kaleb the truth—that Dean was being disrespectful of me (and Kaleb) and wouldn't take my subtle hints. It took some convincing and explaining, but eventually, Kaleb understood that I wouldn't have done anything to intentionally hurt him. Dean clearly got carried away.

Suffice it to say, that was the end of our relationship with Dean and Esther. It was apparent that they weren't on the same page in terms of what they each wanted from the Lifestyle; Dean was more drawn to hooking up with various sex partners whereas Esther focused less on sex and more on making social connections.

"Let's agree to not ever engage with a man or woman without the other being present. This should be about us enjoying things *together*," Kaleb told me.

We reminded each other why we got into the LS in the first place; it was supposed to bring us closer together, emotionally and sexually, not further apart. We promised each other that we had to communicate better or misunderstandings would come between us. *Was it possible? Could we finally find a way to enjoy all that we'd come to love about the Lifestyle without chipping away at our relationship?*

We may have put Annie behind us, but our troubles were far from over. With each new LS experience, we learned a bit more about our own insecurities and how terrible our communication skills could be at times. We vowed to improve. But we were about to be tested, yet again.

31

Unfinished Business

* * *

Three years after moving downtown and re-joining the Lifestyle, my mother passed away from pancreatic cancer. My relationship with my mother had been *complicated*. Growing up, my siblings and I had a closer relationship with her than with our father. Although my mother was equally as strict as my father, she also showed a caring and affectionate side, with her bedtime hugs and "I love you's," which drew me closer to her. She was my source of comfort. As I moved into my teenage years, I began to inwardly direct anger towards my mother, blaming her for not standing up to our father and protecting us children more than she did. As a young adult, I couldn't understand or relate to why my mother would continue to stand by him and enable his selfish ways. This led to our strained relationship that spanned more than twenty years. I didn't realize at the time that my mother was just as afraid of my father as we were. My mother never complained, desperately trying harder to keep him happy. She had been disillusioned with her marriage for years, resigned to the fact that that was the way my father was and she just had to accept it. There was no such thing as divorce in my parents' generation. She accepted her marriage, for better or for worse.

Two years before her death, my mother and I began to slowly reconnect; she would ask me to go to lunch every other Monday (her only day off), and we'd share a big bowl of shrimp wonton noodle soup. Although I never told her this, I enjoyed our time together as we gabbed about extended family. Just as our relationship was getting to a better place, my mother became ill. Her life had been taken away from me suddenly, before I had a chance (and courage) to tell her how I truly felt about her and the sadness I felt about our relationship all those years. Our family never talked about emotions and feelings. I hoped that my mother could see the forgiveness in my eyes as I cared for her in the last few months of her life.

The Swinger in the Mirror

Dealing with the death of my mother was not easy. I was estranged from my father; not having support and comfort from him made it worse. Following her death, I went through a difficult period trying to reconcile how unpredictable and unfair life was. I was already feeling unsettled and unhappy when she passed away. I was, again, feeling disconnected from Kaleb, and I was questioning my own sense of happiness. While I'd been trying to embrace our new LS-outlook since moving downtown, I still struggled from time to time in terms of my emotional connectedness with Kaleb, which only worsened after fights and misunderstandings between us.

I felt angry, overwhelmed and out of control, so I decided that I would put me first for once and do what I needed to be happy. I began to adopt a hedonistic, selfish, and pleasure-seeking attitude. I wanted to enjoy everything that was fun, happy, and spontaneous because my life could end so abruptly, just like my mother's. I wanted to feel *alive*.

So, I immersed myself into my world of sexual pleasures to distract me from the pain and sadness I felt. I made sure we scheduled an outing to the LS club every weekend. I overindulged in drinking and sex to simply forget everything. Even though the Lifestyle brought temporary distraction and fed into my self-indulgent needs, I still felt something was amiss. My emotions were all mixed up. Was I "out of sorts" because my mother had died or because I was unhappy in my marriage? I see now that it was likely both, but at the time, I fixated on Kaleb because he was right in front of me. Was I truly happy with Kaleb? Was he giving me everything I needed in a relationship? I convinced myself that Kaleb was to blame for my unhappiness.

I know now that my state of mind had nothing to do with Kaleb. I was emotionally unprepared to deal with the fallout from my mother's death. And I didn't feel truly supported, not from my father and not from my husband. Not to say that Kaleb wasn't there for me during my time of grief—he did the best that he could for me; however, he didn't know *how* to help me, which left me feeling more disconnected from him. I felt lost without my mother, and I wasn't prepared for the amount of anger I'd been carrying towards my father—anger that I had repressed since childhood.

I began to see a lot of similarities between my mother and myself; she had sacrificed everything for her family, leaving nothing for herself. And, by default, Kaleb had become the embodiment of my father. I projected the anger and resentment I felt towards my father onto Kaleb. I'd become enraged when, during a disagreement about a certain aspect of running our business, I'd perceive him to be frowning upon an idea of mine or he wanted to do it *his* way because he felt it was better, just like my father. I felt like, once again, my voice wasn't being heard. Instead of calmly sharing my feelings with Kaleb, I would start a fight to prove how unreasonable he was being.

"Why are you so stubborn and irritating?" I once accused. "Can't you ever listen to anyone else's opinion, other than your own?"

"What are you talking about? I was telling you what I think!" he exclaimed. "What's your problem?"

It didn't help that Kaleb was defensive and reactive in nature, and he didn't take kindly to my outbursts, especially if he felt they were unwarranted. I would then walk away in a huff and stew in my office. *Did I marry my father?*

I was unhappy and I took it out on Kaleb. I felt that he, like my father, should have stepped up more in our relationship. I focused on everything Kaleb was doing *wrong*. In comparison to some of my play partners, Kaleb got a failing mark when it came to being attentive to my needs, being romantic or making me feel wanted and special. I didn't feel valued or appreciated in our relationship, just as my mother had felt with my father.

My biggest regret is not telling Kaleb how I was feeling at the time and why I was so unhappy. Instead of telling him what I needed most from him, I waited for him to ask me. And when he didn't, I assumed he didn't care about me or our relationship. If I wasn't willing to talk openly and honestly with Kaleb, how could I expect things to change for the better? I should have communicated more with Kaleb, but I didn't. My overwhelming sadness during my time of grieving brought me back to that dark place when Kaleb told me about his affair. All that anger and resentment that Kaleb and I had worked through (or I thought we had resolved), came back. Although seven years had passed by this point, and Annie was no longer in our lives, I hadn't forgotten about the pain and hurt I felt by being betrayed and lied to. The damage from that toxic situation continued to brew underneath, unbeknownst to Kaleb, and was triggered by my mother's death. Deep down inside, I was still hurting and full of anger. My wounds had never fully healed.

Maybe if I had told Kaleb everything that I was feeling during that tumultuous time in my life, things would not have spiraled out of control with us. But I didn't know how to communicate what I needed from him to feel healthy and connected in our relationship. I also assumed that things wouldn't change even if I did say something to him. So, I took matters into my own hands when it came to my own happiness. I was thinking and acting solely from a place of hurt, grief, and pain. My emotionally wounded inner child began to act out as a coping mechanism (Gaba 2020).

This wasn't about *us* anymore; this was going to be all about *me, me, me*! If Kaleb couldn't give me what I needed to be happy, then maybe I needed to go find it for myself. I rationalized that I had a hall pass to act on my selfish impulses, just as Kaleb had done with Annie (clearly, I hadn't forgotten or forgiven entirely). And the Lifestyle provided further opportunities for me to act out, blurring the line between right and wrong and giving me permission to fulfill whatever impulses and needs I was missing.

And then I met Jack.

32

My Emotional Affair

* * *

"I know that you've been going through a lot lately. I'm trying to be there for you, but I feel like you're pushing me away," Kaleb expressed one morning over coffee, approximately six months after my mother's death.

"I don't know what you mean," I replied.

"Babe, we haven't had sex lately and you always seem irritated and distant with me," he stated.

"Well... I've had a lot on my mind," I told him.

"Why don't we go away, the two of us? We could use this time to reconnect."

"I don't know," I replied.

"It'll be good for us, trust me."

So, I did. We decided to book at a couples' resort for the following week. The travel agent found an amazing last-minute deal but warned us that this hotel would be *different* from the typical resort.

"They welcome swingers and LS activities, as well as singles," she told us.

Unbeknownst to the agent, Kaleb and I were more than thrilled to find a tropical LS venue to add to our roster of fun places to meet other like-minded couples.

"Well, I guess it'll have to do," Kaleb told the agent, with a straight face. I couldn't help but stifle a laugh.

Despite my initial reservations, I started to feel excited about this time away, hoping it would give us a chance to reconnect and put the spark back into our relationship. But the night we arrived, Kaleb and I got into a huge fight. I had gone to the bar to grab drinks for us, but I hadn't come back as quickly as Kaleb had expected. He ended up looking for me and became upset when he saw me chatting with a guy at the bar. Truth be told, I was basking in the attention of this young attractive, twenty-something guy, who was flirting with me.

"What took you so long?" Kaleb asked, as I handed him his drink.

"What do you mean?"

"It's been over twenty minutes getting the drinks," he exclaimed.

"I didn't know you were counting," I teased.

Then Kaleb gave me the *look*. "I saw you chatting with *that* guy," he stated.

"Yeah, we were talking while we were waiting for our drinks," I replied. "The bartender was really busy tonight."

Kaleb looked irritated.

"What?" I pressed. "I was just talking to him. It's not like I had sex with him!"

Kaleb stormed off. I reluctantly followed, knowing that a fight would ensue back in our room.

Instead of getting at the heart of what he was upset about, I became defensive and we shot passive-aggressive digs at each other. He was annoyed and I was equally as mad that he was acting childish for no reason. Neither of us was giving in.

As dinner time approached, our attitudes slowly shifted and we were willing to talk calmly to each other. We didn't want to fight on our first day there, and so we kissed and made up to salvage the rest of the evening. But I was still annoyed that Kaleb was jealous over something so stupid and would let it ruin our vacation. *Why did Kaleb have to be this way?*

The next morning, we were both in a better mood and ready to enjoy ourselves. Kaleb and I usually kept the same routine on holidays: a quick coffee before heading to the gym, lunch by the pool, and lounge time on the beach for the rest of the afternoon.

During our beach time on this particular day, while Kaleb read his book, I decided to go for a walk. I enjoyed this solitary time, watching the ocean shimmer in the distance. Eventually, I took refuge on the pier, gazing at the clouds in the sky and daydreaming with my music playing softly in my ears. It was my time to be in my head—thinking about my mom, Kaleb, our marriage ... my life. As I got up to leave, I was startled to see a young-ish man sitting on the pier, a few meters from me. He smiled at me. *How long had he been sitting there?* He was trying to say something to me but I couldn't hear—I forgot I had my headphones on. I quickly removed them.

"I believe you took my spot!" he repeated with a smile.

Was he flirting with me? I felt myself blush. All I could manage to say at that moment was "Oh, I'm sorry."

"I'm just teasing," he smirked. He had boyish good looks with light blue eyes and medium longish wavy brown hair. His tanned body and muscular physique peeked out from under his tank top. He looked to be in his late twenties—way too young for me.

"It's all yours, I was about to leave," I said, feeling flustered. But as I walked away, I could feel his penetrating eyes on me.

The next day, I returned to the same spot on the pier, but he wasn't there. I was surprised to feel slightly disappointed. I put my headphones on, and my mind drifted off with the moving clouds. After a while, I looked at my phone. It was 3 o'clock! I couldn't believe I had been sitting there for close to two hours.

"I better get back," I muttered to myself. I quickly gathered my stuff and started heading back down the pier towards the beach. At the end of the pier, there *he* was, lying on a beach chair. I walked closer towards him, delighted to see him. He greeted me with a warm smile; I felt my heart beating faster. He introduced himself. "Hi, I'm Jack."

"I'm Kim."

"Looks like you took my spot again!" he joked. I laughed.

"I'm territorial that way," I teased.

"Nice to formally meet you," he said.

"Are you on this trip with friends?" I asked.

He mentioned he was at the resort by himself to unwind and get away from his stressful job in investment banking. We discovered that we lived in the same city. Ten minutes into our conversation, I saw Kaleb strolling towards us.

"Hey!" I called out, waving him to come over to join us.

"Been waiting for you to come back," Kaleb stated.

I felt anxious about introducing Jack to Kaleb. I didn't know if Kaleb was going to pull the same jealous bit, like the night before.

"Hey man! Nice to meet you!" Kaleb greeted warmly.

"Likewise," Jack replied. Kaleb seemed in better spirits, which I was relieved to see.

"Babe, we should head back. Beach volleyball starts in 10 minutes," Kaleb reminded me.

"Would you like to join us?" I asked Jack.

"Thanks, but I'm going to sit this one out," he replied.

"Okay, we'll see you around," I smiled.

"How did you two meet?" Kaleb asked, as we walked along the beach towards the volleyball area.

"Why?" I hesitantly asked.

"Just curious," Kaleb replied.

"I bumped into him on the pier yesterday," I said. Kaleb smiled.

"What?" I chuckled.

"Nothing." Kaleb could intuitively sense my attraction to Jack but he didn't say anything else.

We discovered that volleyball had been moved to poolside instead of on the beach, and, to my surprise, Jack was in the pool ready to play! Kaleb and I sat on the lounge chairs and watched the match. Jack waved at me and smiled. I could now clearly see his strong lean body in action as he spiked the ball over the net.

"Let's go back to the room and have a siesta," Kaleb suggested.

"Okay," I said, hoping Kaleb couldn't hear the disappointment in my voice that I couldn't watch Jack play. That was the last time I saw Jack; we flew home the next day.

On the plane, I couldn't get Jack off my mind. I don't know what it was that intrigued me, but there was something about him that I found appealing. Maybe it was his calm energy and quiet confidence, but his gorgeous smile, good humor, playfulness, and tall athletic build didn't hurt either. Although we had chatted only briefly, I felt an instant connection to Jack. It was strange. I have never felt like that upon meeting someone, not even with Kaleb.

Two weeks after getting home, I decided to contact him.

I recalled Jack mentioning that he worked in investment banking at the largest finance firm in our city. A quick Google search had brought me to Jack's company's page, where his email was listed.

Hi Jack. I'm not sure if you remember me from the resort two weeks ago? We met at the pier. No pressure to reply, just wanted to reach out and say hello.

I went back and forth, debating if I should send this harmless and unassuming email to him. Deep down inside, I knew it was wrong to do this behind Kaleb's back but something urged me on. There was such a strong need inside of me to feel special and validated by someone other than Kaleb, which prompted me to act on my selfish impulses.

I quickly pressed *send* before I could change my mind. To my surprise, Jack quickly replied. I took off to a nearby cafe so I could continue messaging Jack without interruption (and Kaleb knowing).

"I guess you found my email!" Jack messaged.

"I hope you don't mind me reaching out to you."

"No, not at all," he replied.

"You know that Kaleb and I are in the Lifestyle, right?"

"I sort of figured that."

"Are you in the Lifestyle?" I asked.

"No."

"Maybe you could bring a girlfriend to the club so the four of us can hook up?" I boldly suggested.

"I don't have one ... unless you want to be my girlfriend?" he flirted.

I blushed reading his messages. I rationalized in my mind that it was okay for me to reach out to this random guy, just as we would on the LS website, to seek out a potential foursome. As long as I was playing inside the LS sandbox, it seemed perfectly acceptable, so I wanted to believe. I was manipulating how I wanted to perceive this situation in order to get what I wanted, and that was Jack's attention and feeling desired. The only problem was that I was breaking one of our cardinal rules—"no secrets and always communicate openly and honestly."

The Lifestyle is all about hooking up with sexy new people, right? Why didn't I just tell Kaleb the truth? Good question. I was afraid to tell Kaleb that I was in contact with Jack, fearful of bringing out that jealous angry side of him. Remember there was the incident with Dean and then the guy at the bar the other day. I knew that Kaleb would lose his shit if he found out that I had gone out of my way to track down Jack and initiate this contact. Kaleb is too inquisitive to not have asked me these questions. The fact that I *knew* Kaleb would be upset should have been a red flag for me to stop what I was doing. But, I forged on ahead anyway. Not thinking, just acting on my impulses.

Then there was the problem of Jack not being into foursomes. He made it clear that he only wanted to get to know me. And since Kaleb had no interest in single males or threesomes, there was no reason for me to continue to talk to Jack under the pretense of an LS connection. However, my brain was dialed to the *selfish-me* mode—I wanted to get to know Jack. He was filling a need that Kaleb wasn't. I knew I was playing with fire, but I didn't want to stop pursuing this lead. I knew that I had to lie and keep this from Kaleb. It was my *secret*; I told nobody. I regressed to my young teenage self, lying and sneaking around in order to avoid getting in trouble. I knew the consequences of getting caught by Kaleb—it would jeopardize our relationship. Yet, despite the risk, I still wanted to seek out a connection with Jack. I wanted my cake and to eat it, too.

"I'd like to continue to talk and get to know you better, if that's okay?" he messaged.

"I'd like that," I replied. "Here's my cell number so you can text me." He gave me his number as well.

"I'm glad you reached out to me. I haven't stopped thinking about you since that day we met on the beach," he messaged.

"I'm happy that I reached out too," I replied. "Message me whenever you want."

"I will. Talk to you real soon," Jack ended his message with a heart emoji.

I grinned from ear to ear. I couldn't believe that I was connecting with Jack, a man that I hardly knew—and he seemed interested in me, too. I was giddy with excitement.

A sudden text from Kaleb changed my mood. "Where are you?"

"Went for a walk. I'll be home soon," I lied.

I better delete these messages before I get home, I thought. That very thought process proves that I knew what I was doing was wrong but I didn't want to stop. I'd been going through such a challenging time that I justified my actions, saying it was all innocent fun. But, of course, it wasn't.

To my surprise, Jack sent me a text the next morning. My heart skipped a beat when I saw his number on my phone.

"Morning, sunshine. Do you have time to chat?" he messaged.

"Sure!" I replied.

Kaleb had gone to the gym so I was able to chat for an hour with Jack; we began with pleasantries and then moved into more flirtatious exchanges. That first week, I went out every day for hour-long walks in the park so that I could message Jack without being caught. We were both feeling more comfortable with each other. We talked about serious and not so serious stuff, flirted, laughed, and shared intimate details of our lives.

Even though we never had a sexual relationship, Jack and I began to form a strong emotional bond over the next three months. I truly felt that he was listening to me and genuinely cared about me. He felt the same with me. Surprisingly, we never video chatted; there was some anonymity and safety hiding behind the wall of our phones, allowing us to go deeper into our emotions. Momentary feelings of guilt and remorse were suppressed by the euphoric feeling of the newness of a relationship.

"I'm glad we met that day on the pier," I messaged.

"It was hard not to notice you," he flirted.

"Were you shocked to get my email message that first time?" I asked.

"I was surprised … and happy too," he messaged. "I had been think-ing about you on my flight home."

"Oh?"

"I felt sad that I might never see or talk to you again since I had no way of contacting you … and here we are now."

"I guess we were destined to meet," I messaged.

I became attached to Jack and our daily conversations; I craved the attention and sense of belonging he gave to me. I also knew, deep down inside, I was distancing myself from Kaleb as I got closer to Jack.

I worked hard to keep my two worlds apart. I got the impression that Jack knew that I was keeping things under wraps with Kaleb, but Jack never asked, and I never shared. I couldn't chance Kaleb finding out, so I made sure to carry my phone with me at all times, even to the bathroom. I didn't want Kaleb to see an incoming message from Jack, and I was diligent about deleting our messages after a conversation, so there was no trail.

But, unbeknownst to me, Kaleb was becoming suspicious of me keeping my phone close at hand. In the past, I often lost track of my phone, often asking Kaleb or the kids to locate it. There was a running joke that my Christmas gift should be a lanyard for my phone to keep me from misplacing it. I made sure to mute my phone so that a text alert didn't sound off. Although I felt excited to receive a message from Jack, there was a dread that I might be caught, so I quickly sought refuge in the bathroom or at a café where I could message him freely and go undetected. Little did I know that this new behavior and constant attachment to my phone had started to raise some eyebrows.

I had orchestrated everything under my control … so I thought. But it was about to blow up in my face. You can only keep your worlds separate for so long.

33

Day of Reckoning

* * *

It was New Year's Eve, and Kaleb and I were looking forward to a night of fun. We had tickets to a LS super party, and we decided to stay overnight at a nearby hotel. As I was getting ready in the bathroom at home, with music playing on my phone, I quickly stepped out to my walk-in closet to pick out an outfit. At that opportune moment, Kaleb dashed into the bathroom and locked the door.

"My stomach's not feeling right," he hollered out.

I had a twinge of fear, realizing that my phone was on the bathroom counter. I had been messaging back and forth with Jack about his plans for the night and how I wished I could be with him. Jack and I had been texting each other daily for three months by this point.

Ten minutes went by ... then fifteen. Kaleb was still in the bathroom. *Was Kaleb checking my phone?* I remained hopeful, telling myself I was being paranoid. But I felt on edge.

"Are you okay in there?" I called out to him.

"Yep, I'm fine," he said casually. Five minutes later, he unlocked the bathroom door.

"I'm feeling better now," he said. "We should get going soon."

I finished getting dressed and we gave a quick hug and kiss good-bye to Samantha and Lucas.

"Let's order pizza for supper," Kaleb suggested in the car ride to the hotel.

"Sure, anything you want," I replied.

I was excited for the NYE party and wanted to enjoy some alone time with Kaleb before heading to the club. After we made love, we lounged in bed and sipped on our wine.

"Will next year be better than this last one?" Kaleb asked.

"I hope so. It can't be any worse, with everything that happened with my mom."

Then *boom!* His next words would hit me like a Mack truck. I didn't see it coming.

"I saw your phone in the bathroom," he said coldly.

I froze, not knowing what to say.

"You've been messaging that guy, Jack."

My fantasy world came to an abrupt end... I was caught red-handed.

"Give me your phone," he demanded. Without questioning, I handed it to him. Kaleb took his time reading over my text messages with Jack (a day's worth that I foolishly forgot to delete), which incensed him. He was not going to give me the chance to explain—there was nothing to say, it was there all in black and white. I looked away in shame, tears streaming down my face. The emotional high of being with Jack all this time came crashing down ... and hard.

"I reached out to him after our trip," I confessed. "I've been talking to him every day for the past three months."

"You've been having an emotional affair! How could you do this to me?!" he shouted. The hatred and anger in his voice jolted me, bringing me back to that little frightened girl who knew she would soon be punished by her father.

Kaleb had every right to be deeply hurt and upset that I kept this secret from him, just as I had felt with his affair with Annie. Now I was the one to devastate the trust and respect in our relationship. I kept quiet, waiting for his ranting to stop. Why hadn't he confronted me at home when he found out? Or in the car ride over? We had just made love... I didn't understand what he was up to.

"It took everything in me to keep my mouth shut in front of the kids," Kaleb uttered. "They don't deserve this shit."

"If you knew, why did we have sex?" I asked, confused.

"I don't know. Maybe I wanted to be with you one last time." Kaleb's eyes filled with tears.

There would be no NYE party for us. The next five hours were excruciating as Kaleb unleashed a roller coaster of reactions and emotions at me. Anger, yelling, tears, sadness, indignation, despair, forgiveness and desperation. We spent the rest of the night in our room, trying to ignore the noise and revelers outside as they prepared for the count down.

Just when I felt things couldn't be worse, Kaleb noticed an incoming text from Jack at midnight, wishing me a *Happy New Year*. Kaleb smirked, "It's your boyfriend."

I cast my eyes downward to avoid seeing his angry smirking face. Kaleb got off the bed and poured himself a drink.

"I assumed we had gotten through the worst, but I guess I was wrong," he continued.

I didn't know what to say ... did it even matter?

"It's over. I'm done ... with us," he said.

"Kaleb, please," I pleaded, his words slicing me like a knife.

"I honestly tried but I can't do this anymore."

I felt dejected and sad, knowing that it might be *finally* over between us. Kaleb had once told me that an emotional affair was far worse, in his mind, than a physical one; the former involved feelings and emotions whereas the latter was merely a physical act. I knew I had crossed the line—there was no hope of coming back from this. I sat on the bed, in silence, waiting for Kaleb to say anything.

He sat on the couch with his head hung low and covered his face with his hands. The last time I saw him this despondent was when he told me about Annie.

It was 1:30 a.m., and I was exhausted but I didn't dare close my eyes in case Kaleb wanted to vent more. Eventually, though, fatigue took over. The last thing I remembered before drifting off to sleep was Kaleb pouring himself another glass of scotch. I kept waking through-out the night, feeling uneasy about what was to come. Kaleb slept on the couch.

In the morning, Kaleb was quiet as he gathered up his belongings and packed. I could see the weariness and despair on his face. I felt the same.

"Come and sit down beside me? Please," I begged.

He walked over slowly and sat on the edge of the bed, keeping his distance. I looked at him and reached out for his hand, not knowing if he would pull it away. He didn't.

"I'm sorry," I said sorrowfully. There were a million things that I wanted to tell him but the words weren't coming out. I had so much to explain to him (and to myself) about why I would ever inflict pain on the man that I once called my soulmate. I didn't know where to begin.

The previous night gave me time to reflect on things. I realized how much unresolved anger and frustration (at my father and my mother) I'd been carrying. And it was now bleeding into my adult relationship with Kaleb. I admitted to myself that I hadn't fully forgiven Kaleb. I was look-ing for an escape from the general unhappiness in my life and then Jack came along ... my utopia. But I was gravely mistaken. I didn't know how I would get through this mess but I knew I didn't want to lose Kaleb, now or ever. It's true that you don't realize how important a person is to you until you are faced with losing them. If I wanted to salvage what was left of our marriage, I had to come clean with Kaleb right there and then, and tell him *everything*. I wanted to fix *us* and I hoped that he would give me another chance, as I had given him seven years earlier.

"I don't want to lose you," I told Kaleb.

"What about your boyfriend?" he said sarcastically.

"I don't want to be with Jack."

"I'm sorry if I don't believe you."

"I know I broke your trust, but I want to get back to where we were before all of this."

"You think it's that easy?" he asked rhetorically.

"No, I know it won't be easy ... but this time, we could go to counseling together. We have a lot to work though, and we can't do it on our own," I expressed. Kaleb stared out the window.

"I don't know if I can try anymore," he said.

"I know you won't believe this, but I do love you," I said.

"Well, you have a funny way of showing it," Kaleb expressed angrily.

Nothing I said made any difference. He was not ready to forgive. Everything I said was lip service. But Kaleb was right about one thing: there was no *us*. I was thinking about *me* all the while I was messaging Jack.

You would think after all the hurt and languish I went through when Kaleb revealed his betrayal, I would be the last person to have an affair. I didn't think I was that person who could subject someone I loved to the same hurtful behavior that I had once endured myself.

"I was messed up, emotionally, this past year. I know it's no excuse for what I did," I expressed. Kaleb was quiet.

"I was feeling lost and I couldn't figure out what to do to make me feel better ... and I made poor choices," I added. I was carrying the wounds of my inner child into my adult relationship (Gaba 2020), unleashing my venom onto Kaleb with my manipulative and destructive behaviors.

"Why didn't you tell me how much you were struggling?" he asked.

"I don't know... I should have," I admitted. "There was so much stuff going on and I wanted to figure things out on my own."

"By starting an affair?" he asked rhetorically.

"I was wrong. I really messed up and made things worse," I said sadly.

"Look. It's simple. Do you want to be with me or not?" Kaleb asked. "No more bullshit."

"I don't want to lose you. I know we have a lot to work through ... *again*, but I want to try. Will you give us another chance?" I asked. There was a long pause, as he processed the intent behind my words. He looked into my eyes and took hold of my hands.

"I don't want to lose you either. I *do* love you," Kaleb voiced. "Maybe counseling will help." I felt relieved.

"I love you," I whispered, as we embraced each other. Then, we packed up and went home to our family.

34

Dr. David

* * *

The next month was a difficult one. Despite my best efforts to work on the emotional parts and intimacy of our relationship, a dark cloud hung over me—would our life ever get back to normal? Kaleb tried to let go of his anger and resentment but it simmered below the surface, ready to go off at any time. I was walking on pins and needles, worried if I would say something wrong and make things worse between us.

They say marriage is hard work; that was an understatement for us. We decided to take a break from the Lifestyle again while we figured out our own relationship. I sent Jack a final message to apologize and explained that I wanted to work on my marriage. He never responded.

Kaleb and I deleted our profile on the *ABC Lifestyle** website and shut down that part of our life. As we continued to try to work through our relationship issues, we found ourselves feeling frustrated and hopeless. The biggest hurdle was the broken trust. Every time I was responding to work emails on my phone, was Kaleb wondering if I was messaging Jack? Or if I had to take my make-up off in the bathroom, could I bring my phone with me and listen to music or did I have to leave it where it was so it didn't raise suspicion? Would Kaleb check my unattended phone? Did he think I was having clandestine meetups with Jack while he was away on business? I knew that Kaleb wasn't able to trust me yet, and it would take time, naturally. I didn't blame him. I know what it feels like to be betrayed and lied to. However, every time these thoughts popped into my head, I questioned whether we were making any headway in rebuilding our relationship.

During this process of reconciliation, Kaleb and I felt disconnected from one another; there were often times we kept our feelings to ourselves. This lack of transparency did not help because we always felt like we were walking on eggshells. No one wanted to say or do anything that would upset the other. Despite our background in mental health, Kaleb and I didn't know how to effectively communicate with each other, and this was a big stumbling block to our healing.

We finally decided to seek professional help and found a psychologist, Dr. David, who offered intensive couples counseling sessions. I contacted Dr. David immediately.

"Most relationships are fixable; it's a matter of deciding if you both *want* to continue in the relationship and if both parties are ready and willing to put in the hard work to address the issues," Dr. David told me on the phone.

I immediately scheduled with Dr. David to begin our three-day therapy for that coming Friday. Our first session would be 3–4 hours, followed by a full 7–8 hours on Saturday and the same on Sunday. This seemed emotionally demanding but we knew this was what we needed if we wanted to fix the underlying problem.

That Friday, we anxiously walked up the steps to the front door, not knowing what to expect. We were greeted by a tall slender man in his early sixties, with prominent gray hair. I was put at ease by his kind demeanor and calm energy. Dr. David led us to his home office, which was situated at one end of his home. Framed degrees and credentials hung on the wall behind his large wooden desk and chair. To my surprise, there wasn't a long couch in the room; instead, we were asked to sit on the two black leather swivel chairs, situated a meter apart. Interesting.

"Over the next three days, I will give you the opportunity to talk honestly about your feelings and more importantly, learn how to *listen* to one another," Dr. David explained.

Kaleb and I looked at each other wearily. Our failed communication is not for lack of trying; we've already tried everything. *Or have we?*

"The aim of therapy is to feel heard and validated by our partner, regardless if we agree with our partner's perception of the situation," Dr. David continued.

We would have to agree to respectfully disagree on any contentious matters that came up. Dr. David explained that his role was to facilitate this dialogue and, if necessary, to mediate any issues that we were stuck on.

"What brought the two of you here today?" he asked.

I didn't know if I should mention about our Lifestyle, which was at the core of our problems. I looked to Kaleb to see if he wanted to say something. He folded his hands in his lap and looked uneasy. I guess he wanted me to speak for us. Although I felt anxious about revealing this intimate part of our lives, I knew that this was why we were here—to share everything if we wanted to deal with our issues, once and for all.

"We've been in the Lifestyle for close to 15 years," I disclosed.

"I don't know much about the Lifestyle. Can you tell me more about it?" Dr. David asked.

And we did. We told him *everything*.

"I would say our relationship really took a dive when we began swinging with our neighbors, Annie and Tom," I said. I told Dr. David about that painful time in our lives, sharing my side of the story while Kaleb sat in his chair and listened patiently.

The crux of the issue for me was that, after all these years, I still felt hurt by Kaleb's betrayal. I didn't feel Kaleb truly acknowledged how much he had hurt me and what his role was in all of it. Although our attempt to resolve these issues on our own in that hotel resort room years ago was a starting point, it didn't resolve the hurt and anger; my resentment continued to fester inside of me, unconsciously. I explained to Dr. David that I still blamed Kaleb for not protecting me in the way that he should have. He had broken my trust and made me question his loyalty to me and to our relationship.

"I'm not sure if you fully took responsibility for your role in it. It had always been all about *her* and how *she* manipulated you to have an affair. I even felt you were blaming me for the fact you had to keep this secret in order for me to maintain my friendship with her. Like you were doing me a favor? Your hands weren't tied ... you had a choice," I expressed angrily.

Kaleb sat up in his chair and became defensive when he heard me say all of this.

"We've been through all of this already! I told you that I was put in a hard situation and I was pressured to lie and keep this secret from you. I wanted out of that stupid foursome long before but you convinced me to stay for the sake of your friendship!" Kaleb shouted.

"See, Dr. David! He's always making an excuse! Why can't you say that you were at fault? Why are you putting the blame on me for *your* affair?" I hollered back.

"What about you and your affair?" Kaleb countered. "You're not the only one who's been hurt!"

"At least, I owned up to it and acknowledged where I went wrong!" I countered.

It was heating up and Kaleb and I felt increasing anger and

frustration with the other's tone and accusations. This back-and-forth quarreling went on for at least an hour, each party trying their best to convince Dr. David to take their side. I didn't realize it until that moment that we had been keeping an unspoken tally over the years of who committed more wrongs and more hurt in this marriage. All the cards were now on the table.

Dr. David remained impartial, simply observing us in our *storming* phase (Tuckman 1965). He let us vent, voice our opinions, and hash out our disagreements, until we were emotionally and mentally done. At that point, we sat back in our seats and took a deep breath. We were now ready to listen.

"I understand there was hurt on both sides. Kim, you were hurt when Kaleb had his affair with Annie and protected her secret." Turning to Kaleb, he stated, "And you were equally as hurt when Kim chose to pursue an emotional relationship with Jack. You both were lied to, and this betrayal broke your trust in each other." He validated each of our feelings and perceptions, one not being worse than the other.

"Let's call a spade a spade. You both made mistakes in the marriage and you both need to acknowledge that. Not to me but to each other. There's no use in pointing fingers; there's fault on both sides."

Dr. David was right. We continued to harbor anger and resentment after the other's affair, not fully accepting an apology and forgiving the transgression. Instead, we hung onto that hurt and anger and then unleashed it onto our unsuspecting partner whenever we felt misunderstood, mistreated, or misjudged. Instead of moving forward and growing from the experience, our unresolved anger was keeping our relationship on pause.

"You're right, Dr. David. I didn't realize how angry I still was. I thought I had forgiven him but I guess I haven't," I expressed.

"I should have told Kim how bad I felt for keeping that secret from her. I know it was my choice and my choice alone to lie, and because of that, I hurt her," Kaleb added.

"I want you to look at Kim and tell her this," Dr. David urged.

Kaleb turned to me and took my hand. "I'm sorry that I didn't tell you what you needed to hear from me. I should not have lied to you. Period. There was no excuse to break your trust. I regret that I hurt you and I hurt *us*."

"And I'm sorry too ... for everything I've done to hurt you," I told Kaleb.

34. Dr. David

My eyes filled up with tears. Kaleb reached over and gave me a hug.

"Let's take a break and continue tomorrow," Dr. David suggested. "There's a lot for you to process from today."

We agreed.

"Now, I want you guys to do something *fun* tonight, okay? Save the serious stuff for tomorrow," he added.

So, Kaleb took me out to dinner that evening and we focused on talking about happier moments in our lives—about the kids, when we first met in school and some funny awkward moments in the Lifestyle. It was nice to be normal with each other and not argue.

The next day, we started bright and early. We took our spots in the leather chairs.

"I want you to now face each other and hold each other's hands. Kim, you're going to start first. I would like you to share with Kaleb everything you've been holding in up to this point. Talk to Kaleb and tell him what you *need* in this relationship," Dr. David directed. "Kaleb, I want you to simply listen. No interrupting. After Kim is done, you'll have your turn to speak." Kaleb nodded.

Kaleb and I swiveled our chairs to face one another and awkwardly took hold of each other's hands. I looked into Kaleb's eyes and I found myself getting emotional. This was the first time I felt I would be able to say what I needed to, without being afraid of the possibility that Kaleb might become angry, defensive, or explode into an accusatory rage. There was a sense of safety knowing that Dr. David was there with us to mediate.

Kaleb comforted me by giving me a gentle squeeze of his hand to let me know that he was listening. There had been so many feelings and emotions I had bottled up since his affair. I didn't know where to start. I was scared to say out loud all of these feelings to Kaleb. Would this help or make our situation worse? Tears streamed down my face as I began to speak openly to the person who had hurt me so deeply.

"I believed without a doubt, I was the most important person in your life, always. When you lied to me in order to keep *her* secret, I felt like I didn't matter. I wasn't important to you," I said. "*She* was more important to you."

I continued to express to Kaleb how his affair had greatly affected my perception of him and where his loyalties laid. I no longer felt safe to commit to our relationship as I had before. I was afraid he could lie and hurt me again and I wanted to protect myself.

"Although I told you I had forgiven you, there was a part of me that couldn't trust you again. I didn't think you would ever let me down like

235

that so it sent me into a tail spin. I've never felt so disappointed and hurt like that, except with my father. I didn't expect you would ever do that to me." Tears welled up in my eyes. "My childhood really messed me up emotionally."

Kaleb got up from his chair and gave me a hug. "I'm sorry that I hurt you like that. I didn't realize at the time that by keeping her secret, I was protecting her interests and not yours ... or our relationship. You're right; I wasn't there for you like I should have been. I know I let you down but I'm not going to be like your father," Kaleb expressed, tears appearing in his eyes, too.

I felt he finally heard me. I knew at that moment that he was truly sorry for what he had done to me.

"I know that I've hurt you and let you down as well," I voiced to Kaleb. "I didn't realize I was still holding on to anger and pain from my childhood. I was searching for an *out* of the unhappiness I felt in my life and I ended up taking it out on you. I was selfish when I reached out to Jack behind your back."

It wasn't easy for me to bring up Jack's name because our conversations always ended up in arguments whenever I mentioned his name. I never felt comfortable to fully share with Kaleb the reasons why I had searched outside of our marriage to fulfill my unmet needs ... until this session.

"I want you to know that I didn't connect with Jack to get back at you," I explained.

"So why did you?" Kaleb asked.

"Okay, maybe I did a little bit. But I was mainly looking for some way to lessen this deep sadness I was feeling in my life ... with my mom dying and being estranged from my father. I didn't think you could help me. I wanted to believe that Jack was the answer and he would save me. Now I realize it wasn't Jack that I wanted ... it could have been any Joe Schmoe on the street. I did wrong by not sharing with you what I was going through. I turned to Jack as an easy quick fix to my unhappiness," I explained.

This dark period in my life was a perfect storm of all my unresolved issues colliding together—a culmination of unprocessed grief after the death of my mother, unspoken expectations within my marriage, lingering anger from Kaleb's affair with Annie, blurred lines created within the Lifestyle, and unresolved anger and frustration with my father redirected to Kaleb. This all left me in a state of confusion and emotional distress; I was acting out of a desperation to try to make sense of my life and feel some semblance of happiness, no matter what the cost.

"I should have told you how I was feeling and I regret not doing that," I admitted. "Our relationship suffered as a result."

"I now understand the pain you must have felt when I told you about Annie," Kaleb replied. "When I read the text messages on your phone, I was devastated. It broke me. I didn't know if I could ever trust you again."

Kaleb went on to explain how the past few months had been difficult for him to navigate his emotions; there was so much anger and hurt that clouded over his hope of reconciling our relationship. There was an internal struggle within him whether he could ever get over my emotional affair and truly forgive me.

"It would have been far easier for me to get past the affair if it had only been sex. When I saw your texts that you had connected with him on an emotional level, in my mind, it was game over. I was ready to walk away from our marriage."

"What kept you from walking away?" Dr. David asked.

"When I saw the remorse and sadness in Kim's eyes in the hotel room that night, I knew she still loved me," Kaleb replied. "And under all of this hurt and anger, I know I still love her. I don't want to throw away what we have and that's why I'm here."

We both acknowledged that there was a lot of hurt and pain on both sides and that we needed to continue to work on our communication and rebuilding our trust in each other.

On the final day of therapy, Dr. David discussed strategies on how we could improve our communication style and allow the other to feel that they were being heard. We practiced role-playing to help us. Dr. David's intensive therapy threw us a lifeline but we knew there was still work ahead of us. But we were 100 percent committed to making this relationship better—no half trust, no half loyalty or half-ass attitude. It was going to be hard work, but we were ready to do better.

Following the intensive therapy sessions, we continued to see Dr. David from time to time, whenever we needed a tune-up. Despite our best efforts to communicate, of course there were times we didn't handle our problems in the best *Dr. David* way, often defaulting to raised voices, exchanging of cross words or our go-to strategy—storming out or evoking the silent treatment.

I also felt it was important for me to see Dr. David on my own in order to work through my unresolved childhood issues, mostly around my tenuous relationship with my father. I wanted to heal my wounded inner child and not let it affect (and transfer) into my relationship with

Kaleb. I didn't realize how much of an impact my feelings towards my father had on how I viewed and reacted to Kaleb. That was truly an *aha* moment for me.

During this time, Kaleb and I stayed out of the Lifestyle so that we could focus on rebuilding our relationship and I could continue to heal emotionally. We didn't know when we would return, if at all. Our break would last two years. One thing I came to realize was that I shouldn't blame being in the Lifestyle (and the choices we made with Annie/Tom and Jack) for the problems that surfaced in our marriage. Foursome or no foursome, our relationship would have been tested at some point. It was a wake-up call for us. The Lifestyle highlighted even more so the non-negotiable need for communication, honesty, trust, compromise and reciprocal effort between two people to maintain a healthy, strong and thriving relationship.

Prior to Kaleb's and my affairs, I surmised that engaging in the Lifestyle could circumvent couples from cheating on each other. I mean why hide and cheat when you and your partner can pursue your sexual desires and fantasies, *freely and openly*, without guilt, secrecy or con-sequences, right? However, we proved that that is not always the case Cheating can happen with any couple, whether you're in the Lifestyle or not. It happened to us. I was cocky enough to think that nothing could ever go wrong with our marriage, even if we were tempting fate by swap-ping partners. Now I realize, swinging was not the problem. It was our communication style (or lack thereof). The foursome circumstance only brought to light the cracks that were underneath and beginning to surface.

Dr. David helped us to see the real *us* again, and only when we felt confident in our communication skills could we entertain getting back into the Lifestyle. And eventually we did ... and better for it too.

Epilogue

*   *   *

At the time of this writing, it's been almost 11 years since Kaleb and Annie's affair, 3 years since my affair with Jack, 17 years since Kaleb and I first discovered the Lifestyle and 24 years since we exchanged our wedding vows. Kaleb and I are happily together and still living downtown. Our adult children are unaware of our *alternative* lifestyle practices. As parents, our first inclination is to hide (or protect) our children from the *messy* bits of our relationship. Kaleb and I are still undecided as to whether or not we will ever share our story with our son and daughter. If and when we do make that decision, it will be disclosed with great care, consideration, and purpose.

After everything we've been through, I would say Kaleb and I are at the healthiest and most stable we've ever been in our relationship. Sure, we have our good days and our bad days; it's not perfect. However, we do have a better understanding and awareness of how the other is feeling, and we're able to communicate with more openness. As we grow older, we're mellowing out and becoming more patient with each other. I'm still working on my deep-rooted issues of being tentative in sharing with Kaleb what I'm truly feeling inside, especially if it is negative and might be upsetting to him ... my daddy issues. I didn't realize how important it was for me to know that Kaleb loved and accepted me unconditionally, with all of my imperfections and insecurities. Couples counseling helped Kaleb to understand how my past childhood and broken relationship with my father filtered down into our own relationship. We still reach out to Dr. David for guidance from time to time, especially when we get stuck and can't see the other's point of view. For the most part, we've been getting along and we are much better communicators than we were at the start of our LS journey.

We have both changed for the better as partners and that's because the Lifestyle forced us to face situations that we might not have had to

239

deal with as overtly as we did. Although some of the experiences of the past have been painful, these moments made us realize that our marriage wasn't as foolproof as we had once thought. As a couple, we can't sit idly by and put our relationship on cruise control.

After all is said and done, I have no regrets about being in the Lifestyle. The turmoil caused by the monogamous foursomes and our subsequent affairs happened in our lives for a reason—it taught us that our relationship is not static but a work in-progress that needs to be nurtured *every single day*. I'm still learning to express and be clear about my needs. Kaleb is trying to be more compassionate and aware of how to help me, as much as he can, so my issues don't play out to the detriment of our relationship. We feel grateful that we're still together and we have been able to overcome some major obstacles. We didn't stay together for the sake of our children; we did this for *us*.

As for the Lifestyle, Kaleb and I continue to explore this alternative way of living as a couple. We renewed our membership with *ABC Lifestyle** but we're not online as much as when we first joined. When the mood strikes, we enjoy a Friday or Saturday at the LS sex club or go through our rolodex of couples to arrange a *play date*. After all these years of swinging, we have yet to find our *perfect* foursome where Kaleb and I are equally attracted to our sex partner. There's no such thing as a perfect partner or spouse—there's varying degrees of compatibility or dare I say, acceptability or tolerability. The same applies with a four-way connection.

Nowadays, Kaleb and I tend to place more emphasis on personality than physical appearance when considering a couple. After all the dates, flirting, messaging and bed hopping, we realize one thing ... we don't want the drama! We prefer to play out our sexual fantasies and hook up with random strangers at a club. It's easier—no strings attached, no names, no expectations, just fun! Trying to find a compatible couple we both are mutually attracted to, have great personalities and that we want to spend time with in and outside of the bedroom has been next to impossible. Yet, we haven't given up all hope. We may never find our perfect couple but that's okay because we're enjoying this journey of meeting new and sexy like-minded couples, which keeps us soulfully connected.

The Lifestyle isn't about having lots of sex—it was never about that, at least for us. It's the lessons and experiences that Kaleb and I have gained with each couple we've met. From our numerous meet-and-greet dates to the raunchy orgies in the back rooms of the sex club, Kaleb and I have come across a lot of fascinating couples over the years. Their individual personalities and sexual idiosyncrasies have helped me to discover and embrace my sexual identity, expanded our sexual horizons, taught us how to verbalize our likes and dislikes and has allowed us to enjoy the hedonistic sexual pleasure in each and every situation.

Now Kaleb and I are doing things differently than we did at the beginning of our LS journey. We are focused on having more fun. We're putting ourselves first and making sure to protect our relationship every step of the way. We want to be true to ourselves and not let other couples dictate what is in our best interest, both in and out of the Lifestyle. We still don't like to commit to one couple, like we did with Natalie/Steve and Annie/Tom. Now we're enjoying meeting new couples and the perks of having multiple sex partners ... possibly all in one week!

I'm not in the Lifestyle because Kaleb wants me to be or vice versa. We're both drawn to the spontaneity, excitement, and sexual freedom that the Lifestyle has to offer. I wouldn't be surprised if we were still swinging in our 70s or 80s—provided we *both* have the desire to engage and our anatomical parts still function!

And while sex undoubtably plays a dominant role in my story, it extends beyond sex and into the realm of human connection; it highlights the complexity around establishing and maintaining healthy relationships with important people in our lives. In this narrative, it centers around my relationship with Kaleb and that of my parents; both have significantly affected me as a person and the choices I've made in and out of the Lifestyle.

In the last year of writing this memoir, my father passed away from COVID. During the previous three years, I had no communication with my father since he remarried and moved to another country after my mom's passing. Our relationship had cycled between superficial pleasantry and distant avoidance. When my twin sister called, weeping uncontrollably as she relayed to me that our father had died, I felt numb. I didn't know how to process the news. *Was I supposed to cry and feel sad because he was our father?* The only emotions I felt were anger and indifference. Tears welled up in my eyes, not from sadness, but from years of tolerating hurt, resentment and disappointment. Perhaps there was a sense of relief that my father could no longer let me down. It wasn't so much what my father *didn't* do for us kids (providing unconditional love and acceptance that we desperately needed), it was what he *did* do to us (he had the power to take away my voice). I never had the courage to tell

Epilogue

my father how I truly felt and how he made me feel so unaccepted and unlovable through the years. Everything I ever hoped to say to my father (or for him to say to me) in order to repair our fractured relationship is now forever gone. It's hard to be sad or miss a relationship you never had to begin with.

I know I have more healing to do, particularly around my childhood. Strangely enough, I do love my father, even though he was never able to say those words in return. I'm still learning to trust my *voice* to tell me what's best for me.

My LS journey has been full of ups and downs. *What have I learned from all of this?* We're all human, complicated, and fallible, trying to navigate our way through life as best as we can, making missteps along the way that force us to learn and grow. Annie and Kaleb made mistakes and I did too. I'm not angry anymore. Although the affair was an extremely painful experience to live through, it was truly a blessing. It opened up my eyes to what was missing in my relationship with Kaleb and forced us to work at it so we could be where we are today ... *together.* And I am forever grateful for that.

Appendix:
Swinging 101 Primer

* * *

When Kaleb and I started our LS journey in the early 2000s, I wished I had done some research and had a handy guide to swinging before we nosedived into this strange, yet fascinating world. We fell into swinging by accident and made some good and not so good choices along the way. I really could have benefited from an *Idiot's Guide to the Lifestyle* or even a psychology course in college (Swingers 101). There were so many times I had wanted to know something but didn't know where to turn. Where do you find other swingers? How do you connect and hook up with other couples (on Craigslist)? Are there any swingers near us? Was this all legal? Is there a hidden code for swingers to indicate you're one of them? Are there LS clubs and websites? Are there rules or LS etiquette that you need to abide by or does *anything* go? What do you do on a foursome meet-and-greet date? What are the boundaries or expectations with LS couples? Are you supposed to put out on the first date? I've heard of *soft* and *full* swap but what does that mean?

I had a lot of questions at the beginning, but no one to ask. Hopefully, I can share some of my experiences and the things I do know, particularly if swinging is something that you and your partner are curious about and you want to start your own LS journey.

Let's start off with the basics. What is a *swinger*? According to the Collins English Dictionary (www.collinsdictionary.com), swingers are people who are in a long-term relationship and who enjoy (and crave) having sex with other people's partners. This is different from a *polyamorist*—one who gets involved with two or more people at the same time in sexual *and* romantic relationships. Although a swinger and a polyamorist both have sex with other people's partners, a swinger does not (and should not!) necessarily become emotionally or intimately attached to anyone other than their long-term partner. For Kaleb and me, we engage

243

in swinging purely for the variety and enjoyment of having sex with someone else *and* we have no intentions of getting emotionally attached to our sex partners. Period.

There is other important LS terminology that should be mentioned:

Bull: a male who is looking for casual sex with a female, who is either single or part of a couple (men who are *bulls* are usually well-endowed)

Double Penetration (DP) or *Double Vagina* (DV): both involve one female and two males; DP is vaginal and anal penetration simultaneously and DV is two penises in the vagina simultaneously

FMF (Female, Male, Female): 2 women with 1 man in a threesome

Full Swap: when a couple sexually engages fully with another couple, including intercourse

Girl-Girl or *GG:* when only the women "play," while the men watch and/or join their own partners but don't engage with the other person's partner

MFM (Male, Female, Male): 2 men with 1 woman in a threesome

Newbies: people new to the Lifestyle or to the LS club/resort

Swinger Name or *Handle:* a nickname to identify and/or describe a couple's personalities that doesn't reveal their true identity—e.g., FOXYFLIRTS or SEXYLOVERS

Soft Swap: limited to swapping orally and/or heavy petting

Unicorn: for swingers, this refers to a single woman who sexually engages with the male and/or female of the couple

Vanilla: this refers to something that is non–Lifestyle or people and/or activities that are not geared towards sex—e.g., "We're busy this weekend with our vanilla friends."

Over the years in the Lifestyle, Kaleb and I have come up with a number of important rules of engagement. We didn't decide to sit down one Sunday afternoon and come up with a bunch of rules; we had a few basic ones to start with but many more were added over time. Some rules were obvious, others came to light with particular incidents that we had to work through, and some had to be reworked while other rules were reinstated or reiterated.

Disclaimer: we haven't always followed these rules, especially in the moment, which has occasionally led to some major blowout fights. But we do our best to remember them and follow them.

These rules have evolved over time and they were instrumental in helping us navigate through some tricky LS situations over the years. The LS playbook rules will be different for every couple. You and your partner have to decide on what boundaries and parameters you feel comfortable with and, most importantly, to keep checking in with each other to see if rules need to be added, deleted or modified.

The following are rules that Kaleb and I have added to our evolving list:

Rule #1: No romantic or deep intimate connection with our sex partners or engaging outside of the foursome relationship without each other's knowledge and consent. Keep sex and emotions *separate,* a philosophy that we follow to this day. That's the single most important rule for us—Kaleb and I view crossing this boundary as having an affair.

Rule #2: No secrets between us; always communicate openly and honestly. For us, it couldn't work any other way being in the Lifestyle.

Rule #3: Play in the same room. Kaleb and I enjoy having sex with another couple(s) in the same room because watching each other is part of the sexual exhilaration and fun! This allows us to be voyeurs as well as engage with our sex partner.

Rule #4: Talk about details before we act. Kaleb and I discuss our boundaries and what our expectations are every time we go out; for example, are we in the mood to play only with each other? Or are we going to the LS club's back room to have sex with multiple partners? These are extremely important details for us to discuss beforehand to avoid any potential disappointment, resentment or misunderstanding playing out.

Rule #5: Don't assume. This has been a source of many fights. Even though we might have agreed on something earlier on, in the moment, something can get inadvertently changed by one of us without asking the other. Kaleb and I agree that it's extremely important to continually check in with each other to make sure we are still feeling OK about a given situation; wants/needs can change on the fly, especially when it comes to emotions.

Rule #6: Use a safe word/phrase. We now signal to each other (discreetly) if we are feeling uncomfortable about a situation, not interested in engaging with the intended couple, and/or simply want to go home *right at that moment*. We used to say, "We should check in on our daughter, she just called." Now we keep it short and simple by interjecting "Pizza Pizza" in the conversation.

Rule #7: Find a moment to check-in with each other to see if it's a green/red light to potentially hook up. This is similar to **Rule #5** (don't make assumptions). Kaleb and I have to ask each other if we're both feeling a mutual connection with the intended couple, and if we're OK with soft or full swap and any other details that might come up.

Rule #8: Don't take one for the team. There have been times (not often) when one of us was not as attracted to our sex partner but we still engaged in play; the person taking one for the team is less than satisfied with the sexual experience.

Rule #9: Always use a condom. This is non-negotiable for all our LS play; regardless we ask couples if they regularly test and are HIV and STI negative.

Rule #10: No open relationships. Although some couples prefer to open up their relationships to casual sex with other partners and it works for them, Kaleb and I don't want to fool around (no pun intended) with this scenario. For us, engaging in LS play is something we enjoy doing together. For us, open relationships are potentially *complicated;* going out on separate dates and having casual sex and emotional attachments with other partners may lead to issues of infidelity or feelings of jealousy or mistrust and/or the other partner possibly wanting a more committed relationship from you. We don't need or want unnecessary emotional drama in our life. We've had our fill!

Rule #11: Kissing and oral sex are required for play. These are a must for us to truly engage in the sexual experience.

Rule #12: No single males or "unicorns." We do not enlist any single individuals (i.e., threesomes) into our sex play; Kaleb and I enjoy watching each other with another sex partner where we both are engaging in intercourse *at the same time*—that way, there isn't an odd man out, so to speak.

Rule #13: No more monogamous couple relationships. After our bad experiences, Kaleb and I vowed never again to engage only with one couple at a time; it gets complicated and dramatic dealing with the couple's jealousies and expectations and excluding other couples from joining in. Our unrestricted approach allows us to engage with multiple couples at the same time, and it allows us to have the final say as to how we spend our time and with whom.

Rule #14: Our Golden Rule: If one partner disagrees with a decision/behavior, then it's a no go! If it doesn't work for one partner, then it doesn't work for anyone! We're in this relationship *together* so both parties have to agree when it comes to an LS situation.

When creating these rules, we've had to account for differing views on some of the areas covered. For instance, I have always fantasized about a threesome with a male. However, Rule #12 (no singles) was initiated by Kaleb because he isn't keen on a male having sex with me while he sits back and watches. For swinging to work, we always have to default to any feelings of discomfort one person may have, so fulfilling this fantasy of mine is far less important than Kaleb's comfort.

These rules regularly change. The list I've included show the most up-to-date version. Compromise is an essential part of any good relationship. You're in this together; if one partner isn't okay with an idea, then it shouldn't happen. If one partner feels a rule is unfair or they have been forced to concede, then resentment will build up over time and the rule may get broken. Kaleb and I have to feel that a rule makes sense; if it doesn't work anymore, we either get rid of it or we modify it so both of us are happy.

Every couple's rulebook will be different. You and your partner will have to decide what rules feel right for you.

Further Reading

* * *

Brach, Tara. *Radical Acceptance: Embracing Your Life with the Heart of a Buddha*. New York: Bantam Books, 2003. This author's inspiring quote taught me that I don't need to subscribe to other people's expectations or ideology of how they think I should live; I can choose to set boundaries (or not) in my own life.

Davis, Shirley. "The Wounded Inner Child." CPTSD and Inner Child Work, CPTSD Research. July 13, 2020, https://www.cptsdfoundation.org/2020/07/13/the-wounded-inner-child/. This author's work from 2020 described the signs of a wounded inner child (a concept first introduced by psychologist, Carl Jung) and how it influences your behaviors, emotions and the decisions that you make.

Gaba, Sherry. "Carrying a Wounded Inner Child into Your Relationships?" *Psychology Today*, Dec. 16, 2020, https://www.psychologytoday.com/ca/blog/addiction-and-recovery/202012/carrying-wounded-inner-child-your-relationships. This author's work in 2020 informed my thinking on how my parents' behavior, particularly my father's lack of unconditional love, affected my behavior and emotions and transferred over into arguments and conflict with my husband.

Kneisl, C.R. "Healing the Wounded, Neglected Inner Child of the Past." *The Nursing Clinics of North America*, 26(3): 745-755, 1991. This author's work in 1991 informed my thoughts on the benefits of healing my wounded inner child and how unresolved childhood issues impacted on my adult relationships.

Tuckman, B.W. "Developmental Sequence in Small Groups." *Psychological Bulletin*, Vol. 63, No. 6, 384-399, 1965. This author's work in 1965 informed my thinking on the 5 stages of teamwork or group development: forming, storming, norming, performing and adjourning. I discussed how the storming phase took centre stage during our couples counseling with Dr. David and how it affected our ability to effectively communicate with one another during the session.

Tyagi, Kajal. "Romantic Relationships and the Wounded Inner Child." *Therapy Route*, Mar. 4, 2023, https://www.therapyroute.com/article/romantic-relationships-and-the-wounded-inner-child-by-k-tyagi. This is an interesting article, written in 2023, which discusses how our inner child wounds can be strongly triggered in our relationships whereby unrealistic expectations are placed upon our partners to fulfill our unmet needs and longing; however, only we can heal our own selves.

Index

BDSM 10
betrayal 58, 64, 179, 183–191, 229–234; emotional affair 219, 227–228, 237
bisexuality 46, 77
Brach, Tara: *Embracing Your Life with the Heart of a Buddha* 4

Carrying a Wounded Inner Child into Your Relationships? 218, 229, 249
condoms 13–14, 38, 55, 88, 95, 105, 246; *see also* safe sex
couples counseling 232, 239

Davis, Shirley: *The Wounded Inner Child* 249
Developmental Sequence in Small Groups 234
dissociating 61

Embracing Your Life with the Heart of a Buddha 4

foreplay 11, 25, 35, 55, 79, 87, 109

Gaba, Sherry: *Carrying a Wounded Inner Child into Your Relationships?* 218, 229, 249
glory hole 39, 44

Healing the Wounded, Neglected Inner Child of the Past 188, 249
hook up 13, 40, 77, 113, 150, 198, 207, 223, 240, 243, 246

jealousy 27, 29, 44, 96, 112, 198, 200, 210, 213, 246

Kneisl, C.R.: *Healing the Wounded, Neglected Inner Child of the Past* 188, 249

LS connection 223; foursomes 15, 21, 64, 196–198, 200–208, 223, 240; threesomes 26–27, 35, 90, 165, 223, 244–247

LS rules 6, 13, 43, 56, 61–63, 92, 95, 122–127, 131, 151–152, 209–210, 223, 243–247
LS websites 3, 201, 204, 210, 223

monogamous LS relationship 1, 45, 61, 102, 105, 150, 189, 196–198, 204–208, 240, 246

newbies 3, 40–42, 244

open relationships 111, 246
orgasms 27, 74–89, 96, 207

Romantic Relationships and the Wounded Inner Child 249

safe sex 6; *see also* condoms
sex clubs 5, 7, 35–39, 45, 151, 195, 205, 240–241
sex toys 10, 26; Barney 75
sexual identity 241; bisexuality 46, 77
soul encounters 3
soul mate 1, 22, 24, 228
STI 105, 246; *see also* safe sex
swapping 21, 42, 55, 57, 64, 72, 147, 190, 238, 244; full swap 55, 200, 243–246; soft swap 200, 244

Tuckman, B.W.: *Developmental Sequence in Small Groups* 234
Tyagi, Kajal: *Romantic Relationships and the Wounded Inner Child* 249

unicorn 244, 246

women empowerment 74
wounded inner child 188, 218, 229, 237, 249
The Wounded Inner Child 249